ESSENTIAL
EARLY
YEARS

LOUISE DRYDEN

RUTH FORBES

PENNY MUKHERJI

LINDA POUND

ESSENTIAL
EARLY YEARS

RITA CHAWLA-DUGGAN

URMI JOSHI

CLARE MENON

LYN TRODD

Hodder Arnold

A MEMBER OF THE HODDER HEADLINE GROUP

Acknowledgements

The authors and publishers would like to thank the following for permission to reproduce material in this book:

Pages 2, 13, 33, 42, 66, 80, 85, 92, 112 and 159, Bubbles; pages 21 and 174, Hulton-Deutsch Collection/CORBIS; page 26, Voisin-Phanie/Rex Features Ltd; pages 28, 70, 122, 132, 167 and 221, John Walmsley; pages 44 and 55, Edith Palmer; pages 56 and 141, BDI Images Ltd; page 59, John Powell/Rex Features Ltd; page 62, Giles Shewell; page 98, Mary Evans Picture Library; page 99, reproduced by permission of the People's History Museum; page 108, Sipa Press/Rex Features Ltd; page 110, Tom Kidd/Rex Features Ltd; page 142, Michel Tcherevkoff/The Image Bank/Getty Images; page 148, Valiant Technology Ltd www.valiant-technology.com; page 152, SUNSET/Rex Features Ltd; page 156, Roy Peters/reportdigital.co.uk; page 180, Alix-Phanie/Rex Features Ltd; page 186, PA Photos; page 191, Will Mcintyre/Science Photo Library; page 226, Melanie Friend/Photofusion.

Every effort has been made to obtain necessary permission with reference to copyright material. The publishers apologise if inadvertently any sources remain unacknowledged and will be glad to make the necessary arrangements at the earliest opportunity.

Orders: please contact Bookpoint Ltd, 130 Milton Park, Abingdon, Oxon OX14 4SB. Telephone: +44 (0)1235 827720. Fax: +44 (0)1235 400454. Lines are open from 9.00–6.00, Monday to Saturday, with a 24-hour message-answering service. You can also order through our website www.hoddereducation.co.uk.

British Library Cataloguing in Publication Data
A catalogue record for this title is available from the British Library

ISBN–10: 0 340 88877 6
ISBN–13: 978 0 340 88877 3

First published 2005
Impression number   10 9 8 7 6 5 4 3
Year   2007 2006

Copyright © 2005 Louise Dryden, Ruth Forbes, Penny Mukherji, Urmi Joshi, Rita Chawla-Duggan, Clare Menon, Linda Pound, Lyn Trodd

Typeset by Pantek Arts Ltd, Maidstone, Kent.
Printed in Dubai for Hodder Arnold, a division of Hodder Headline, 338 Euston Road, London NW1 3BH.

CONTENTS

ABOUT THE AUTHORS

Louise Dryden is Senior Lecturer in Early Years Language and Literacy at London Metropolitan University, where she lectures on a range of undergraduate and postgraduate courses. Previously, she taught in schools and further education colleges. Her current responsibilities include a role as academic liaison tutor, working alongside three partnership colleges running Early Years Sector-Endorsed Foundation Degree programmes.

Ruth Forbes is a Children's Centre Manager for the Dorset Sure Start Unit and is an experienced early years author. Working in a rural area she is responsible for the delivery of the national agenda for Children's Centres, managing a multi-agency partnership to promote and deliver better outcomes for children and their families. Previously she was co-ordinating and lecturing the Early Years Sector-Endorsed Foundation Degree in Early Years at Swindon College.

Penny Mukherji is a Senior Lecturer at London Metropolitan University and teaches child health topics on the Early Childhood Studies Scheme. Penny has had many years' experience teaching early years practitioners on Higher Education courses and helped to set up the Sector-Endorsed Foundation Degree in Early Years at London Metropolitan University. She is an experienced early years author.

Linda Pound is an early years consultant, undertaking a wide range of development work in the UK and overseas. She has worked with experienced practitioners in three universities and was a local education authority inspector for ten years. Prior to that she was a nursery school headteacher. Linda writes widely. Her most recent book, co-written with Chris Harrison, is entitled *Supporting Musical Development in the Early Years*.

Rita Chawla-Duggan is a Lecturer in Early Childhood Studies in the Department of Education at the University of Bath. She has taught in preparatory, primary and middle schools. Rita's research interests are child poverty and education, the social influences on children's learning, and the study of early years' education. She has conducted ethnographic research in England, Japan and India. She has recently conducted an evaluation of a local Sure Start programme.

Urmi Joshi is a Senior Practitioner and Co-ordinator of the Foundation Degree in Early Years at Hackney Community College. Her research on aspects of the Foundation Degree have been published widely. She is currently completing her thesis on the Foundation Degree, focusing on employer perception and with reference to widening participation and social inclusion.

Clare Menon is Information Technology Manager with responsibility for quality at Milton Keynes College. Previously she was the New Learning Technologies Manager at West Herts College, where she lectured on the Post-Graduate Certificate in Education and the Early Years Sector-Endorsed Foundation Degree programmes in collaboration with the University of Hertfordshire. She has taught in both England and Malaysia.

Lyn Trodd is Senior Lecturer in Education (Early Years) at the University of Hertfordshire. She is the Link Tutor for the Early Years Sector-Endorsed Foundation Degree and a new Foundation Degree in Playwork that are offered in the Consortium formed of the four Hertfordshire Colleges and the University. Lyn is the Vice Chair of the National Network of Early Years Sector-Endorsed Foundation Degrees, a member of a DfES Children's Workforce working group developing the status of Senior Practitioners, and undertakes Subject Reviews of foundation degrees for the Quality Assurance Agency.

INTRODUCTION

Essential Early Years is designed as a comprehensive and accessible introductory textbook for students on Early Years courses, particularly those studying in Higher Education. The original author team consisted of lecturers involved in the management and delivery of the SureStart Sector-Endorsed Foundation Degree programme at all levels, and in a range of different institutions. Each author brings a different subject specialism, and an insight into the workings of the programme as it is delivered in their particular institution. As the project evolved, we invited other authors to contribute their own unique perspectives to the book. We hope that readers will find the wide range of experience among the author team both refreshing and stimulating.

The book provides an overview of the core subject areas which are most commonly studied in Early Years programmes. Each chapter explores the major issues related to each subject area, providing an ideal stepping-off point for further study. Throughout the book, the authors discuss important historical and theoretical perspectives, current debates and relevant equality issues.

We begin with a chapter entitled Launching into Learning by Lyn Trodd, which considers how your new programme of study can help to enhance your skills as a reflective practitioner. Chapter 2, by Penny Mukherji, considers the importance of health for children and their families, and Chapter 3, by Louise Dryden, focuses on the development of language and literacy.

Chapters 4–6 look at curriculum matters relating to the three distinct age ranges which make up the early years. Ruth Forbes writes about working with the under-threes, Linda Pound considers the Foundation Stage, and Rita Chawla-Duggan discusses children's experience of transition from the Foundation Stage to the Key Stage 1 classroom.

Chapters 7–11 are concerned with broad topics which relate to working with children across the early years. Clare Menon examines the use of technology in child care settings. This is followed by Linda Pound and Urmi Joshi's chapter on management and leadership issues in the context of early years teams. In Chapter 9, Linda Pound considers early years policy as we begin the twenty-first century. In Chapter 10, Urmi Joshi and Penny Mukherji explore issues relating to special educational needs and disability, and, in the final chapter, Ruth Forbes considers the important topic of child protection.

In the appendix, there is a chapter on study skills for those students who are returning to education after a break and may need to re-establish their study habits, or for existing students who would like to refresh their current habits!

Clearly, it would be impossible to provide all the information students need, but our intention is to whet the appetite of the reader, and thus to stimulate interest for further reading and debate. Each chapter includes *pause for thought* and *reflective activity* boxes, designed to encourage the reader to make links between the text and their own experiences. Finally, we conclude with a list of suggested further reading on key topics raised in the chapter.

We hope that you will enjoy reading this book as much as we have enjoyed writing it, and wish you all the very best in your course and your career!

1 LAUNCHING INTO LEARNING:
BECOMING A REFLECTIVE PRACTITIONER

Two roads diverged in a wood, and I –
I took the one less travelled by,
And that has made all the difference.
—Robert Frost, 'The Road Not Taken', 1916

IN THIS CHAPTER WE WILL CONSIDER THE FOLLOWING TOPICS:

* Becoming a learner
* Gathering evidence to inform personal and professional development
* Evidence-based practice and the place of research.

BECOMING A LEARNER

gladly would I learn and gladly teach
—Chaucer, *The Canterbury Tales*, c.1387

If you are currently studying for a degree in early years, one of your hopes may be that people see you differently. If you are already working as an early years practitioner, you may feel ready to assume more challenging responsibilities in your work with children. Whatever your situation, you will have certain expectations and aspirations for the future. As Maslow's hierarchy of needs illustrates (see below), human beings yearn for much more than just safety and comfort.

PAUSE FOR THOUGHT

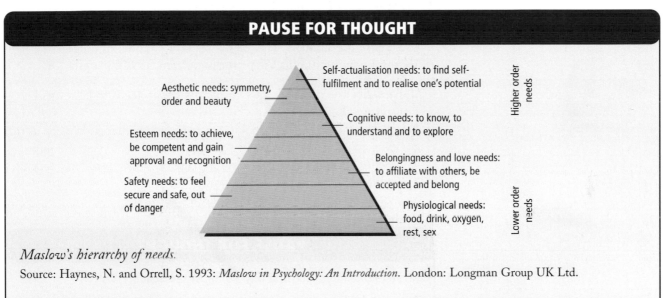

Aesthetic needs: symmetry, order and beauty

Self-actualisation needs: to find self-fulfilment and to realise one's potential

Cognitive needs: to know, to understand and to explore

Esteem needs: to achieve, be competent and gain approval and recognition

Belongingness and love needs: to affiliate with others, be accepted and belong

Safety needs: to feel secure and safe, out of danger

Physiological needs: food, drink, oxygen, rest, sex

Higher order needs

Lower order needs

Maslow's hierarchy of needs.

Source: Haynes, N. and Orrell, S. 1993: *Maslow in Psychology: An Introduction.* London: Longman Group UK Ltd.

Using Maslow's hierarchy of needs as a starting point, consider how studying for and achieving your early years degree will meet your needs.

Most learners find it helpful to their motivation and understanding to clarify their needs, goals and intentions and to review them regularly. As part of this process it is a good idea to draw up your own action plan for professional and personal development. The most effective action plans draw on a variety of sources of evidence and should help you assess your current level of knowledge, understanding and skill in your role in an early years setting or as a higher education student.

The reflective practitioner: thinking critically

As an early years practitioner you have to take responsibility for the way you work with children, families and colleagues, in the same way as those in other professions do, such as doctors and lawyers. Like other professionals you have to work fairly autonomously and any outside monitoring of your actions is largely retrospective. As a reflective practitioner you will be professional and competent and will continuously seek to improve your practice. Throughout both your studies and your training your aim should be to develop a reflective and critical approach to working with children that will continue throughout your career. This will enable you to manage change by thinking

> ## REFLECTIVE ACTIVITY
>
> Draw up two lists showing where you might obtain evidence that would help you assess your effectiveness in your job role and in your student role.

critically, drawing on evidence to ensure the validity and currency of your practice in the future. Early years practitioners who have learned to think critically and reflectively will question assumptions and actively challenge accepted values and practices if they are no longer relevant or beneficial to children. This questioning and reflection is an important part of ensuring that children's real needs are met.

The Pause for Thought task below reflects a model of critical reflection known as the DATA process (Peters 1994):

D – describe the problem, task or incident that needs to be looked at and possibly changed

A – analyse the description, looking at assumptions that were made at the time and also any that are being made about how to respond now

T – theorise about a range of ways to respond to the problem, task or incident

A – act using one or more of the theories above.

PAUSE FOR THOUGHT

Can you remember *your* first day at nursery or school? (D)

What were the beliefs and values that influenced your experiences on that first day? (A)

In what ways would you meet children's needs on entry to a new setting differently now? What has changed? Why has it changed? How could it be improved further? (T)

How could the improvements you describe be put in place? (A)

As you think, apply Peters' model of critical reflection.

A rather different approach to critical reflection has been described by Brookfield (1995), who suggests that we look at reality from:

- our own viewpoint
- our colleagues' viewpoints
- the viewpoints of learners
- the viewpoints offered by theoretical literature.

These are the four critical lenses to look through and ask ourselves, 'What were the assumptions made by each perspective?'

Another approach to critical reflection is critical incident analysis. This approach is similar to case study research. You examine a typical incident or example – one that illustrates a general point – and identify problems or issues to explore further. An example would be to

PAUSE FOR THOUGHT

Think about the first day for children in your setting:

- What assumptions do you make about the needs of children on their first day in your setting? Where do these assumptions come from?
- What views do your colleagues have of children and their needs on the first day in your setting? Where do these views come from?
- Are these views different from those of parents? Where do you think the parents' views come from?
- What assumptions do the children make? Do they perhaps assume that you and your colleagues live in the setting and do not go home at night?
- What about the assumptions of theories of children's development and concepts of childhood? In what ways do these theories underpin our expectations of children on their first day in a new setting?

investigate the experience of a child with a mobility difficulty when he or she plays outside. We might be able to identify barriers to inclusion that could be removed. This process should also help increase our awareness of any hidden assumptions that we might hold about mobility difficulties.

Dewey (1933) describes the process of reflection as follows:

1. We recognise that a problem or thought-provoking event has happened.

2. We try to interpret the event using existing knowledge and understanding.

3. We use our intelligence and skills to describe and explain the event thoroughly.

4. We use our thoughts from stage three to change our perceptions and expectations.

5. We alter our approach or thinking in order to improve or change things.

When students read a description of Dewey's stages in reflection, it often reminds them of Piaget's notion of schemas and the processes of adaptation, assimilation, accommodation, equilibration and organisation (Piaget, Garbain and Garbain 2001). Just as Piaget thought that children actively construct knowledge and understanding as they manipulate and explore the world, Dewey thought that individuals develop, deepen and evaluate their knowledge and understanding through reflection.

The examples above are not a definitive list of approaches to critical reflection, but they do help to illustrate how practitioners use informal theory to guide and shape their practice. We often find it hard to describe or articulate this informal theory, even though we use it all the time; we perceive it as common sense. Schön (1983) called this underpinning theory translated into action 'knowledge in action'.

In addition to informal theory, there is a whole body of formal theory that we use to guide our practice. For example, we may expect to describe children's development in a linear, sequential way because many theorists such as Freud, Piaget and Erikson have described developmental change in stages. If you have used a developmental checklist in the last few weeks, your assumptions were underpinned by Freud, Piaget and Erikson's theories of development!

Another very important aspect of reflection is an awareness of yourself – especially your own thinking. A central part of reflective learning is about the uncovering and questioning of assumptions or informal theories. Schön (1983) argued that 'surfacing' assumptions and learning is an important dynamic in personal growth and self-awareness. You can learn to treat yourself as an object of knowledge and evaluation and develop your self-awareness and thus your ability to act in a professional, safe and consistent manner. Eventually this mindset, or habit, becomes an important aspect of critical reflection – it is sometimes described as reflexivity (Usher and Edwards 1994). You can develop your own self-awareness through reflection on the explicit or implicit feedback that you receive from your work with young children, their families and your colleagues. There are many sources of such feedback and in the next section we will look at some of them.

GATHERING EVIDENCE TO INFORM PERSONAL AND PROFESSIONAL DEVELOPMENT

Self-assessment

to thine own self be true

—Shakespeare, *Hamlet*, 1600

Tools for self-assessment

There are several tools for self-assessment that can supply useful evidence for self-evaluation and also contribute to your professional understanding. Many have been influenced by Kolb's Learning Styles Inventory (1984), which identified the possession of four different abilities:

- concrete experience abilities (feeling and intuition rather than thinking)
- reflective experience abilities (understanding and meanings rather than practical application)
- abstract conceptualisation abilities (thinking rather than feeling)
- active experimentation abilities (influencing and changing rather than reflection or understanding).

For instance, the Belbin questionnaire may help you as an early years practitioner to highlight your preferred team role; in addition, it might help you to see the range of potential roles in a team and the dynamics that might be experienced within it (Belbin 2003). The Belbin questionnaire suggests that a team containing members with a range of team role preferences is more likely to be successful in achieving its goals. Many early years practitioners who use the Belbin questionnaire find that they have high scores in the category 'Team Worker'; in other words, they can assume any role that is needed in order to achieve the group goals.

Another example of a tool for self-assessment is the Honey and Mumford questionnaire (1992). This classifies preferred learning styles as:

- activist
- pragmatist
- reflector
- theorist.

Another questionnaire, designed by Dunn and Dunn (1978), is particularly useful because it uses the preferred sensory stimulus to describe learning styles as:

- visual
- auditory
- kinaesthetic.

Awareness of learning styles is also very useful when supporting and enabling children, and when planning and differentiating in order to maximise learning.

Using a learning journal

As an early years practitioner, you regularly use the professional skill of observation of children, and this means that you are well aware that a factual narrative can be a rich source of analysis and reflection. In the

---

REFLECTIVE ACTIVITY

If this kind of personal exploration to help you to become more self-aware interests you, do some Internet research on the following:

- Six thinking hats
- Cattell 16PF Profile
- Myers Briggs Type indicators
- Douglas McGregor's Theory X and Theory Y
- Herzberg's Motivation Hygiene Theory
- Assertiveness
- Johari Window
- Covey's Seven Habits
- The 7S Framework
- Transactional Analysis
- Situational Leadership
- Tuckman's stages of group development
- Gardner's theory of multiple intelligences.

same way, a regular journal can be a very useful source of evidence for your professional and personal development action plan. It can help you to become more self-aware and reflective and can provide evidence of progress to develop your self-esteem, professionalism and confidence. You may find that you need to keep this journal entirely private in order to enable you to write it in a frank and honest way and remain true to yourself. An example of a journal entry is shown below:

> **30 August 2004**
>
> It is so frustrating that I can't get on with my interviews for my research on what parents think about homework for children younger than 7. I really should have planned things better and carried out the survey before the term ended and everyone disappeared for the holiday. Talking to my sister Louise today I realised that people have different ideas about what actually constitutes homework. Louise thinks that homework includes my niece, Georgina, pairing up socks and counting them in twos as well as learning the two times table by heart (as set by her teacher). Maybe I should have defined what I meant by *homework* more clearly before starting…

Portfolio-building

Obviously, assessment methods vary considerably across the wide range of foundation and undergraduate early years degree courses. However, many courses will require some element of portfolio-building as part of the assessment process. The work-based assessment aspect of your programme is a very significant feature. Generally, a list of learning outcomes is provided by your university or college. You should be able to meet many of the learning outcomes using evidence generated from your existing work role. This evidence will need to be collected together and organised in a portfolio. The process of creating, organising and cross-referencing a portfolio is a challenging task. If you have already taken an NVQ you will have some experience of portfolio-building. Many students take great pride and pleasure in ensuring that their portfolio is of a high quality.

You will need to be determined, alert to opportunities and very organised in your pursuit of evidence. Your university or college tutor will advise you about what constitutes valid and acceptable evidence for your portfolio. Generally there is a requirement that evidence is sufficient (for the learning outcome or competence being claimed) and authentic (directly attributable to the candidate). Usually the portfolio will include witness statements, signed observations of you, child observations, supervisor reports, 'products' such as policies and other working documents, photographs, minutes of meetings, letters, reports, videos, reflective accounts, work plans and samples of children's work.

Top tips for starting your portfolio:

- Buy a large A4 lever arch file NOW.
- Colour coordinate the file or select a particular font or type of paper. Having your own distinctive style can encourage your sense of ownership of your portfolio.
- Decide where the learning outcomes and evidence will go and how you will separate them – using dividers or index tabs.
- Design and set up a template or pro forma on your laptop or computer that can be used to record your evidence.
- Spend half an hour each week reviewing your portfolio and planning how to get the necessary evidence – what you have, what you still need.
- Talk to your mentor, line manager or critical friend (see p. 10) to hear their ideas about how you could provide the evidence needed.
- A potential employer may be interested in seeing your portfolio. Bear this possible audience in mind as you create it.

Evidence from others

To see ourselves as others see us
—Robert Burns, 'To a Louse', 1785

Feedback

Your lists in the Reflective Activity box (see p. 3) probably included feedback received from your line manager when you were last appraised or observed, as well as comments from children, parents, peers, family, friends, tutors and other students. It might also be interesting to ask for feedback from colleagues whom you manage. The important thing is to see the feedback as a gift from someone who has your best interests at heart – to invite it and welcome it.

As well as learning to receive feedback constructively you may need to develop your skill in giving feedback to someone else. The principles are generally the same. You should check that:

- the receiver wants and is ready to receive the feedback
- there is an appropriate length of time to discuss it fully
- the context is conducive, relevant and non-threatening
- the feedback has been heard correctly
- the feedback is expressed in descriptive rather than evaluative or judgemental language

REFLECTIVE ACTIVITY

At story time you notice that your early years colleague tends to direct their questions about the book towards the boys, and ignores the girls. After a peer observation of the colleague during story time you give feedback. Role-play this situation with a fellow student or write a script to show how you would communicate the feedback, including your observation about your colleague's gender bias when asking questions.

- the feedback is delivered in a 'sandwich' or layered approach, that is:
  - a statement of intention to be helpful and supportive
  - positive comments and acknowledgement of strengths
  - an area for development
  - an opportunity for the receiver of feedback to comment
  - a restatement or summary and thanks
  - the receiver of the feedback has the last word.

Unfortunately, now you are aware of this widely used approach, you will expect areas for development to follow positive comments!

Being and having a critical friend

Fellow learners on your degree programme can be a valuable source of feedback too, particularly if you enter into an informal contract as 'study buddies' or 'critical friends'. The fullest definition of a critical friend, and the one quoted frequently by writers on the subject, is:

> A person who asks provocative questions, provides data to be examined through another lens, and offers critiques of a person's work as a friend. A critical friend takes the time to fully understand the context of the work presented and the outcomes that the person or group is working toward. The friend is an advocate for the success of that work.
>
> (Costa and Kallick 1993: 50)

A critical friend can be seen as someone who not only has a different perspective on the piece of work from its author, but also assists that author to see the familiar in a new light. A critical friend's viewpoint assumes even greater credibility if it is informed by an understanding of the situation.

'Critical' can appear to have unhelpful, negative connotations, and 'friend' could imply non-professionalism, but together they describe a role that combines the elements of non-judgemental support, benevolent support and assistance implied by 'friend' and, at the same time, provision of an external perspective and challenge implied by 'critical'.

A critical friend is someone who:

- has 'a licence to help'
- brings a particular perspective which is informed by an understanding of the situation, but maintains an element of detachment
- builds and maintains a relationship of trust
- balances friendship and critique, with the emphasis on being a *friend* to people as people, and a *critic* of actions

- motivates and reassures
- seeks to enable those they work with to become more self-sufficient and skilled at self-improvement
- from a transactional analysis (see glossary, p. 15) viewpoint, seeks to operate with inter-adult relationships.

The overall aim of a critical friendship is to support improvement through empowerment, by demonstrating a positive regard for people, and providing an informed critique of processes and practices. In carrying out this role, the higher education critical friend will:

- observe, listen and learn
- demonstrate positive regard for their colleague/fellow student
- help identify issues and explore alternatives
- offer sources of evidence and/or expertise
- work collaboratively and encourage collaboration and the sharing of ideas
- offer a thoughtful critical perspective

but will not:

- assume a directive role
- offer solutions to problems, or provide 'quick fixes'
- rush to judgement
- have hidden agendas or impose their own agendas.

Mentoring

As with different assessment methods, you will find that individual courses have different requirements in terms of mentoring. You may have both specific journal mentoring arrangements and also more informal ones.

A workplace mentor can be a very useful source of feedback. The mentoring relationship will vary from learner to learner and will be shaped by the expectations of both mentor and 'mentee' or protégé. It is difficult to define mentoring other than in a very general sense, but, fundamentally, it is a process that enables the mentor to use their experience to help the mentee to learn more quickly, more reflectively or more deeply than they would have done otherwise. In general, the skill of mentoring: '...involves primarily listening with empathy, sharing experience and learning (usually mutually), professional friendship, developing insight through reflection, being a sounding board, encouraging' (Gardiner 1998).

> **REFLECTIVE ACTIVITY**
>
> Think about the role, function, attributes and benefits of a critical friend, as described above. Now write down three ways that a fellow student could have helped you improve a recent assignment by being a critical friend. Alternatively, you could write down three ways that a critical friend might have helped you resolve a difficult workplace situation.

> The word 'mentor' comes from Greek mythology. In Homer's *Odyssey* (*c*.800 BC), Odysseus set off for war and left his son, Telemachus, in the care of an older man called Mentor. He asked the older man to use his experience and wisdom to guide the child.

Colwell (1998) noted that mentorship has a crucial role in the 'socialisation process' of an individual into workplace culture. Other recent work on mentoring mentions dialogue, challenge, critical examination and reflection on practice.

Pollard (2002: 381) establishes the link between reflection and mentoring in the context of teaching:

> Reflection is the process through which teachers become aware of the complexity of their work and are able to take actions which impact positively on this. Mentoring provides a stimulus, drawing on accumulated professional knowledge and experience, which can help teachers to reflect with purpose and focus. Taken together then, reflection and mentoring help to inform and build a culture of professional learning.

In your education and training to work with children you may have come across Bruner's analogy of 'scaffolding' learning (Bruner 1975). 'Scaffolding is a process in which students are given support until they can apply new skills and strategies independently' (Rosenshine and Meister 1992). Mentoring can be seen as a way to scaffold your learning as an early years professional.

A mentoring relationship is dynamic and evolving, based on trust and mutual respect. It can be extremely valuable for the mentor and mentee to draw up an informal contract, outlining how the mentoring relationship will work. This will help you both to agree your expectations, and to establish any specific goals, as well as setting boundaries. You may need to decide how frequently and for how long you will meet and the kinds of topics and activities you will discuss within the mentoring relationship.

If you work in a school setting it is possible that someone on the staff has already had a great deal of experience being a mentor to teaching practice students or newly qualified teachers. Quite often, however, your mentor is new to the role and may feel quite daunted by it. They may feel responsible for you and your success on your degree programme. What matters when you are looking for a mentor is that they take on the role freely and gladly, that they wish to see you succeed and that they can support you but also challenge you – in much the same way as a critical friend. It is an added bonus if your mentor can use their influence to open doors for you so that you can gain further experience. You can support your mentor by sharing information about your programme, your assignments and your work-based portfolio. Mentors often report that they pick up new ideas and improve their own practice through the mentoring relationship. One of their motivations for being a mentor may be that they were helped by someone who was a mentor to them when they were starting out in their career.

While you are being mentored you are also learning how to be a mentor.

One of the more difficult aspects for mentors and mentees is that in some early years degree programmes the mentor supports the student but also assesses them in the workplace. The mentor can feel that there is a conflict of roles in such circumstances. Remember that the mentor is accountable to your organisation for the supervision of your practice and must try to ensure that you work with children in a safe, sensitive and effective way, as well as liaising with your university or college tutors.

EVIDENCE-BASED PRACTICE AND THE PLACE OF RESEARCH

'Faith' is a fine invention
When Gentlemen can see –
But Microscopes are prudent
In an Emergency

—Emily Dickinson, 'Poem 185', 1860

The development of evidence-based practice is a key professional skill for all early years students and practitioners. Action research is intended to solve an everyday problem, and it accepts that the research outcome will only be true for the specific context that is researched. It is carried out by you as a practitioner, for yourself and other practitioners, in order to improve the way you work with children.

The approach is generally cyclical:

- the issue is identified
- there is clarification of what can be changed
- action is taken or data is collected
- the results are evaluated
- your practice is revised
- another issue is identified.

Ethics in evidence-based practice

Adopting a clear and accepted code of ethics is absolutely central to the development of evidence-based practice within early years settings. It is also a vital part of your professional mindset, geared towards promoting children's well-being and protecting them in every way possible. A comprehensive code of ethics for early years practitioners must examine the acquisition and use of evidence gathered from children and the contexts where they live, play and work.

It goes without saying that the development of evidence-based practice should not harm children or their families and that the action researcher should be sensitive, respectful, open and honest in the way that they seek and use information. There are many grey areas in research, however, so the key safeguard is your ability as a practitioner to be reflective and reflexive about your role, responsibilities and relationships (Aubrey *et al.* 2000). An ethical approach to evidence-based practice also helps to develop critical reflection and reflexivity because it requires you as a practitioner to consider the impact of your actions upon others and to examine the values and assumptions that shape your research.

You should always ask yourself the following questions:

- Why am I carrying out this action research? Who will it benefit? Do the potential benefits justify the research process?
- Am I seeking the truth and acting in good faith?
- Have I obtained informed consent from all participants from whom evidence is gathered? (or their parent/carer)
- How will I ensure that confidentiality is maintained at all times?
- Have I complied with the Data Protection Act (1998)?
- Have I identified all possible risks to the well-being of participants and eliminated these from the process of research?
- Does my research respect the participants' rights and treat them with respect and sensitivity?

Research is not a separate activity from work with children but something that can be integrated within it. When you use your own research and code of ethics to inform your practice you will be in a better position to challenge some of the 'received wisdom' with which early years practice is imbued. You will also avoid making old-fashioned or unhelpful assumptions about working with children. Being reflective, both as a student and as a practitioner, will help put you back in charge of the way you work.

GLOSSARY

Case study research An empirical investigation of one specific situation or case.

Critical incident analysis This used to be a means of gathering data, but it is also a tool to enable reflection and learning by practitioners who are asked to recall a specific incident or moment from their recent experience and to critique it, with the focus on the critique, rather than the incident.

Critical perspective Applying one's own views and approaches, rather than simply accepting other people's information, attitudes and judgements. This is seen as higher-level thinking than simply learning facts or describing.

Learning style The variety of approaches, preferences or methods learners can bring to being learners.

Received wisdom Knowledge or understanding that is generally accepted as being right or correct because it is based on non-specific authority or has never been questioned.

Reflective practitioner Someone who engages regularly in the process of reflecting on their own practice and experience, and who seeks to learn from such reflection.

Socialisation process The means by which new entrants or children learn to adopt or adapt to the behaviour patterns or norms and values of the surrounding culture.

Transactional analysis A method of understanding people's behaviour by analysing the 'transactions', relationships or social interactions which go on between them. The analysis uses a theory that describes three ego states (parent, adult and child) which coexist in the personality and are linked to feelings and behaviours that were formed in childhood and that may now hinder a person's development.

KEY TEXTS

Atkinson, T. and Claxton, G. (eds) 2000: *The Intuitive Practitioner: On the Value of Not Always Knowing What One Is Doing*. Maidenhead: Open University Press and McGraw Hill Education.

Hillier, Y. 2002: *Reflective Teaching in Further and Adult Education*. London and New York: Continuum.

Pollard, A. 2002: *Reflective Teaching: Effective and Evidence Informed Professional Practice*. London and New York: Continuum.

Schön, D. 1983: *The Reflective Practitioner: How Professionals Think in Action*. New York: Basic Books, Inc.

THE IMPORTANCE OF HEALTH 2

INTRODUCTION

In this chapter we will be looking at child health. Over the last 20 years, the UK has seen increased prosperity and overall improvements in the health of both adults and children. However, it is evident that great inequality still exists and the health of the nation's children is a matter of concern, not only to individual children and families, but also to society in general.

As we investigate various aspects of child health we will discover that ill health can affect all areas of a child's development, not least their ability to learn and fulfil their potential. Various government and local agencies are involved in promoting child health and it is increasingly apparent that, in order to improve child health, agencies must work in partnership. This means that as an early years practitioner you have a key role in promoting child health, alongside agencies such as the National Health Service, Sure Start, DfES and local authorities.

THE MEANING OF HEALTH

If you ask your friends or colleagues to explain what 'health' means to them you will inevitably get a variety of responses. For some people, being healthy means that they are not ill. For others, being healthy means that they are well enough to carry out the tasks of everyday life. Other people take a holistic view that includes not only the absence of disease, but also the presence of good social support and a meaningful spiritual life.

What do children understand by the concept of being healthy? Traditionally, the views of children have not been sought. According to Mayall (1996, cited in David *et al.* 2003), children are the *objects* of health care and their views and opinions have not been seen as important. However, in a study of five- to six-year-old children, Mayall

REFLECTIVE ACTIVITY

Talk to the children you work with. What does being healthy or unhealthy mean to them?

noted that children did have an understanding of health, formed through informal learning at home.

Definitions of health

Health professionals use a variety of definitions to describe 'health'. One of the most influential definitions was formulated in 1946 by the World Health Organization (WHO). Health was defined as 'a state of complete physical, mental and social well-being and not merely the absence of disease or infirmity'. Although this definition was welcomed at the time for implying that health is more than simply not being ill, it was also criticised because, using this definition, a state of health is almost impossible to achieve. In 1984 WHO widened the definition to include the idea that health is a resource related to how well individuals can adapt and change. Health was defined as:

> the extent to which an individual or group is able on the one hand to realise aspirations and satisfy needs; and, on the other hand, to change or cope with the environment. Health is, therefore, seen as a resource for everyday life, not the objective of living; it is a positive concept emphasising social and personal resources, as well as physical capacities.

Generally, most health practitioners would agree that the concept of health is broad, meaning not just the absence of disease, but including the presence of social, cultural, spiritual, mental and emotional aspects.

The framework, *Birth to Three Matters* (DfES 2003) takes 'a healthy child' as one of its main themes. The components of this theme reflect the wide definition of health, as taken by early years educators, and consist of:

- emotional well-being
- growing and developing
- keeping safe
- healthy choices.

Measuring health

The government gathers statistics from a variety of sources in order to monitor the health of the nation. Hospitals, GP practices and registers of births and deaths all contribute information, as does the census that is held every ten years. Without such information the government would be unable to plan to meet health needs effectively. The information can also be used to make comparisons across time and across different communities. For instance, you may read that the infant mortality rate is higher in one country than another, or has been steadily improving over the years in this country.

Infant mortality

The infant mortality rate for a country is a good indicator of the overall level of development. For instance, in 1998 the infant mortality rate (per thousand births) for industrialised countries was 6. In sub-Saharan Africa, an area of extreme poverty, the rate was 107. The average infant mortality rate for the world was 59 (UNICEF 2000).

The figures for the UK in 2002 were as follows:

· Infant mortality dropped from 5.6 deaths per 1000 live births in 2001 to 5.2 deaths in 2002 in England and Wales.

· 68 per cent of these deaths occurred in the first month of life, the main causes being prematurity and congenital abnormality.

· Within the UK as a whole Northern Ireland had the lowest infant mortality rate (4.7) and Scotland the highest (5.3).

· Within England and Wales the lowest rate was 4.3, in the East and South-west. The highest was 6.6, in the West Midlands (Office for National Statistics 2004b).

The Office for National Statistics (2004a and b) also collects data about children's health from a variety of other sources.

REFLECTIVE ACTIVITY

Investigate The Health of Children and Young People website at http://www.statistics.gov.uk/children (accessed October 2004). There are 12 overviews which summarise the data in the reports. One of the overviews looks at social inequalities. What information does it give for differences in health between children from minority ethnic groups? Can you think of any reasons why these differences exist?

FACTORS THAT INFLUENCE HEALTH

As an early years professional you should have a good understanding of the factors that affect children's health. Without such an understanding it is difficult to formulate effective health promotion programmes for children and their families.

Tones and Tilford (2001) consider that 'the major determinant of health and illness is a complex web of social, psychological and structural interactions'. One way of understanding these interactions is to use the 'health field concept model' (Lalonde 1974). In this model, health and illness are seen to be influenced by four factors:

· genetics
· the environment
· lifestyle
· medical services.

Genetics

We all know that some illnesses 'run' in families. That is, the individual may be *genetically predisposed* to become ill. Sickle cell disorders and cystic fibrosis are examples of diseases that affect children, and which can be inherited from their parents. In these conditions, children with a particular genetic make-up will inevitably become ill. In some diseases the genetic influence is more subtle. In order for a disease to become manifest, certain environmental triggers need to be in place as well as genetic factors. For instance, a child may be born with the tendency to have allergic reactions, but these reactions will show themselves only if they come across triggers in the environment.

The environment

The environment has an influence on our health from the moment of conception. The developing foetus is at risk from the adverse effect of:

- drugs, alcohol and other toxins
- radiation
- infections
- poor maternal health and nutrition.

Once we are born, our health can be compromised by factors such as:

- inadequate nutrition
- poor housing
- infections
- drugs, alcohol and other toxins
- radiation/effects of the sun
- accidents
- stress.

One of the main contributions to improved child health in the last century was the provision of clean water. This single measure has had more of an effect on child health than the provision of up-to-date medical services. Both national and local government have a responsibility for public health, from refuse collection to environmental services that monitor hygiene in food outlets. In countries where there is no, or inadequate, public health enforcement, infant and child mortality from disease is much higher than in the UK.

Within the UK there are areas where the environment has a particularly detrimental effect on child health. Inner-city, industrialised, deprived areas generally have higher rates of infant mortality. In some rural areas children can suffer from the effects of agricultural spraying and polluted rivers.

Lifestyle

Most of us have a good idea of the lifestyle choices that affect our health; it is hard to escape exhortations to eat a balanced diet, drink alcohol in moderation, take exercise, not smoke or abuse drugs and attend regular health and dental check-ups. Yet many of us knowingly make health choices that may harm us, or find it very difficult to change our behaviour. Although there is much health promotional activity designed to encourage behavioural change, there is an increasing realisation that things are not as straightforward as they seem. For example, the average person eats less now than in the 1950s, but rates of obesity are rising. Our lifestyle has changed dramatically. Immediately post-war there were very few cars on the road; people used public transport, cycled or walked. Few households had television, so the population tended to sit in one position less, especially children, who would play outside. Many household tasks were labour intensive, burning more calories. Simply in the normal tasks of living people were more active.

Much media attention is being given to the problems of childhood obesity and the lack of exercise. There is a danger that a 'blame culture' is developing, whereby parents are held solely responsible for the inappropriate diets and lack of exercise of their children. However, unless we look at the influence of other factors, such as the use of modern technology and changes in the way we live, we will find it difficult to find effective interventions.

Household tasks used to burn more calories.

PAUSE FOR THOUGHT

What is the relative contribution of the NHS to the nation's health? What proportion of deaths can be prevented by good medical treatment?

Health and medical services

The National Health Service was set up in 1948, with the aim of providing free treatment throughout our lives.

The answers to the questions in the Pause for Thought activity may surprise you. The most important contributions to the nation's health are public health measures such as the provision of clean water, sanitation and decent housing. Adequate nutrition is also important. According to Jacobson *et al.* (1991), only about 5 per cent of deaths in the UK can be prevented by good medical care. Ewles and Simnett (1999) consider that the NHS has had disappointingly little impact on the nation's health. Only recently the Select Committee on Health reported that the NHS had, up until now, been unsuccessful in preventing and treating obesity. It made recommendations that involved a wide range of initiatives and government departments, not just the NHS (The UK Parliament 2004).

One area of the National Health Service that does have a direct effect on children's health is the programme of screening and surveillance that aims to detect potential difficulties early on so that appropriate measures can be put in place. The immunisation programme has been highly successful in reducing the incidence of mortality and morbidity among young children.

HEALTH INEQUALITIES

There is clear evidence of the importance of a 'healthy' environment in the early years in order to protect current health and prevent future ill-health. One factor that cannot be overlooked in providing a 'healthy' environment is an adequate income...

(British Medical Association 1999)

In recent years various reports have emphasised the link between relative poverty and ill health. In 1980 the Conservative government published the Black Report, outlining how the health of an individual could be affected by social inequalities.

In 1997 the newly elected Labour government asked Sir Donald Acheson to update the report. He found that there were noted inequalities:

- across classes
- between different racial, cultural and religious groups
- between the sexes
- across the age range
- between different geographical regions in the UK.

As a result of the Acheson Inquiry, the government made tackling health inequalities a priority, and in 2002 the cross-cutting review was published, outlining progress made. At that time it was found that wide-ranging inequalities were still exerting a powerful influence on the nation's health (Hyder and Mukherji 2004).

In July 2003 the government launched 'Tackling health inequalities: a programme for action'. The main aim of the programme was to reduce inequalities of health outcomes by 10 per cent, as measured by infant mortality and life expectancy at birth.

In response to the 2002 cross-cutting review, the Health Inequalities Unit was set up to oversee the cross-governmental programme. One of its aims is to support families, mothers and children. Key initiatives under this aim are the Sure Start initiatives and the introduction of Child Tax Credit.

The link between poverty and ill health
Infant mortality

Infant mortality is one of the most sensitive indicators of a nation's health (Spencer 2000). The 2002 cross-cutting review noted that infant mortality was highest in the lowest social classes. There are multiple factors that contribute to this difference in infant mortality, including:

· higher rates of smoking in social class V compared to social class I
· poor maternal nutrition in lower social groups
· maternal age, with higher infant deaths reported for teenage mothers
· poverty, lack of social support, parental ill health, drugs and alcohol problems.

Diet

Poverty affects the nutritional status of children with direct effects on their health.

· The number of mothers breastfeeding their children is related to indices of disadvantage. Younger mothers, those with less education and those from lower social classes tend to breastfeed less than more advantaged mothers (Hamlyn *et al.* 2000).
· Children living in poverty often do not get adequate nutrition, with a lack of fresh fruit and vegetables and an over-reliance on foods high in sugar and fat. This can adversely affect children's ability to learn, can increase the risk of infection and can lead to children being either overweight or underweight. Poor nutrition in childhood is also linked to cardiovascular disease in adulthood (Graham and Power 2004). In a

study of 55 families on a low income it was found that 28 per cent of children never ate green vegetables or salad and 10 per cent of children never ate fruit. The study showed that to eat healthily costs significantly more than to eat unhealthily (NCH 2004). The government-sponsored School Fruit and Vegetable Scheme is one initiative aimed at increasing fruit and vegetable consumption in young children.

- There are well-documented links between disadvantage and dental disease in children, related to poor diet and lifestyle factors. In 2000 it was reported that young children living in the poorest (non-fluoridated) communities suffered almost six times as much dental decay as children in better off or fluoridated communities (NAEDH 2000).

Accidents

Children from disadvantaged families are much more likely to be involved in accidents than other children. Children aged up to 14 from unskilled families are five times more likely to die in an accident than children from professional families, and 15 times more likely to die in a fire at home (End Child Poverty 2002).

Environment

David *et al.* (2003) note that disadvantaged families are often adversely affected by the environment in which they live, as they are more likely to live in polluted, industrialised areas. Poor housing is another factor that can compromise the health of children and has been linked to higher rates of illness (Thompson *et al.* 2001).

CHILD HEALTH SURVEILLANCE

The health and development of babies and children is monitored from the time that women know they are pregnant until children leave school. Child health surveillance consists of three elements:

1. Surveillance. This involves periodic checks on a child's developmental progress, with the aim of detecting illness or abnormality so that interventions can be implemented as soon as possible.

2. Screening for specific conditions. Screening tests are procedures that are designed to be brief, cheap and reliable, so they can be undertaken on all children. Screening tests include procedures to test for dislocated hips in newborns, and blood tests to find out if new babies have thyroid deficiency.

3. A planned schedule of immunisations.

Screening/surveillance

Until recently child health surveillance was based primarily on a medical model, with the emphasis on screening for disorders. Recently the Royal College of Paediatrics and Child Health published a report, *Health for all Children* (Hall and Elliman 2003), in which proposals were made to place greater emphasis on health promotion and targeting children and families at risk.

The proposals include:

- targeting families most in need
- a core programme of screening, developmental checks, immunisation and health promotion advice for all families
- additional inter-agency support for families in need
- more emphasis on promoting a healthy lifestyle
- using the skills of other professionals, such as early years practitioners, to promote healthy living messages and to observe child development.

Your role as an early years practitioner is key to these proposals, and senior practitioners with the foundation degree will be at the forefront of new initiatives.

Immunisation

According to Karnes (2004: 694), 'immunisation has become a triumphal success in reducing morbidity and mortality during the last 50 years. The administration of vaccines during infancy has saved lives and improved quality of life by preventing diseases and their complications'. Globally, immunisation is the most cost-effective medical treatment available. It has been so effective in the case of smallpox that this disease has been eradicated and children no longer need to be immunised against it (Hyder and Mukherji 2004).

There are many parents who worry about their children being immunised because, on very rare occasions, children have been damaged by the treatment. Recently there has been a scare about the combined measles, mumps and rubella (MMR) vaccination. In 1998 the medical journal *The Lancet* published a report by Dr Andrew Wakefield and others from the Royal Free Hospital in London, outlining a link between the MMR vaccination and the onset of autism. This was taken up by the media and, as a result, many parents became fearful about having their children vaccinated. Despite many further studies to the contrary, some parents remain convinced that the immunisation is harmful. Sadly we are seeing a rise in the number of children contracting measles, a trend likely to lead to increased morbidity and mortality.

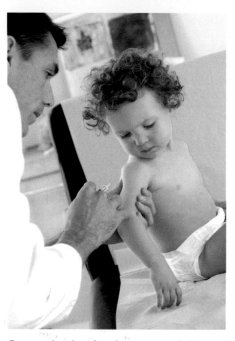

Immunisation has been successful in reducing illness in children.

What is the role of the early years practitioner in all this? You are seen as an expert in health matters by the parents of the children for whom you care, and you may be asked about whether or not a child should be vaccinated. Whatever your personal opinion, you have a professional responsibility to point out that none of the latest studies have shown any links between the combined MMR and autism. The NHS has put together a website to answer questions that parents may have about MMR (http://www.mmrthefacts.nhs.uk accessed November 2004).

EMOTIONAL WELL-BEING

At the beginning of the chapter we discussed the *holistic* nature of health. As an early years practitioner you have a responsibility to monitor a child's mental health and to promote emotional well-being.

Factors affecting the mental health of children and young people

In 2001 the DfES produced a report entitled 'Promoting children's mental health within early years and school settings'. The report defines mental health as being 'about maintaining a good level of personal and social functioning', and highlights some experiences that can potentially result in an increased risk of mental health difficulties:

- loss or separation – resulting from death, parental separation, divorce, hospitalisation, loss of friendships (especially in adolescence), family breakdown (when a child has to live elsewhere)
- life changes (e.g. birth of a sibling, moving house, changing schools)
- traumatic events – abuse, violence, accidents, injuries, war or natural disasters.

Although we have an understanding of what may contribute to a lack of emotional well-being, it is difficult to predict which children will be affected. Two dimensions, risk and resilience, have been proposed by researchers Rutter and Smith (1995) to explain these differences (as discussed below).

Risk factors

Risk factors increase the probability of a child developing mental health problems – they may be within the child themselves, within the family or within the wider environment. Risk factors in the child can include illness, special needs or difficult temperament. Risk factors in the family can include parental conflict, child abuse, illness or inappropriate parenting.

Resilience/protective factors

A child's ability to be resilient depends upon the protective factors that enable them to overcome difficulty. Again, they may be within the child themselves, within the family or within the broader environment. Resilience factors in the child include being female, of high intelligence, with good communication skills. Resilience factors in the family include at least one good parent–child relationship, clear, firm discipline and support for education.

Good quality early years care and education are an effective way of promoting emotional well-being for children. Many children, who may otherwise have become mentally ill, have been protected because of the warm, stable, affirming relationships built up with their early years practitioners. Protective factors within settings include:

- stable childcare arrangements so that children interact with just a few caregivers in one day; an efficient key worker system
- low staff turnover so that children are cared for by the same adults over several years
- good staff training in child development
- adequate child to staff ratios
- positive behaviour management
- an atmosphere that values difference and promotes self-esteem.

A warm relationship with an early years practitioner can promote emotional well-being.

Well-being and the curriculum

The Curriculum Guidance for the Foundation Stage sets out key principles for early years practitioners in relation to children's personal, social and emotional development:

- establishing constructive relationships with children, with other practitioners, between practitioners and children, with parents and with workers from other agencies, that take account of differences and different needs and expectations
- planning activities that promote emotional, moral, spiritual and social development alongside intellectual development
- providing support and a structured approach to achieve the successful social and emotional development of vulnerable children and those with particular behavioural and communication difficulties.

In *Birth to Three Matters*, one of the components of 'a healthy child' is emotional well-being. The important factors are:

- being special to someone
- being able to express feelings
- developing healthy dependence
- developing healthy independence.

PAUSE FOR THOUGHT

How important is the concept of well-being in your setting? Look at all aspects of the care and education that the children receive. Is there room for improvement? If you work with very young children you may have a key worker system, but does it work in practice? Observe a child during the course of one day. How many adults is the child interacting with? Is it considered important that key workers undertake all the routine activities with their key child?

NUTRITION

Poor nutrition in childhood not only contributes directly to ill health but also contributes to ill health as an adult. Diets that are high in fat, sugar and salt, low in fruit and vegetables and are unvaried can lead to anaemia, dental decay and obesity in children. Children who receive an inadequate diet are more likely to suffer diabetes, heart disease and cancer as adults (Hyder and Mukherji 2004).

Models of nutrition

The medical model involves looking at nutrition in terms of food groups, physiology and biochemistry. It concentrates on looking at the foods we need to eat to prevent illness (Fieldhouse 1996). However, many of the decisions we make about what foods to eat, or what foods to give to infants, are influenced by social and cultural factors. The cultural model of nutrition recognises that food has great cultural and social significance. As an early years practitioner you need to be aware of this significance, and be sensitive to the various views and attitudes about food that you will encounter.

Nutrition in pregnancy

Low birth weight often occurs because of poor maternal health and nutrition and poor foetal health. In the UK maternal nutrition is usually adequate, although teenage mothers are at risk of poor nutrition and having a baby of low birth weight. This is because they are still growing and their bodies compete with the foetus for the nutrients they both need. Mothers who are obese in pregnancy are at significantly increased risk of complications during pregnancy and have a greater risk of still birth (Sebire *et al.* 2001). Obesity in mothers has also been related to a 30–40 per cent increase in the chance of giving birth to a baby with major birth defects (Deckelbaum 2002).

Infant feeding

Human milk is the appropriate food for human babies. The World Health Organization recognises that infant feeding is the 'cornerstone of care for childhood development. Worldwide about 30 per cent of children under five are stunted as a consequence of poor feeding and repeated infections' (WHO 2004). The organisation recommends that babies are exclusively breastfed up until the age of six months, when the baby can gradually be introduced to other, appropriate foods. Breastfeeding should continue up to two years or beyond.

In the UK there has been a rise in the number of mothers who breastfeed. The latest infant feeding survey of 2000 reported that 70 per cent of mothers in the UK commence breastfeeding (Hamlyn *et al.* 2000).

The benefits of breastfeeding

Breast milk is the most appropriate food for babies for the following reasons:

- it has the correct composition, changing to meet the nutritional needs of babies as they grow
- it changes composition during a feed, the first milk being designed to quench thirst with the hind milk being richer, satisfying a baby's hunger
- it temporarily passes on the mother's immunity to some infections
- it gives long-term health benefits to the baby (breastfed babies tend not to be overweight, have a higher IQ and have less heart disease as adults)
- it helps mothers to regain their figure, reduces fertility, is convenient and cost-effective.

Bottle-feeding

Some mothers may find establishing breastfeeding difficult or may have been advised not to breastfeed for health reasons. In the minority ('developed') world, a mother who is HIV positive will be advised not to breastfeed because there is a risk of the virus being transmitted to the baby via breast milk. In parts of the world where it is difficult to bottle-feed safely because of poor hygiene conditions, it is safer for the baby to be breastfed. (The risk of dying from a gastric infection is higher than the risk of contracting HIV.)

For some mothers, bottle-feeding fits in better with their lifestyle than breastfeeding, and it must be recognised that many millions of babies have been successfully bottle-fed and have grown up to suffer no obvious ill effects. As an early years practitioner it is your role to supply mothers with up-to-date information about the benefits of breastfeeding and to encourage it, but you should also respect a mother's decision to bottle feed and not make her feel guilty. If she does decide to bottle-feed, the following factors must be taken into consideration:

- Only modified cows' milk should be used. Cows' milk that has not been altered to make it suitable for babies must not be used until the child is at least one year old. No baby should be put onto non-milk products such as Soya baby milks unless this has been expressly advised by a paediatrician.

- More expensive follow-on or progress milks designed for babies of over six months of age are not needed.
- Cows' milk can be used from one year, but it must be full fat.
- Strict hygiene must be used in the making and storing of feeds.
- Bottle-feeding should always be carried out in such a way that babies are given the same close comfort as they would have if they were breastfed.

Weaning

The term 'weaning' has two distinct meanings in infant nutrition:

- the cutting off of the infant's access to human milk (weaning off the breast)
- the gradual process of accustoming children to foods eaten by adults.

Weaning off the breast

The process of weaning a child off the breast is bound by social and cultural factors, and the age at which a child is weaned is subject to great variation. The World Health Organization recommends that breastfeeding should continue until the infant is two years old (or older). In the UK only a small minority of babies are still breastfed by four months. Mothers who persist in breastfeeding until their children are two are considered to be a little 'unusual'. Mothers who breastfeed until the third or fourth years are often met with condemnation, the situation being perceived as 'not quite nice'. Expectations are very different in other countries, where babies are breastfed until the next child is conceived (often not until the first child is three because of the contraceptive effects of breastfeeding). If the baby is the last in a family it is often much later (Karnes 2004).

Weaning onto adult foods

The World Health Organization recommends that weaning onto foods other than milk should not occur until the child is six months of age. The age when weaning is initiated, the process and typical weaning foods are, again, subject to great cultural variation. In most cultures the first solid food that is introduced is usually a 'staple', such as a grain, tuber, root or fruit, which has been cooked or softened with milk or cooking liquid.

As an early years practitioner you may be involved in weaning babies. The following are factors to consider:

- Weaning should occur when the child is about six months old. By then, babies have used up stores of some nutrients that they were born with, which cannot be replaced by a diet of breast milk only. In particular, babies of this age need extra protein, vitamins A and D and iron.

- Because they are growing, babies need increased energy. The volume of milk needed to supply this energy is too much for their small stomachs to deal with, so more concentrated forms of energy are required.

- Chewing helps the development of speech, and for that reason weaning should not be left much later than six months. In addition, there seems to be a critical period when infants are particularly ready to experience new tastes and textures. Babies who are not weaned until the end of the first year often do not take to it very easily as the process is lengthened.

- Weaning is a gradual process. Although the child needs extra nutrients, it is not a 'life or death' situation. One can afford to be relaxed and let the baby take the lead. The main goal is that the baby is eating family food, more or less, by about a year.

- It is recommended that first foods are puréed fruits and vegetables and non-wheat cereals. No sugar, salt or egg should be offered to the baby. It is important that 'baby' cereals are used. There have been occasions where babies have become very ill or have even died because they were fed an adult cereal with high salt levels.

- Over the next few months the proportion of solid food to milk increases, but at one year old a child still needs one pint of full-fat milk a day. The texture of the foods will vary from runny, at first, to mashed, chopped and finally cut up.

- Babies should be offered drinks in addition to milk. They should be given in a cup, not a bottle and should be restricted to water or diluted pure fruit juices. No tea, coffee or sugary drinks should be offered.

Nutrition and the under-fives

It is during these early years that many of our attitudes towards food are laid down. Children are affected by the attitudes and behaviour of those who care for them. If mealtimes become a source of conflict and stress, children will not learn the pleasures of enjoying food in a social situation. Instead food may be seen as an agent of control or punishment. This could lead to distorted attitudes towards eating as an adult. Erratic mealtimes or allowing a child to fill up on sweets and biscuits may lead to a child never experiencing hunger or enjoying a nutritious balanced meal when it is offered. The following guidelines may help to ensure mealtimes are a happy, relaxed time for all involved.

- Children should enjoy mealtimes and relish the opportunity to socialise with other children and adults in an unhurried, relaxed manner.

- Children should be encouraged to choose what they would like to eat from a range of healthy options and should be given the knowledge to be able to choose healthy food. Family, religious and cultural preferences should be honoured.

- Children should be encouraged to be adventurous eaters and sample different foods and combinations of food.

- Let children eat their food in the way they feel most comfortable with. Some families do not use cutlery – instead children are taught to eat neatly with the fingers of one hand. Forcing children to eat with a knife and fork can cause distress. If staff eat with the children and model how to use cutlery, children will soon follow.

- Do not expect very young children to sit at the table for too long. Make sure food is ready before you sit them down and allow toddlers to leave the table when they have finished.

- Involving children in food preparation and laying the table will encourage them to be adventurous in trying food.

Mealtimes should be happy and relaxed

Guidelines for children under five

- Because children have small stomachs, the food they are given should be nutritionally dense. They need a higher proportion of fat in their diet than adults and they should only be given a little high-fibre food such as whole-wheat pasta and brown bread and rice. It has been found that fibre in food prevents the efficient absorption of some nutrients.
- Children under five need small, frequent meals. A nutritious snack mid-morning and mid-afternoon is recommended, such as a banana or a small cheese sandwich.
- Children need iron-rich foods such as meat, well-cooked eggs, pulses and leafy green vegetables. Food rich in vitamin C, such as an orange or kiwi fruit, should be offered at the same time, as this aids the absorption of iron.
- Unless a child is eating well and receiving the nutrients they need, vitamins A, C and D should be given as a supplement.
- Children need one pint of full-fat milk a day from the age of one year. If children are the correct weight for their height they can be given semi-skimmed milk from the age of two years. Skimmed milk should only be given to children over five, and only then if they are thriving.
- No added salt or sugar should be used in children's meals. Pre-prepared food often contains high levels of salt and sugar and should be avoided. In addition, pre-prepared food contains many additives. We should aim to give children food that is as free from added chemicals as possible.
- Children should be encouraged to drink water or milk if they are thirsty. They should not be given tea or coffee, nor should they be given sugary drinks or those containing artificial sweeteners.
- Above all children need a balanced diet. A balanced diet is one where children are encouraged to eat a variety of foods, in different combinations, from the four main food groups each day.

PAUSE FOR THOUGHT

Review the way your setting provides for children's nutritional needs.

HEALTH PROMOTION AND THE EARLY YEARS PRACTITIONER

It is clear from an analysis of the factors promoting health that as an early years practitioner you are in a good position not only to influence positively the health of the children in your care, but also to be a positive influence on the health of the families who use the setting. Unfortunately, research undertaken for the Health Education Board for Scotland (HEBS) in 2003 revealed that, in a study of early years practitioners in Scotland, practitioners were taking a rather narrow approach. There were four main areas of concern:

1. There was too much reliance on discrete health education themes rather than taking a holistic, unified approach.

2. Health initiatives tended to focus on the physical aspects of a child's development, neglecting the social and emotional aspects of keeping healthy and making healthy decisions.

3. Early years practitioners had a narrow understanding of health.

4. Early years practitioners failed to see how working more closely with parents is crucial if health messages are to be reinforced in the home.

Defining health promotion

Any definition of 'health promotion' will need to be wide, to encompass its holistic nature. Downie et al. (1996) suggest that health promotion is essentially about preventing ill health and encouraging positive health. The World Health Organization's definition (1984) states that 'health promotion is the process of enabling people to increase control over, and improve, their health.' According to Naidoo and Wills (2000), there are five main approaches to health promotion:

1. medical or preventive

2. behavioural change

3. educational

4. empowerment

5. social change.

If we consider these approaches in relation to childhood obesity, the *medical* approach would be to search for appetite-suppressing drugs or surgical interventions to prevent food being digested.

The *behavioural change* approach would focus on helping the child change eating behaviour (e.g. always eating at the table, not eating in front of the TV, using a smaller plate, keeping only healthy snacks in the fridge). Taking more exercise would also be part of a behavioural change approach.

The *educational* approach would concentrate on educating the child about eating five portions of fruit and vegetables a day, explaining about the role of the various nutrients in the diet and how to choose less fattening foods.

REFLECTIVE ACTIVITY

As an early years practitioner, outline ways in which you and your colleagues could promote good dental care for children in the foundation stage. Use the five approaches to health promotion to help you. Try to use the findings of the HEBS research as an additional guide.

The *empowerment* approach would be to help the child be assertive and ask parents and school to provide suitable food, and to be able to choose a healthy meal when out with friends instead of a fatty burger and chips.

The *social change* approach would look at local and national initiatives (e.g. providing healthy food in schools, legislating to prevent parking near schools so that parents are encouraged to walk children to school). Legislation to reduce the advertising of unhealthy foods during children's TV programmes would be an aspect of social change, as would any initiative to reduce inequalities within society.

Developing a health promotion programme

There are several steps to take when planning a health promotion programme in an early years setting:

- the identification of needs and priorities
- setting aims and objectives
- deciding on the best way to achieve these aims
- identification of resource needs and available resources
- evaluation
- action plan.

The identification of needs and priorities

These will be different for every setting. They may originate from observation of a particular child or group of children's needs, or be part of a locally or nationally driven initiative. Sure Start areas and local health authorities all have priorities for health promotion objectives and you may be involved in an initiative that involves other establishments in your area. National health promotion initiatives may also guide your identification of priorities.

It is at this stage that you will need to involve all interested parties in planning meetings. This will include not only the staff, but also parents and representatives from outside agencies who may be involved, or who may be willing to help.

Setting aims and objectives

In any health promotion campaign you need to be clear about your aims and objectives. These need to be incorporated in your short-, medium- and long-term planning. Aims and objectives should not only focus on the individual child, but should also include the wider community of the setting and the parents. In the case of healthy eating, you may decide that one of your aims is to redesign the setting's menus and to introduce healthy snacks instead of sweets and crisps. An aim that involves parents may be to encourage parents to provide healthy lunch boxes. Any planning you do will also link into your planning according to the foundation stage curriculum, *Birth to Three Matters*.

Deciding on the best ways to achieve your aims

You will need to consider a meeting with parents so that they can become actively involved. Make use of local experts who may come in to talk to parents. It is especially important to be creative in involving parents who may be excluded, for instance, parents with special needs, work commitments or those who need a translator.

When introducing health promotion activities to children you should be using the same principles that you would use in any other aspect of early years education.

Identifying resource needs and available resources

- Early years magazines, such as *Nursery World* and *Early Years Educator*, often have resources that you can use in health promotion activities with children.
- Local health authorities often have a health promotion library, which will lend out materials for use in early years settings.
- Government websites, such as http://www.healthpromotionagency.org.uk and http://www.wiredforhealth.gov.uk, are useful sources of information, as are the websites for organisations such as the British Dental Association (http://www.bda-dentistry.org.uk/) – all accessed October 2004.

Evaluation

When planning a health promotion campaign you should consider how you will evaluate the success of the campaign. The methods you will use should be agreed at the initial planning stage and should be linked to your aims and objectives. For instance, you may have wanted to help children develop the skills of effective hand washing and to develop appropriate hand-washing habits. An evaluation could involve observing the children at the start of the programme and observing them afterwards to see if there is an improvement in the frequency and efficiency of hand washing.

Action plan

After the evaluation stage the staff team should get together to review how well the programme went. You need to go back to your initial aims and objectives and discuss whether these were met. Inevitably, there will have been aspects of the programme that did not go as well as expected. You may be able to identify specific reasons for this and make suggestions for changes for the next time. Observing the children's learning and involvement will give you ideas for extension activities based on the children's developing interests and needs. Obtaining feedback from parents is important. Parents may want to carry the health promotion programme further and consider acting as a group to elicit change at a local level. From this information you can develop an action plan for future work in this area.

Personal care routines

Many of the factors that contribute to keeping healthy are habits laid down in early childhood. Early years practitioners have an important part to play in helping children establish health routines that will stay with them throughout life.

Health routines include:

- efficient hand-washing after going to the toilet and before preparing and eating food
- independent self-care when going to the toilet
- the correct use of tissues when coughing or nose-blowing
- correct teeth-brushing technique and oral hygiene
- independent dressing skills and protection from the sun
- routines surrounding mealtimes.

Care routines need to be carefully considered. Children learn these routines by copying other children and adults, so it is important that adults are good role models. For instance, children need to see you, as a practitioner, washing your hands efficiently and disposing of used tissues appropriately.

REFLECTIVE ACTIVITY

Identify a care routine in your workplace. Break down the routine into the various steps involved and the key skills that you are trying to teach. Look carefully at the way routines are organised to see where significant changes could be made. Sometimes changes will open up new avenues of learning.

GLOSSARY

Incidence The number of new cases of a disease occurring over a particular time.

Infant mortality rate The number of deaths in infants under one year per thousand live births registered.

Morbidity Information about specific diseases.

Mortality The ages at which people die and the causes of death.

Screening Brief, simple, cheap and reliable tests or procedures on a large group of individuals to check for the presence of a treatable condition.

Surveillance The process of watching over. In child health, surveillance consists of the periodic assessment of children's developmental progress.

KEY TEXTS

Bradshaw, J. 2002: *The Well-being of Children in the UK*. London: Save the Children.

David, T., Goouch, K., Powell, S. and Abbott, L. 2003: *Birth to Three Matters: A Review of the Literature*. Nottingham: DfES Publications, ch. 6.

End Child Poverty 2002: *Child Poverty and Health: A Briefing Paper*. http://www.ecpc.org.uk (accessed October 2004).

Graham, H. and Power, C. 2004: *Childhood Disadvantage and Adult Health: A Life Course Framework*. Health Development Agency NHS: http://www.hda.nhs.uk/evidence (accessed October 2004).

Parliamentary Office of Science and Technology 2003: *Improving Children's Diet*. POST: http://www.parliament.uk/post (accessed October 2004), Report 199, September.

LANGUAGE AND LITERACY

3

> **IN THIS CHAPTER WE WILL CONSIDER THE FOLLOWING TOPICS:**
>
> ✳ Learning to communicate
> ✳ Being bilingual/multilingual
> ✳ Playing with language
> ✳ Developing literacy.

This chapter explores the development of communication during the early years. Language learning as a process continues throughout our lives – even as adults we continue to extend the vocabulary of our first language, become familiar with words from other languages and try out new modes of written and spoken communication. Young children are only at the very beginning of their personal journey; they must learn to use a variety of different means of communication in order to express themselves and respond to others. We will consider how children establish reciprocal communicative relationships with those around them. Then we will look at how speech gradually develops – often in a number of different languages – and consider how formal literacy is acquired. We will consider your role as practitioner in this process and, most importantly, examine the exploratory and playful ways in which children practise their linguistic and literary skills.

LEARNING TO COMMUNICATE

First language acquisition

All babies are born with natural communication strategies. From their very first days, babies begin to communicate with those around them through crying, eye contact and bodily movements. Research also shows that newborns can recognise their carers' voices, and can discriminate between their mother tongue and other languages (Karmiloff and Karmiloff-Smith 2001). Communication gradually becomes more reciprocal in nature: the five-month-old baby is capable of communicative turn-taking with another person. Babies have been shown to take part in what are known as proto-conversations: the baby will coo, pause for a reply and then wait for the respondent to stop before they continue with the next stage of the 'conversation'. In this way the baby demonstrates a fundamental aptitude for interaction with others.

Babies are surrounded by sound in the environment. They hear spoken language, adult conversation, songs and rhymes and, simultaneously, they begin to experiment with their own capacity to produce sounds (cooing). As their speech begins to develop, babies

enjoy practising (often even when alone), using a range of random sounds that can be found in languages from around the world (Gopnik *et al.* 1999). Gradually, as they hear their carers talking, they begin to distinguish those sounds particular to their home environment and stop practising the sounds they do not hear.

In this way, all babies begin babbling at around six months in an international tongue, but slowly lose this capacity as their first proper language develops. Eventually the speech patterns, rhythms and intonations of their home language are also evident in their babbling, even though no individual words are recognisable. At this stage adults often attempt to make meaning from the sentences and respond as if they understand what is being said. This encourages the young child to continue these attempts at conversation and in so doing helps to develop these vital skills. Babies are great mimics, and from around eight months they begin to repeat simple sounds (echolalia) as part of a game with adults.

Young children are excellent communicators long before they are able to utter their first words. Their wishes and needs can be communicated, pre-linguistically, through pointing with a finger, making eye contact by gazing at the desired object or trying to move towards such an object physically. Before children can utter more than a few recognisable words they already understand a vocabulary of more than 50 words (known as receptive language). At around one year, they are capable of responding to simple instructions relating to frequently used vocabulary.

Expressive language use begins in their second year of life, when they begin to employ a limited number of words to express their needs and interests. A child's first spoken words often relate to food, toys and favoured adults. The term 'holophrase' refers to the use of single words alongside gestures and eye-movements that babies use to get across their message (Bee 1997). Once they become interested in speech and understand that everything in their environment has a name, toddlers enjoy acquiring new vocabulary by requiring those around them to name objects. They will point to things that interest them and expect adults to name them; this vocabulary is then stored for later use (Gopnik *et al.* 1999). These strategies enable children to begin to gain a little more control over their own environment. Once they begin to use single words to name items, they will overgeneralise their use (known as overextension). For example, all animals might be referred to as 'cat' and, of course, all males are 'Daddy' (which has been known to cause some embarrassment!).

Between 18 months and 2 years of age, once they have an expressive vocabulary of at least 50 words, they begin to produce two-word sentences such as 'Mummy's cake'. These utterances, often comprising two nouns, can represent a statement of fact, a question or even a demand. Facial expression, intonation and gesture all assist interpretation of meaning, and in this way children are able to communicate with those around them in a very simple yet effective way.

The next phase is termed telegraphic speech because, like an old-fashioned telegram, it uses only the bare minimum of words (Karmiloff and Karmiloff-Smith 2001). All the most important elements of a sentence are used, but indefinite articles, plural endings, auxiliary verbs and connectives are missed out. This produces sentences such as 'Granny go shop?' The average three-year-old will have a working vocabulary of more than a thousand words, but it takes a further two years before children fully integrate the grammatical constructions used by the adults they converse with.

Current debates

There are a number of different theories relating to the acquisition of language. Whitehead (1997) discusses four types of approach:

- behaviourist
- nativist
- cognitive
- social-interactionist.

Behaviourist approaches – sometimes referred to as learning theory (Garton and Pratt 2002) – suggest that children learn to speak in an imitative way. In keeping with traditional behaviourist theories, children's attempts at imitation of the speech they hear around them are reinforced – they receive adult approval or have their demands met. This approach suggests that children cannot form innovative sentences, but can only repeat what they have already heard.

The behaviourist stance has been challenged by those assuming a nativist approach, such as Noam Chomsky, who believe that the human brain is programmed to produce unique utterances. Chomsky considers that humans are born with an inbuilt disposition towards acquiring language patterns and grammar; he terms this the 'language acquisition device' (LAD) (Chomsky 1965). He believes that this helps to explain why children are able to make up unique sentences which they have never heard. He also considers this to be the explanation for children's misuse of grammatical constructions, such as 'I goed over to my friend's house and then I comed home'. It is unlikely that a child would have heard these particular conjugations of the verbs 'to come' and 'to go' in adult speech; nor would they have received specific instruction in grammar! What they have done is to listen to the numerous English verbs which do end in 'ed' when describing past events and then overused the rule. Children all pass through this phase before they finally grasp correct grammatical constructions.

The cognitive approach suggests that language development is maturational and that, in a Piagetian manner, children's ability to communicate ideas develops alongside their cognitive understanding, with even the simplest of two-word utterances being imbued with deeper complexities. On the other hand, the social-interactionist approach concentrates on the fact that children learn to communicate within a social context. Bruner (1985), believing that language development is supported by adults (and more able speakers), coined the term 'language acquisition support system' (LASS). In this approach, language development is a result of interpersonal communication.

It is clear that all the approaches have some merit and, as with so many debates, there is no right or wrong answer. A number of important research projects in the 1980s focused on the social-interactionist perspective (see Wells 1987; Tizard and Hughes 1984; Heath 1983) and are still worthy of consideration. These studies investigated the use of children's language in the home and other settings, and they all acknowledged the important influence of the social interaction that takes place within the family unit.

Functions of language

REFLECTIVE ACTIVITY

Make a list of all the different types of conversation you had yesterday. Consider *who* you spoke to, the *context* and the *content* of each exchange.

When you look at the list you will notice that you used a wide range of different types of communication, such as the following:

- a chat with a friend/colleague
- an argument with your partner
- giving instructions to a child or adult
- a formal telephone conversation
- a discussion on practice/policy at your workplace
- an interview with a parent/carer.

We adjust our way of talking to take into account the relationship we have with the person with whom we are communicating, the context in which the conversation takes place and the subject matter.

Consider the tone, content and type of language you would use when talking to a colleague about:

- a child's behaviour
- an Ofsted report
- the recipe for a special dessert
- plans for a wedding party.

Thus we can see that speech has many functions, and as a practitioner you must recognise that children need to experience and experiment with language and conversation in a wide range of contexts and with multiple purposes. Halliday (1975) and Tough (1977) have considered the development of children's ability to express themselves for different purposes. Halliday's seven 'Phase 1 functions' have attempted to categorise the early social use of language. These include the instrumental function ('I want') and the regulatory function ('do as I tell you') (Halliday 1975: 19–21). Even at the earliest stages, when using just three-word sentences, a child is, for example, able to convey a message of regulation – 'Mummy no go!'

Children need opportunities to talk to different audiences, to explain, describe, ask, instruct and problem solve. Tough (1977: 44–45) describes four functions relating to language use for three-year-olds: directive, interpretative, projective and relational; each helps the child to achieve different communicative purposes. At first children find it easier to converse with adults, who are better able to interpret their meaning, but gradually their conversational skills become an essential part of their social interaction with their peers. Furthermore, to engage in complex cooperative play situations, particularly imaginative scenarios, children need to be able to communicate ideas, discuss and negotiate with each another. The most verbally fluent child often gets to direct the action!

REFLECTIVE ACTIVITY

Posing questions:

Most children will pass through the 'why stage', asking for explanations of everything until adults are frequently exasperated. However, recently a student who had been observing children's use of language in her workplace was astonished to realise how difficult children of nursery age found it to compose a question. Children in the nursery were routinely given the opportunity to talk on a subject of interest as part of a 'show and tell' session. The nursery staff decided to introduce the concept of asking questions to get further information/clarification from the speaker. They were astonished to find that given this specific forum, even the most vocal of children could not think of a single question to ask the child who had given the talk. The student had to model several questions herself before any of the audience grasped the concept. As a result, the staff decided to repeat this type of activity and ensure that children were given more opportunities to engage in dialogue and discussion.

Language and thought

Language is regarded as a tool not just for communication, but also for thought. Vygotsky and Piaget held some conflicting views on this question (Wood 1988). Piaget (1959) considered that, at first, language is used internally, as a set of symbols, representing their actions as the young child plays and explores, adjusting their understanding of the world. Thus in his view, language and thought develop simultaneously. On the other hand, Vygotsky (1986) considered that children first use language to think aloud, processing their ideas, and that it is a later stage of development when children become able to internalise these thoughts. A useful analogy here is when young children first begin to learn to read, they find it very hard to read silently. Similarly, children can often be heard talking themselves through an activity or procedure, and this appears to aid their concentration and problem-solving skills.

It is clear that language facilitates cognitive development. Without language, expressing time, feelings and beliefs (decontextualised thoughts) is very difficult. Sacks (1990) discusses the difficulty for profoundly deaf children in expressing themselves beyond the here and now. Without language, conversations using facial expression and gesture have to be conducted in the present. This is remedied for such children once they begin to use a sign language, where full expression is possible. However, Sacks warns that some deaf children can find problem solving difficult as they may not have had as many opportunities to speculate and consider issues across time and space.

Cultural influences

Since language develops in a social context, it is clear that cultural influences will affect children's use of language. Language wields power, and the way that people speak and the vocabulary and grammar they use can affect their confidence and indeed their status within society. 'Received pronunciation' (known as 'RP') has been associated historically with education and status, and until quite recently people with regional and non-RP accents felt compelled to alter their speech patterns if they wished to move on professionally.

Bernstein (1975) discussed two different types of language code used by families, the 'elaborate' and 'restricted' codes. This view suggested that the use of an elaborate speech code includes descriptive and explanatory uses of language within the family context, while those households using a restricted code tend to be more regulatory, with a great deal of conversation relating to instructions and rules. However, Tizard and Hughes' (1984) study of four-year-old girls demonstrated that it was the richness and frequency of the interactions between mothers and their daughters that was important, rather than the speech code used within the family setting.

Different groups within British society enjoy sharing a particular vernacular, which can be used to express their community's character and reinforce the cohesion of a social group. For example, there are numerous accents which are associated with geographical locations in the Greater London area. These subtle differences in accent may be missed by people from other parts of the country, but a Londoner can usually tell whether someone lives north or south of the River Thames! Similarly, cockney rhyming slang was a dialect used to set people from the East End of London apart from their neighbours, although it is not commonly used anymore.

Cultural references are an important way of helping people to feel part of the community, and how people express themselves linguistically is a significant part of their identity. Some groups in society may use a specific vocabulary to set themselves apart from others, and even deliberately to confuse or exclude outsiders. All these variations on 'standard English' (defined below) contain cultural references, and over time a number will be absorbed into the mainstream language.

- Standard English: the language of public communication (DfEE 1998).
- Dialect: a regional variation of a language with some unique vocabulary and syntax.
- Patois: a language which combines the vocabulary of one existing language with the grammar of another.
- Pidgin: a simple language that develops when two or more communities need to communicate, historically for trading purposes.
- Creole: a pidgin language that has evolved into mainstream usage and becomes the first language of a community.
- Slang: informal vocabulary particular to a group of people.
- Received pronunciation: a prestigious accent which is considered to reflect the higher social and educational background of the speaker.

Recent curriculum reforms have emphasised the requirement for familiarity with standard spoken and written English within the educational context. This means that children need to be able to produce standard English in school, even if they do not speak it in their home context.

BEING BILINGUAL/MULTILINGUAL

Home languages

We live in a multicultural and multilingual society and this must be reflected in the way we approach language development in early years settings. In many communities in Britain, families speak a number of languages other than English in their homes. Language diversity should be considered an asset rather than a challenge (Cummins and Swain 1986), with positive aspects for all children in a community.

Some children develop two languages from the moment they begin to communicate. These children are known as 'simultaneous bilinguals' and often have parents who have different languages of origin. These children are fortunate in developing an enhanced capacity for language acquisition and often go on to speak numerous languages. Simultaneous bilinguals enjoy a rich verbal environment where language 'mixing' and 'switching' take place within the home (Alladina 1995). Family members frequently mix vocabulary from their shared languages in their conversations, often producing sentences made up of words from several languages. Language switching is the term used to describe conversations where speakers use different languages in response to one another. For example, a mother was overheard talking to her bilingual children. When discussing things of a personal nature, she spoke in French, but her daughters responded in English. This mixing and switching is done in an unconscious manner, but even very young children soon recognise who speaks which language and will adjust to their audience.

Early years settings can provide the perfect environment for acquiring new languages at a time when children are at their most receptive. Crèches and nurseries enable young children to hear and respond to new languages in a natural setting, where languages acquisition is contextualised.

Very young children entering early years settings while still developing their home languages(s) can be supported in communicating in a variety of ways. It is helpful for staff to learn some key words in the child's first language, particularly words of comfort and those pertaining to the child's physical needs. In general, communication will be established using exactly the same methods used with babies from homes where English is the first language (through the use of gesture, facial expression, pointing/signing and use of visual materials where appropriate). Thus, for these very young children, an understanding of English develops alongside their home language(s), and becomes an additional means of communication in the child's expanding repertoire.

Children who come to early years settings fluent in their home language(s) are known as 'emergent (sequential) bilinguals'; it is important to remember that they have already acquired these languages and will soon learn to speak English. Most young children quickly begin to understand a new language when surrounded by it at nursery or school. However, while some children are happy to communicate with a limited vocabulary, others may be responsive but remain in a silent phase (Baker 2002) for a considerable time, lasting anything from a couple of weeks to a year. Krashen (1981) suggests that people's personality traits can affect their confidence with regard to developing spoken language. For example, introverted emergent bilinguals may be more reluctant to express themselves in the new language than their extrovert peers.

The stages of second language acquisition to some extent mirror those of first language acquisition discussed earlier. Emergent bilinguals begin by tuning in to the sounds of English in the environment, listening to the tone and rhythm of speech and rhyme. They begin to learn single words, gradually building up a responsive vocabulary before they start to speak themselves. Hester's 'stages of English learning' (1990) chart the gradual development of confidence and competence as the child moves from being at Stage 1 – new to English – towards Stage 4 – a fluent user. The framework includes a detailed set of criteria which helps to describe, and effectively communicate to others, the stage of development reached by an individual child.

A number of writers have looked at how bilingual children bridge the linguistic worlds of their home and school. Drury (2004) describes an interesting example of a girl who is new to English and uses one- and two-word utterances to communicate in the nursery. At home she is heard rehearsing her English during a play sequence with her two-year-old brother. She employs language-switching, using Pahari, the home language, to engage the participation of her younger sibling, and practises her knowledge of simple English phrases as part of the dialogue.

Finally, it is very important not to neglect the other home languages of bilingual children who are completely fluent in English. Use of their other languages should still be encouraged within the early years setting.

Involving parents

It is important that workplace policies demonstrate to staff and parents that all languages are respected and that their use is encouraged. Children should be made to feel that their home languages are valued whether or not anyone else speaks them in the setting. It is important to collect information about the languages spoken and read in the home when children first enter your setting (for example, Hall 1995), and, when possible, to find other children or staff who can converse with them in their home language or dialect. Strong partnerships with parents will enhance children's early experiences of participating in a new linguistic community, by bringing their first languages into the setting. Many parents tell their children only to speak English in nursery or school as they believe that this immersion will be the fastest way for their children to become fluent in the new language. It is therefore very important for you, as a practitioner, to discuss the setting's policy, and to explain to parents the reasons why they should encourage their children to use their first languages in the setting (Siraj-Blatchford and Clarke 2000).

Parents may be willing to volunteer their time, translate notices and captions, or provide examples of books, taped stories or music in the child's home language. In this way, all the children's languages can be shared with other members of the group. Care needs to be taken when

REFLECTIVE ACTIVITY

How do you welcome children who are new to English into your setting?

List the strategies you could use to introduce the child and their family into your nursery/class.

50

making these requests since many people can speak languages in which they are not literate. Kenner (2000) has described a number of cases where parents have become involved in the literacy practices of a nursery. For example, parents were encouraged to write letters to their families abroad while seated in the nursery writing area. This set an example for the children who were becoming biliterate.

Cognitive benefits

It is important to ensure that cognitive challenges are rich and stimulating for emergent bilingual children. It is crucial for their cognitive development that they are encouraged to think in the language they find most useful – it can be very limiting intellectually to be restricted to a basic English vocabulary when ideas can be expressed more clearly in their home language/s.

Cummins discusses a 'common underlying proficiency' model (CUP) and uses a graphic analogy of an iceberg (Cummins and Swain 1986). This diagrammatic explanation depicts two peaks of an iceberg as the separate languages, clearly identifiable, while below the surface the main body of the iceberg is where cognition is taking place in an abstract, shared context.

Learning to express themselves in a variety of ways increases the intellectual capabilities of bilingual children and stimulates their cognitive powers. Some research suggests that 'balanced bilingual' children (equally confident in two languages) may develop long-term cognitive advantages over their monolingual peers, as they may have acquired a greater capacity for divergent and creative thinking (Baker 2002). It is evident that emergent bilinguals rely on contextual clues and experiences to help establish their use of the new language. The most difficult learning experiences are where the task is cognitively demanding but the context is reduced (Siraj-Blatchford and Clarke 2000).

REFLECTIVE ACTIVITY

Consider the situation where a child who is very new to English is attempting to build a simple electric circuit using wires, a bulb and a battery.

How would you support their learning? Think about the way in which children use thought to learn new concepts (discussed earlier). Would you consider taking a Piagetian stance, where the child is left to discover alone, perhaps using their first language internally to work through the new concepts? Or would you adopt a Vygotskian viewpoint that the adult needs to support the child's understanding through social interaction?

Ideally, someone who speaks the same language (child or adult) would be on hand to discuss the concepts in the child's home language, though of course this is not always possible.

Delay

Discussions with parents can help to clarify whether a child is experiencing a delay in their first/home language; if the child has fluency in one language, then the capacity to learn a new language exists and the child simply needs more time. However, if there is evidence of a more general language delay, professional help should be sought from a speech therapist. Language delay in a child's first language may also be a symptom of a more general learning difficulty.

Some older children who are still in the early stages of learning English can be misdiagnosed as having a learning delay/impairment. Wright (1991, cited in Hall 1995) discusses the false-positive and false-negative diagnoses that may be attributed to emergent bilinguals when they are failing to make progress in school. If an emergent bilingual is making slower progress than their peers, one has to consider the situation very carefully to ensure that these children are not unfairly diagnosed as having a learning impairment. If a child is still acquiring English, a false assessment may result in them being placed erroneously with children who have learning difficulties (false-positive). On the other hand, sometimes children are not given the extra learning support they need because the learning deficit is masked by their inability to use English (false-negative).

There is no evidence to suggest that children get confused or that proficiency in one language has adverse effects on acquiring another. Nor does the brain have a finite amount of space for linguistic storage (Alladina 1995). However, the 'threshold theory' (Cummins 1976) suggests that children do need to achieve a certain level of expertise in a language before they can reap cognitive benefits. There is some debate (Baker 2002) as to whether a person can be equally fluent in a number of languages or whether, ultimately, one will be stronger than another. However, the evidence suggests that taking everything into consideration, being bilingual is an asset.

PLAYING WITH LANGUAGE

Enjoyment of language

Young children soon become fascinated by the power of language. As discussed earlier in this chapter, they use it to control their world, to organise their thoughts and to problem-solve. However, they also enjoy language for its own sake: they take pleasure in playing with sounds, enjoy puns and begin to understand verbal humour.

From infancy, most children are both entertained and soothed by nursery rhymes and songs. These experiences help children to learn the patterns of their home language and to engage in a variety of joint language experiences. However, recently some practitioners have expressed concerns about the language development of some of their new entrants. These reports suggest that a growing number of children arrive with poorly developed language skills (*Guardian* and *Independent* 4 March 2003), are unfamiliar with rhymes and songs and that their conversational skills have been underutilised in the modern family environment. The continuous background noise of radios and televisions may hamper children's power of concentration and mean that they are not picking up on the general conversations around them. However, experience suggests that in the absence of any serious congenital language delay, this deficiency can be addressed quickly by providing children with regular opportunities to engage in playful language-learning experiences, including learning rhymes and singing in small groups (www.ican.org.uk – accessed October 2004).

Children take delight in humorous rhymes, puns, tongue-twisters and alliterative games (such as finding descriptive words which start with the same first letter as their names). These episodes may be instigated by adults, but are frequently part of spontaneous playfulness between children. They often take place while children are engaged in other activities; the playful exchange of humorous phrases and nonsense words causes great hilarity and brings a sense of camaraderie. This awareness of rhyme and playfulness with words prepares children for other forms of communication, and research suggests that children who demonstrate an interest in rhyme go on to learn to read more quickly than their peers (Bryant *et al.* 1989). As children mature, this interest will be transferred to poetry as a genre.

Playing together

All forms of play provide diverse opportunities for language. Communication between babies and adults begins with playful interactive episodes and continues as children begin to respond to spoken language. In Chapter 4, Ruth Forbes discusses the way in which recent brain research has helped us to consider the importance of social interplay and its links to higher thinking skills.

Vygotsky and Bruner (Wood 1988) consider that children use spoken language to express their thoughts when playing alone (as discussed earlier in this chapter). In their view this is the precursor to internal thought and can be seen in early years settings when children frequently talk or sing to themselves as they play, providing a running commentary on their actions. Whitehead (1997) explains that the appearance of imaginative play demonstrates the developing ability of children to represent their thoughts symbolically. At first this may be a solitary occupation, but gradually children start to play cooperatively with others and begin to be involved in socio-dramatic play, in pairs or larger groups.

Children extend their conversational skills with their peers during social play: playing in pairs and groups necessitates constructive dialogue, including explanation, negotiation and reconciliation skills. Thus most play experiences provide children with important opportunities to hone their expressive language.

Imaginative play is particularly rich in language opportunities. Children can move beyond the here and now and either revisit past experiences or rehearse future ones. The dialogue that is produced in these scenarios encourages children to practise a variety of different forms of communication. Once engaged in particular scenarios, children recognise the modes of speech that characterise a range of different roles. For example, in home-corner play, children frequently replay episodes witnessed at home and take on the forms of adult speech they have overheard, switching to their usual register when out of role. In this way, children demonstrate a sophisticated understanding of language and how it varies according to context.

Hall and Robinson (2003) reflect on how the production of narratives in socio-dramatic play is similar to the later production of written texts. They suggest that while children's written narratives have an end product, play-scripts leave a memory. Many writers – in particular, Vivian Gussin Paley (1981, 1986) – have documented the importance of narratives and socio-dramatic play in children's lives and recognise their ability to sustain interest in particular episodes over very long periods of time; small groups of nursery-age children can remain engaged in a particular dramatic reconstruction on a daily basis.

Many practitioners are wary of encouraging children to bring popular cultural and media-influenced play into their settings. This is unfortunate as children's communication skills are developed within an environment rich in these influences (Marsh and Millard 2000), and lively play which encourages verbal expression should be nurtured.

REFLECTIVE ACTIVITY

Watch out for a group of children in your work setting who you feel rarely get involved in the organised activities. You may discover that they are actually engaged in a form of highly organised socio-dramatic play of their own devising. These groups often search for a secluded area, as some of these activities may involve behaviours which are not condoned by adults, such as super-hero and gun play. However, this type of role play is rich in narrative and encourages the linguistic participation of the children in a deeper way than many of the more formal learning experiences which we provide for them.

Try to observe the group without being seen and make some notes. You may wish to structure your observation, for example, by using the seven functions described by Halliday (1975). Consider the use of dialogue and the 'text' of their narrative. If you watch over a series of days you should notice that some of the script remains the same, while there may be further plot developments.

Retelling stories

Reconstructions of familiar stories encourage children to engage in language-rich experiences. Puppets, small-world toys, figurines and storyboards all give children opportunities to revisit a favourite story and retell it in their own words. These experiences are particularly useful for children who are new to English, as they have the opportunity to retell the story in their home language or practise familiar English catchphrases from a book they have recently heard.

The work of Paley (1981, 1986) demonstrates that children's own narratives are an extremely important part of their daily lives and their emotional and intellectual development. One of the techniques she employs is to ask individual children to tell her their stories. She sits quietly with them and scribes their exact words; these are used later as play-scripts for groups of their peers to re-enact. In this way she demonstrates that adults take seriously even the very simplest of their storylines.

DEVELOPING LITERACY

Early encounters with literacy

Many wonderful books are produced which appeal to babies and toddlers. Colourful, clear illustrations and particular formats which include items to be discovered (characters and items hidden behind flaps or that pop up) engage very young children's interest and curiosity. It is never too early to introduce books to babies. The *Bookstart* initiative, which began during the early 1990s in Birmingham, has now been adopted by the government and the project has been funded nationally by the government since 2004. Under the scheme, health visitors distribute a literacy pack to new parents to encourage the idea of sharing books with their babies. Follow-up research from the original project suggested that engaging the parents at this early stage had long-term benefits, with families maintaining their enthusiasm for literacy as the children grew older (Moore and Wade 1998).

Very young children become familiar with books through initially sharing them with adults and older siblings. These episodes provide an opportunity for quieter, intimate moments between children and their carers. These practices that begin in the home will then be continued when children move into group childcare settings. An adult can sit with a small group of two or three children to share in the delights of a favourite text; the children are included in the process while the adults read the story, interjecting their thoughts, asking questions and thoroughly engaging in the storytelling process.

Environmental print

From the moment children are born, they are surrounded by incidental print, and are being gradually inducted into the world of literacy (Hall and Robinson 2003). Food, cosmetics and cleaning products around the home are all labelled, and even a child's clothing is frequently decorated with letters, numbers and logos (Hallet 1999).

Children soon begin to build up a sight vocabulary of the signs and symbols that surround them. As with the acquisition of speech, the first logos and print that the child recognises will usually relate to their basic interests and needs. For example, they soon learn to recognise the symbols which refer to a favourite drink or snack, and enjoy helping to find items when out shopping by looking for the familiar illustrative clues. The advertising industry has coined the phrase 'pester power' and understands that it can target young shoppers long before they are able to read in the conventional sense. Recognising and interpreting a variety of forms of incidental print is an important first step towards literacy (Nutbrown 1997). Outside all our homes, the local streets are filled with advertising hoardings, traffic signs, shopfronts and posters on bus shelters, to name but a few, and in multilingual homes and communities, children are likely to become familiar with an even greater variety of alphabets and scripts.

All these literary incidents help children to recognise the purpose of the printed word (Hallet 1999). They subsequently begin to distinguish

between pictorial information and print. Children will have seen adults reading printed materials such as newspapers, books, television guides, catalogues and bills, and will have witnessed people writing cards and letters. Many literacy events are promoted through daily household chores (Rivelland 2000), such as reading recipes, following DIY instructions and making shopping lists. Thus even if their home does not appear to foster a strong literary focus, the pre-school child does already have a strong concept of what constitutes print and what its purpose is. Once their interest in print has been stimulated, children will be looking out for examples in their environment and will frequently ask adults to read signs and posters to them. Fred Sedgwick (2001) confides that his son's first sight-words included the name of a pub which they regularly passed on a car journey!

It follows that when children enter a childcare setting, they should encounter the same sort of print-rich environment, where literacy is context related. Historically, it was considered that the acquisition of reading was exclusively through books and that writing was developed by school-age children in formal settings. However, this view has changed radically, as we shall see later in this chapter.

Current debates

In recent years, a sociocultural perspective on the development of literacy has become popular. Bourdieu (1977, cited in Barratt-Pugh 2000) suggests that literacy is 'cultural capital', and believes that children who move into adulthood with good literary skills will have enhanced opportunities in life. He argues that children from middle-class homes come to school with cultural capital, which means that they have linguistic and literary advantages over children from less affluent homes. His work implies that it should be the school's responsibility to address any deficit in order to enrich children's future prospects. Heath's research (1983) into the literacy practices in two working-class communities in the USA showed the different attitudes towards books, reading and writing held within the groups; the children she studied received very different messages about the purposes of literacy from their home communities.

Narrative

Narrative is an important part of our lives; from bedtime stories to classic novels, from comics to television soaps, the majority of adults and children are entertained by it daily. Children across the world listen to stories from their earliest years; some have the stories read to them from books, while others are part of a rich storytelling tradition. Narratives can be funny, scary, intriguing or even moralistic, but all are essentially entertaining.

Generally, the language used in narrative is far richer than in other spoken communication. Transcripts of our everyday conversations highlight the fragmentary way in which most of us express ourselves. In general conversation our speech frequently leaves sentences, and even thoughts, incomplete. Narrative, however, is crafted; every word is carefully selected and none can be omitted. Stories in book or oral form have a patterned language which children begin to recognise early on. Children enjoy the repetition of catchphrases and recognise that a story has a prescribed set of conventions (Meek 1991); there will be a set of characters and an unfolding sequence of events, and finally an expectation of a satisfactory conclusion. The quality of the vocabulary and the descriptive nature of stories make them much richer sources for linguistic development than language in everyday use.

Stories also have an important role in the emotional life of children (and adults). Children never tire of hearing their favourite stories retold, and these narratives frequently have at their core an important message which has individual significance for the child (see, for example, Bettelheim 1975). In addition, children who are read to at bedtime are likely to associate stories with comfort and intimate family moments.

Reading

Reading is a very important skill in our society. As already mentioned, we are surrounded by print throughout our daily lives, and those who are unable to access the written word are somewhat disadvantaged. Historically, children have been taught to read using specially devised primers, which are more concerned with form (in particular, phonetic structures) than with content. This type of reading material often contains a thin storyline and can become a chore rather than a delight. While many current reading schemes have been designed with entertainment as well as instruction in mind, the best start on the journey to literacy is still the real story book that will grab children's interest.

Many, but not all, children will be fortunate in having been introduced to a wide variety of story books and other literature in their homes from a young age. These children come to formal schooling with an expectation that they, too, will be able to crack the literacy code. Dombey (1992) suggests that in order to learn to read children need to have had considerable experience of a wide variety of texts, many of them read aloud. She asserts that children need to adopt a set of attitudes which include recognising the pleasure and satisfaction to be derived from texts, being confident in the belief that they will be able to learn to read and being persistent in attempting to do so. They also need a range of knowledge and strategies which help them to understand the conventions of print.

There was a widely held myth (Nutbrown 1997) that children needed to be taught to recognise letters before they can begin to read words.

This standpoint ignores the fact that children build up a sight vocabulary before any formal phonic training begins. Written English has an extremely complex phonic system. While many other languages can be very simply taught through a direct correlation between the alphabet and the sounds the letters make, in English, spelling rules are much more complex. Consider, for example, the phoneme *f* in the words 'fate' and 'philosophy'; and say aloud the words 'enough', 'ought' and 'bough', and listen to how differently the *ough* is pronounced. This certainly makes it harder for children to become fluent readers in English, and this is why statistical comparisons of reading fluency with other countries are often very unhelpful.

In the early stages, children can be taught how to deconstruct simple words using basic phonic knowledge. However, as their reading competence grows, they need to be able to call on other reserves of perceptual knowledge (using visual clues) (Riley 1999). As adults, we do not split up every word phonetically when we are reading the newspaper; we generally revert to phonics only when we come across an unfamiliar word (perhaps in a textbook!). Competent readers skim across the top of the words. (You can try this yourself, by covering the bottom half of the words in the following sentence with a piece of card.)

Thus children need to acquire two sets of skills – they must be able to decode unfamiliar words using their phonic knowledge and have a growing bank of memorised vocabulary. However, these skills need to be accompanied by comprehension of the text. Children's books often have illustrations, which can provide valuable clues to the written content, and the competent reader is also able to anticipate probable words in a sentence because they know what is likely to come next grammatically. Unfortunately, children who rely solely on phonic knowledge often 'bark at print', in other words, they are not reading for either meaning or enjoyment. In addition, if the child is reading aloud without comprehension they will not be able to self-correct.

Apprenticeship approach

Many experienced practitioners have questioned the traditional, behavioural approach to teaching reading. Waterland (1988) came to the conclusion that an apprenticeship approach, in which the child is an active partner in the reading process with a supportive adult, would be more productive. She contends that the most important element of learning to read is the child's engagement with the material, and that selection of appropriate texts should be a cooperative venture where the adult acts as a 'guiding friend' (Waterland 1988: 16) so that the child is not too challenged by their choice. This requires the careful selection of a wide range of texts for every nursery and early years classroom. Rather than listening to children read, the adult *shares* the book with the child. To begin with, the adult reads the book to the child, but on subsequent readings the child takes a more active role until, gradually, they can take over and read it for themselves.

This apprenticeship approach can be taught to parents and provides a much more meaningful experience for children when they take books home. Without this emphasis, a significant number of parents can make reading a test of their child's skill, which results in tears all round. Also, it is important to recognise that there are different patterns of home literacy within the community (Heath 1983), and that in some cultures books are so revered that parents may be fearful of letting their children handle them.

Despite the popularity of the apprenticeship approach during the 1980s, the National Literacy Strategy (NLS) (DfEE 1998) has resulted in a return to a largely phonic-based approach, where texts are selected to meet specific learning objectives. However, the shared reading aspects of the 'literacy hour' do use 'real' books, and the literature selected by teachers for individual and guided reading generally incorporates well-designed, imaginatively illustrated texts. The NLS requires children to be introduced to a wide range of genres, including non-fiction texts and biographies.

Thus it can be seen there are strongly contested viewpoints on how children should learn to read. Like many such debates, this issue does not have one single solution. However, many practitioners recognise that using a combination of methods helps to address the different learning styles of the children they teach. When children are experiencing difficulties in acquiring reading skills, individual support from within the school can help to address underachievement. Clay (1991) pioneered the Reading Recovery programme, which gives targeted children regular intensive help from an adult for a limited period of time to help them to catch up with their peers. This intervention has proved effective, but it is costly.

Becoming a writer

Children across the world, whatever their circumstances, begin to make marks in the same way. Kellogg (1979) describes how children's drawing begins with scribbling. Studies show that children are not restricted to using writing implements: a baby may begin experimenting using their own fingers (such as making patterns in pools of food during mealtimes), and in less affluent societies children of various ages (and adult narrators) may compose their drawings with sticks in the dust. Early mark-making and drawing by even the very youngest children enable them to express their ideas and understandings in a symbolic manner (Matthews 1994).

While writing and drawing may appear to be human inventions rather than innate skills, some researchers have investigated their natural antecedents. Sheridan (2004) has suggested that there are neurological links between early scribbling behaviours and babbling, and research by Kennedy (cited in Zalewski 2002) showed that people blind from birth were still able to draw realistic interpretations of everyday objects. These ideas suggest that there may be an innate capacity in humans to develop mark-making skills as a form of communication.

Current debates

Developmental and maturational perspectives on early writing development consider that children can be taught a series of age-related skills.

Historically, writing was thought to be a skill which should be formally taught, and copy-writing was considered to be the best starting point. This meant that early emergent writing was dismissed by adults, totally ignoring the plentiful instances of children's early mark-making.

Children's first attempts at writing may have many of the characteristics of 'real' writing, even though no recognisable letters are in evidence. They may, for example, draw lines across the page from left to right to mimic English script. As children become aware of environmental print, they begin to incorporate some letters into their drawings. Gradually emergent writing begins to become more letter-like, including some recognisable interpretations of familiar letters. Children are often particularly interested in their own name, and their initials or other letters from their name are often incorporated into their early drawings (Godwin and Perkins 2002). Practitioners should be aware that for bilingual children, the first signs of literacy may be in the alphabet/script of their first language.

Writing for a purpose

Early years settings provide children with a wide range of opportunities to represent their ideas symbolically. The Foundation Stage guidance (DfEE/QCA 2000a) describes the importance of engaging children in discussions about their early attempts at representation and mark making. It also emphasises that, like parents, practitioners are important role models for children, as they can demonstrate the purposes of written representations in everyday life.

It is fundamentally important for children to recognise the purpose of writing by engaging in meaningful experiences. Role-play activities particularly lend themselves to literary resources. There has been a great deal of interest in the past few years in resourcing imaginative play areas to encourage literacy development in realistic scenarios (Hall and Robinson 2003). In these scenarios, children can make lists, write down food orders or write prescriptions as part of their role-play activities, using emergent writing. For some children a blank piece of paper can seem intimidating; by designing interesting materials for

> ### PAUSE FOR THOUGHT
>
> **Think about any writing you have done in the last week.**
>
> **Britton (1972, cited in Browne 1999) describes the functions of three types of writing – 'expressive', 'transactional' and 'poetic'.**
>
> **Your list will probably include examples of expressive writing (e.g. making lists, writing a diary, writing a note or email to a friend) and transactional writing (e.g. writing instructions or a report, or lesson planning). However, you are perhaps less likely to have written anything poetic, of artistic merit.**

these activities, such as decorated forms and pads incorporating picture clues, as practitioners you can encourage children's early attempts at mark-making.

Involving parents in the writing area of a nursery is another way of encouraging interest in literacy practices. As was mentioned earlier in the chapter, Kenner (2000) describes how biliterate parents came into a nursery setting and sat with the children, writing letters to relatives abroad, for example. This encouraged the children to become aware of different scripts and also to recognise writing as a form of communication with people far away.

Recent curricula documents (DfEE/QCA 1998, 2000a, 2000b) recognise the importance of introducing children to different writing genres. Children can be encouraged to begin to write in a variety of different styles: making lists, labelling diagrams, writing letters and instructions, in addition to the traditional classroom activities of composing captions for their pictures. As their skills progress, they can begin to compose pieces of writing of greater length and complexity. They must begin to understand the concept of communicating with an unseen audience, and be encouraged to plan and draft prose and poetry before it is deemed to be complete.

Spelling

It is generally accepted today that reading and writing develop alongside one another. As children begin to develop a sight vocabulary they are often able to write down these memorised words. Similarly, as phonic understanding develops, they can use this knowledge to spell out words. Bissex (1980) describes how her son tired of her inattention and, noticing how she was always reading, got so exasperated that he printed the sentence, 'R U DF' (Are you deaf?). This is a marvellous example of a child using emergent spelling to good effect!

As discussed earlier in the chapter, English spelling is very irregular and does not conform to phonic rules. This makes learning to spell correctly a lengthy process. It is important that children are encouraged to write without worrying too much about spelling in the early stages. This is recognised in the SATs at key stage 1, where marks are neither awarded nor lost for spelling in the composition tasks. This encourages children to be adventurous with their composition and not restrict themselves to a finite memorised vocabulary. However, children are expected to consider the conventions of grammar and punctuation at seven years old, and are tested separately on their spelling knowledge.

CONCLUSION

The rapid advance of technology means that in the future, the current generation of children may abandon the pen in favour of electronic methods of communicating. The prolific use of mobile phones suggests that there is plenty of verbal communication taking place, and 'texting' is encouraging people to write to one another (though there are fears that this is not helping young people's spelling!). Computers and word-processing are increasingly part of most people's working lives. Therefore, as a practitioner, it is your responsibility to encourage the use of all forms of ICT, in order to facilitate children's understanding and development of appropriate technological skills. Without sufficient access to communication technology, some children (for example, those who do not have a computer in their home) could be disadvantaged.

Language and communication in whatever form is of fundamental importance to people in every society. Language enables people to share information, ideas and emotions. As a practitioner working with young children, you must ensure that you support the development of speech and literacy, through engagement in exciting and culturally diverse linguistic activities.

KEY TEXTS

Browne, A. 2001: *Developing Language and Literacy 3–8* (2nd edn). London: Paul Chapman Publishing.

Hall, N. and Martello, J. (eds) 1996: *Listening to Children Think. Exploring Talk in the Early Years.* London: Hodder and Stoughton.

Marsh, J. and Hallet, E. (eds) 1999: *Desirable Literacies. Approaches to Language and Literacy in the Early Years.* London: Paul Chapman Publishing.

Whitehead, M. R. 1997: *Language and Literacy in the Early Years* (2nd edn). London: Paul Chapman Publishing.

USEFUL WEBSITES (All accessed October 2004)

www.clpe.co.uk – Centre for Literacy in Primary Education (CLPE)

www.ican.org.uk – charity concerned with children with speech and language difficulties

www.literacytrust.org.uk – National Literacy Trust

www.makaton.org – Makaton Vocabulary Development Project

www.naplic.org.uk – National Association for Professionals Concerned with Language Impairment in Children

WORKING WITH YOUNG CHILDREN (0–3 YEARS)

INTRODUCTION

We will begin by identifying the most important aspects of normal growth and development. It is important for students and practitioners alike to have a good understanding of child development. A curriculum for young children should be based on their development, focusing on what they are able to do, either with support or on their own. It should not be about what we think they should be doing by the time they are a certain age (Manning-Morton and Thorp 2001).

One of the most important elements of a high-quality play and learning environment for babies and children up to the age of three is the adult. We will examine the critical role of the adult and the need for close and constant relationships. We will examine work from educators and practitioners, such as Bowlby, Bower and Goldschmied. We will also look at the work of theorists, including Piaget, Bruner and

Vygotsky. We will explore how their work still influences our practice and provision today and how our views of babies and young children as 'competent learners' (DfES 2002) and not 'blank slates' have developed.

The chapter will conclude with an exploration of the wider issues of working with other people's very young children in settings outside the home, exploring some of the questions that educating and caring for other people's children raises. What are the implications for society? What is the cost? What sort of guidance and regulation should be in place for settings? What are the provision and policy in other countries, and how do they differ from our own?

The work of practitioners and the needs of very young children in a range of settings will be considered throughout the chapter. The recognition and response to children's individual and specific needs must underpin our practice, ensuring all children are encouraged and supported to fulfil their potential, no matter how complex those needs may be.

GROWTH AND DEVELOPMENT

In this section we will identify the key aspects of development of children up to three years of age. We will consider normative development and what this means to the learning and play of young children.

Nature and nurture influence and affect young children's growth and development, and people, families, social and cultural experiences and opportunities help to make and shape us. This is particularly important in our knowledge of development and learning in the early years. The research and new information about the developing brain have changed our thinking and appreciation of babies' and young children's learning and development. This new knowledge of how the developing brain literally makes new pathways (neural connections), using the baby or young child's everyday experiences, means we have to rethink our ideas about their development. All the adults involved really do influence and shape children's development.

Adults working with other people's children have a responsibility to ensure that they have knowledge and understanding of how babies and young children grow and develop. Families may sometimes seek your advice as an early years practitioner, or you may become part of a wider network of professionals and specialists working with children and their families. Your opinions may be asked, you may become involved in discussions about how a child is developing, whether they are in the 'accepted normative scales'. Whether the discussion involves a parent asking about potty-training or working with a speech and language therapist to support a child with language delay, an understanding of what is 'normal' and when you should be concerned or seek further advice is essential.

Normative development

'Normative development' is the traditional method of studying development. This involves using stages of development, matching ages to ability or skills and using the 'milestones approach'. It is important to consider that although there are recognised sequences in children's development, children will develop in different ways and at varying rates, and are influenced by their environment and culture. The broad areas of development are helpful, but they should be used to support and influence your work with very young children, not to direct or dictate the planning and provision offered.

Mary Sheridan's (1973, 1997) rigorous observations and sketches of babies and young children who attended her clinics contributed to a comprehensive checklist of stages and sequences of development. These were originally written for the purpose of supporting families of children with complex needs to identify what these children could do – and then identify ways of supporting them to reach their potential. Sheridan identified specific developmental areas, including gross motor, posture, hearing and vision and fine motor control. She also identified methods of assessing children's development.

Most early years students are used to thinking about child development under specific headings (e.g. **PILESS**: Physical, Intellectual, Language, Emotional, Social, Spiritual; **SPICE**: Social, Physical, Intellectual, Communication, Emotional). However, Bruce and Meggitt (2002) suggest that in order to think about young children's development in a holistic way, 'cultural and symbolic behaviour' should also be considered.

The English *Birth to Three Matters: A Framework to Support Children in their Earliest Years* (DfES 2002) recognises that children's development is not linear and can be uneven. In this way, it values babies and children as individuals who develop and progress at their own pace.

It might be more helpful for you as a practitioner to look at the significant shifts in development – sitting, standing and becoming more mobile – instead of the checklist approach of developmental milestones, where the focus is on the age and related ability or skill the child should have achieved.

The framework identifies the four broad bands of young children's development as follows:

- heads up, lookers and communicators: 0–8 months
- sitters, standers and explorers: 8–18 months
- movers, shakers and players: 18–24 months
- walkers, talkers and pretenders: 24–36 months.

It is also helpful to consider the characteristics of babies and young children in relation to their growth and development. The framework identifies these as:

- a skilful communicator
- a strong child
- a healthy child
- a competent learner.

Using the framework headings and the broad areas of development can help you as a practitioner to plan and organise the environment, resources and routines you offer to young children.

Valuing and supporting difference

Any discussion about young children's development has to recognise that some children may have specific needs or disabilities, with varying degrees of complexity. However, as Bruce (1987) reminds us with her principles of *Early Childhood Education*, we start with the child and what they can do. The checklist model and the medical model (particularly in relation to children with disabilities) of assessing and monitoring children's development can result in a deficit model or view of the child. It can become a list of things they *cannot* do yet. The deficit model view of the child may also lead to the sort of planning that focuses on adult-led activities in order to 'plug the gap' or test whether the child has developed a skill or acquired 'knowledge'.

Principles for good practice

Experiences and opportunities for young children should reflect the rapid development and learning that occur and focus on the child rather than on the 'end product'.

- Principle 2: Babies and young children are whole people who have feelings, ideas and relationships with others, and who need to be physically, mentally, morally and spiritually healthy.
- Principle 6: There are times when babies and young children are especially able to learn particular things.
- Principle 7: What babies and young children can rather than cannot do is the starting point of the child's play, learning and education.

(Adapted from Bruce 1987)

The ten principles are helpful for all practitioners of high-quality early years education (and care) and have been adapted in many forms. *Birth to Three Matters* (DfES 2002: 4) and the *Curriculum Guidance for the Foundation Stage* (QCA 2000: 11) have adopted a set of principles which underpin both sets of documentation and which should be evident in high-quality and effective practice.

Young children's interests and learning supported by an encouraging adult (principles 6 and 7)

REFLECTIVE ACTIVITY

Read this observation and think about which principles the practitioners were applying to Harry's play and learning experience.

Harry, aged 9.5 months, had become a 'cruiser': he was using furniture to pull himself up and move along the length of it. He was spending a lot of time leaning over one particular piece of nursery equipment, bending right over the back of the locker and exploring the patterns of the maple frame. Several times he gracefully slid right over the furniture on to the floor as he overbalanced, so involved was he in the exploration of the patterns in the board. The practitioners responded to his interest in textures and patterns and made a collection of many other textiles for him to explore. They also ensured he had access to different heights of nursery furniture to pull himself up on and practise walking along, sometimes with one hand, other times using both.

Only three of Bruce's principles are set out above. Look up the others and use them to see how the practice in your setting reflects them or is influenced by them.

Principles 2, 6 and 7 are particularly important when considering the growth and development of babies and young children. Can you identify a specific element of your practice that responds to these three principles?

Bruce's principles and those in *Birth to Three Matters* (DfES 2002) can offer support in identifying the different developmental stages of individual children and providing good and effective practice. They can be used to highlight and illustrate good practice, and explain to families and visitors the ethos and beliefs of the setting in a practical way.

Brain development

There has been an ever-increasing amount of research into the development and function of the brain over the last ten years. It is now widely recognised that the period of very early development in children under three is critical to the growth and development of the brain.

We have discovered more about the workings of the brain in recent decades than ever before, through the use of magnetic resonance imaging (MRI), functional magnetic resonance imaging (fMRI) and positron emission topography (PET) scans. The brain is very complex and divided into three parts:

· the brainstem (sometimes referred to as the reptilian brain at the base of the brain, near the neck) – the cells here determine the brain's level of alertness and regulate our breathing, heartbeat and blood pressure

· the limbic system – where sight, smell, hearing and memory are laid down (many of our basic instincts for survival are generated here)

· cortex – the thinking, planning, organising and communication area of the brain, with two hemispheres covered by tissue called the cerebral cortex (the human cortex is the largest of any species and is what gives us the potential for learning).

(Carter 1999 pp. 16–17)

However, it is the link between neuroscience and early education that has significantly raised awareness of early brain development.

Neurones and synapses

Babies are born with approximately 100 billion neurones – these are the brain cells that create brain activity. Most of our brain cells are called glials – simple cells that are responsible for repairing and servicing tissue and cells, lining cavity surfaces and maintaining balance around the neurones while protecting them from potentially toxic chemicals. Neurones account for about one in ten of the total number of cells.

At birth, few of the neurones are connected; however, they begin connecting with each other through a process of sending and receiving electrical signals or messages. There are two kinds of branches: those that *send* signals (axons) and those that *receive* information (dendrites). What has interested neuroscientists is what happens at the gap where the dendrite meets the axon. This gap is called the synapse. So that the electrical signal or message from the cell can cross the gap, neurotransmitters are secreted by the axon. This causes a chain reaction from the neighbouring cell, which also fires, and there is simultaneous activity in millions of connected cells (Carter 1999; Blakemore 1998).

It is here that the brain becomes wired and networks of synapses are laid down. The connections are made from life experiences, so everything that parents, practitioners or other significant adults in young children's lives do will have an effect on the hardwiring of their brain.

Making connections

During the first eight months of life, connections outpace disconnection and an eight-month-old baby may have one thousand trillion synapses in his brain, about 20 times more than at birth, and twice as many as an adult (Blakemore 1998).

We know that there are crucial times during pregnancy for brain development, when the effects of alcohol and drugs can be particularly damaging. Scientists have gained more precise information about the threats and outcomes to the foetus from exposure to drugs soon after conception, when many mothers are unaware of their pregnancy. This has implications for prenatal preventative work and for those working with women at risk.

The brain does not need all the connections it has begun to make and begins a process of 'pruning' or synaptogenesis. The experiences young children have which are reinforced by the connections made in the brain become permanent, whereas connections that are not used begin to die. It is becoming increasingly clear that maintaining large numbers of synapses or connections requires huge amounts of energy. In the early years the brain has a significantly higher metabolic rate than it will have in later life. We all recognise the incredible speed with which babies move from being almost helpless to beginning to reason, talk, walk, form intentions and carry them out.

As the baby begins to make sense of their world through real experiences, schemas (patterns) develop. Piaget's (1896–1980) stage development theory is based on age-related stages in the child's thinking and knowledge acquisition. Piaget (1962) suggested that true knowledge is when the child knows how and why they can do something – operative thinking as opposed to simply knowing how to do something, which is working at a lower, functional level. He asked many questions of children as they set about his experiments, in order to probe why they did what they did.

We are also finding out from the work of neuroscientists just how important adults are. Vygotsky (1978) identified the social interplay between adults and children as vital in stimulating children's higher thinking skills. Babies and young children begin to store up information and make connections between their actions and the effect on objects or people. They also start laying down the foundations for judging speed, distance and spatial awareness. Think about the things very young children are interested in:

- touching and mouthing everything
- what is this (treasure baskets)? (Goldschmied and Jackson 1994))
- what can it do (heuristic play)? (Goldschmied and Jackson 1994)
- can I hold it?
- will it fit in here?
- can I move it to somewhere else (transporting schema)?
- and what else can I do with it – wear it, eat it, wrap it up in something (enveloping schema)?

ENTITLEMENTS AND RIGHTS OF VERY YOUNG CHILDREN (0–3 YEARS)

What do babies and young children need?

Kellmer Pringle (1980) identified the developing and fundamental needs of children and stressed the importance of the interdependence of the following needs:

- the need for love and security
- the need for new experiences
- the need for responsibility
- the need for praise and recognition.

She maintains that in order for children to reach their optimal intellectual, social, educational and emotional development, all their needs have to be met equally.

Goldschmied and Jackson (1994) advise us to consider babies and young children as people. Until we begin to consider them as part of our society, they suggest, we will always think of them as 'needy' and 'dependent'.

Of course, babies and young children are totally dependent in terms of their *physical* needs – being fed, kept warm and loved and cared for. They also have other fundamental needs, including:

- nourishment – essential for growth and development
- temperature – babies need warmth, from appropriate clothing and coverings

- a safe environment and to be kept secure
- people – babies and young children are very sociable and need contact with other people and the opportunity to develop close relationships, both at home and in outside-the-home settings
- a sense of well-being – emotional literacy
- stimulation and toys (not necessarily the same things – adults or other children to talk to, sing and play games with can be more important than the paraphernalia of unnecessary or inappropriate toys)
- care routines which are flexible and adapted to meet their changing and developing physical needs.

(Kellmer Pringle 1980; Bruce and Meggitt 2002)

Responsibility is something most human beings respond to positively and even children under three years can be given opportunities to take responsibility for themselves or others. By encouraging a young baby to hold the flannel and 'help you' as their face is wiped after a meal or play experience, they are beginning to take responsibility for their own comfort. It helps them to find out about their body, where their face begins and ends, the temperature of a warm cloth, the gentle change in pressure as their face is wiped and the magic of 'all gone'. (Where has that paint splodge gone, or the smear of custard that decorated the cheek?)

PAUSE FOR THOUGHT

Cerys (10 months) was playing alone at a Treasure Basket. The metal measuring cup became wedged under her leg. She made several attempts to get hold of the handle, she vocalised her efforts, raising the tone and level of her voice; she looked to the observing adult, she looked to the object, she turned her attention to another object but then returned to the metal cup. She pulled, pushed, leaned right over into her own lap, nearly over balancing. After more than 5 minutes of using different strategies to retrieve the measuring cup, she succeeded; her vocalisation and the wide smile on her face displayed her delight and pleasure at her own success.

The adult had enabled Cerys to succeed by staying close and supporting her struggle. Cerys' mum after watching the video of her daughter's intense struggle and persistence was amazed and delighted at her strategies and success. In discussion with the practitioners she said that she would have moved in and given the object to Cerys much sooner, and some of the practitioners agreed that they might have done as well, if Cerys had not been part of an action research project on babies' play and learning at a Treasure Basket.

(Forbes 2004: 86)

Think about something you have done for a young child – finished off stacking a block of bricks; taken away their plate or bowl without checking for signs that they have indeed finished; moved a seated baby to another part of the room without warning. Could you have done things differently? How can you encourage and support even very young babies and children to make their own decisions and choices? Have you taken away an opportunity for a child to struggle – an important part of play? Are you denying them their rights to make choices?

Very young babies can be supported to take responsibility for their own learning and to begin to understand how their choices affect others. Later in this chapter we will explore examples of good practice to promote and support this aspect of play and learning.

What are babies and young children like and what can they do?

Ask any group of practitioners to describe the young children they work with every day and they might suggest any of the following: 'the terrible twos'; 'they don't concentrate on anything'; 'inquisitive, dependent yet wanting to be independent, continually trying to talk or show you things'.

Babies and young children are:

- intensely curious – exploring the world around them using all their senses
- physically and emotionally dependent on adults – for 'nourishment', nutrition, warmth, love and care
- skilful communicators – beginning by looking (eye-pointing), gazing intently at people and objects, pre-verbal noises, giving and exchanging objects, mutual touching (Goldschmied and Selleck 1998)
- sometimes noisy, sometimes quiet
- responsive, interactive
- highly imitative
- beginning to get a sense of themselves as individuals ('I')
- beginning to make friends – developing relationships with other children
- concentrators – deeply involved in their exploration and play, as observations at the treasure basket have shown (Goldschmied and Jackson 1994; Manning-Morton and Thorp 2001; Forbes 2004).

If we think about *what the child can already do*, we begin to see a more rounded picture of babies and toddlers, which will support us to think about them as co-constructors of knowledge and to reflect on how we can enable and support them to play and learn.

Babies come equipped for learning. Gopnik *et al.* (1999: 201) tell us that 'Babies are already as smart as they can be… They are designed to learn about the real world that surrounds them, and they learn by playing with the things in the world, most of all by playing with the people who love them'.

There are some 'myths' about the abilities of babies and toddlers. We are sometimes told that babies do not play with other babies and that they are unable to share objects. However, practice and observation have shown that babies at the treasure basket offer objects to each other.

When offered an interesting array of objects to choose from in a well-stocked basket, sharing does not become an issue. If they are not able to grasp the object because the other baby has got there first, babies have been observed gazing intently at the object and at the other baby before returning either to the basket and another object, or returning to the object after the other baby has discarded it after a period of play (Goldschmied and Jackson 1994; Forbes 2004).

Even very young babies can be seen reaching out to touch each other, echoing each other's pre-verbal sounds, imitating the smallest facial expressions, gestures and movements. (Goldschmied and Selleck 1996).

In group settings, as a practitioner you can offer young babies opportunities to begin getting to know each other, communicating through gentle touching and reaching out for each other. It is important to position babies carefully, ensuring that they are safe from more mobile babies and toddlers. Think about background noise as you find a safe space for this early play experience – a quiet area is needed. This is also an ideal time to observe and record early communication and play.

Competent learners

The nurseries of Reggio Emilia in Northern Italy have received worldwide recognition and acclaim for their practice and visionary provision. The '*pedagogiste*' (educators) ask themselves, 'Who is a child?' The central concept and image is that of the 'rich' child; they see children as co-constructors of knowledge, 'rich in potential, strong, powerful and competent and most of all connected to adults and to other children'.

The *pedagogiste* work in an environment based on values and the children. It is shaped not by a method, but by a way of thinking about education.

The framework provided by *Birth to Three Matters* (DfES 2002) suggests that we look at babies and young children through four headings (as identified above): a competent learner; a healthy child; a skilful communicator; a strong child. These four 'aspects' are then subdivided into 'components'. The components provide the detail and description of the aspects.

'A competent learner' identifies young children creating, discovering and experimenting with symbols and marks, creatively exploring and experimenting with sounds and movement, becoming competent and creative, resourceful. It identifies how children begin to imitate, mirror and imagine. It recognises that young children are multi-sensory and use all their senses when they play imaginatively and begin to use gestures, ideas and words. It describes how children make and use patterns and find out about the environment, making connections through the senses and through movement.

The framework highlights and focuses on the developing strengths, abilities and skills of these young children. It celebrates what babies and young children can do, what they are interested in and how adults can promote and encourage this development.

Table 1 (below) identifies the key focus of the component parts (see DfES 2002 for the detail of the aspects and components). The framework views the baby and young child holistically, building on the principal understanding that they are competent learners from birth.

What are very young children entitled to?

It is vital that we think about, value and respect babies and young children for what they can do. The United Nations Convention on the Rights of the Child and the Children Act 1989 set out the rights and entitlements of *all* children. Try looking up the Convention on the web, or go to: www.cirp.org/library/ethics/UN-convention. Article 1 of the UN Convention states that the rights are for all people under 18 years of age. They apply to everybody without discrimination (Article 2).

Respecting and working towards the UN Rights of the Child means ensuring that your practice, the environment and the play experiences that you offer start with the child and what they are entitled to.

Attachment theory

John Bowlby's seminal work for the World Health Organization on homeless children shaped much of the emphasis on attachment relationships. His work has influenced much further research and many expert practitioners and still influences practice today. Goldschmied, who introduced the key person concept and the importance of close

> **REFLECTIVE ACTIVITY**
>
> If you are not familiar with the UN Convention on the Rights of the Child, look it up.
>
> How many countries have signed up to it?
>
> How many articles does it have?
>
> How do the practice and policies of your setting respond to the Rights of the Child?

A STRONG CHILD	A SKILFUL COMMUNICATOR	A HEALTHY CHILD	A COMPETENT LEARNER
Me, Myself and I *Realisation of own individuality*	Being Together *Being a sociable and effective communicator*	Emotional Well-being *Emotional stability and resilience*	Making Connections *Connecting ideas and understanding the world*
Being Acknowledged and Affirmed *Experiences and seeking closeness*	Finding a Voice *Being a confident and competent language user*	Growing and Developing *Physical well-being*	Being Imaginative *Responding to the world imaginatively*
Developing Self-assurance *Becoming able to trust and rely on own abilities*	Listening and Responding *Listening and responding appropriately to the language of others*	Keeping Safe *Being safe and protected*	Being Creative *Responding to the world creatively*
A Sense of Belonging *Acquiring social confidence and competence*	Making Meaning *Understanding and being understood*	Healthy Choices *Being able to make choices*	Representing *Responding to the world with marks*

Table 1

early attachment relationships between practitioners, parents and very young children, was influenced by the work of Bowlby and Anna Freud.

Bowlby documented the distress of children made homeless and being cared for in institutions at the end of World War II. The film made by one of his colleagues (James Robertson, a social worker) of young children separated from their parents while they were in hospital was distressing to all who saw it. (Such is the film's impact that care should be taken when sharing it with students, even today.)

Bowlby's work on attachment theory has helped us to understand some significant aspects of young children's emotional behaviour and development.

Some key points of Bowlby's (1969) theory are:

- babies are born to find secure attachments; they are instinctively looking for comfort, to be close to an adult, physically and emotionally
- babies and young children can become close to a small number of adults
- as we mature we do not need or rely on others so much, except at crisis times or periods of stress in our life (Goldschmied and Jackson 1994).

During the period after the publication of Bowlby's work, it was seen very much as the mother's role to be the close adult. It was thought that those babies and young children who did not spend all of their time with their mothers would have serious problems, developmentally and emotionally, by not forming secure attachments or relationships.

Other researchers, such as Mary Ainsworth, carried out work to assess children's attachments to adults, primarily their mothers. Ainsworth pioneered the 'strange situation'. This was a test where the mother and her baby are playing together in a room. The mother then leaves the baby and returns a few minutes later. The researchers measured how 'anxious' the baby had become and how quickly the mother could reassure her baby. The babies who were more easily reassured by the mother following a cuddle and a greeting, and then continued playing, were seen to be 'secure'. However, not all babies responded securely to their mother's return:

- 'Anxious avoidant' babies were seen to be distressed on the mother's leaving, but avoided her or did not want her attention on her return.
- 'Anxious ambivalent' babies demonstrated a mixture of behaviour: they appeared not to know what they wanted, demanding attention and reassurance at first, then pushing the mother away.

The tests have also been filmed, with Ainsworth sending in a stranger with the mother and baby. The stranger is left in the room with the baby as the mother leaves. The stranger then tries to interact and join in the baby's play, trying to reassure the baby and take the place of the mother. For the 'secure' babies, the distress of a stranger trying to intervene and console them is evident; the anxious avoidant and anxious ambivalent children do not react in the same way to the stranger, putting up with her attempts to pacify and interact with them and then not responding to the return of their mother (Bowlby 2002).

More recent work on attachment by Howard Steele (2001) demonstrated that young children who were insecure or disorganised in a 'strange situation' had raised levels of cortisol up to 30 minutes after the reunion with the parent. (The brain produces cortisol in response to stress or fear.)

We also know from Bowlby's (1988) work that when babies and young children are frightened by something they will want to get close, both physically and emotionally, to the significant adult in their life. For those young children in out-of-home settings, when their parents (or main carer) are not there, the significant adult will be their key person. For the young child, the beginning and end of the day are often challenging times, as parents leave and arrive. Other adults (staff and parents) entering or leaving the room (are they coming back? who are they?), and going to a new area or having something personal done (nappy changing, sleeping, feeding) are also times when babies and young children can feel very vulnerable.

Key person approach

Establishing a close relationship with the child and their family is essential for a practitioner taking on the role of the 'key person'.

Much has been written on the key person approach (Hopkins 1988; Goldschmied and Jackson 1994; Elfer *et al.* 2003) and the importance of relationships between practitioners, parents and children (you will find further reading on p. 96).

PAUSE FOR THOUGHT

Read some of the literature on the key person approach and emotional development of very young children before you respond to the following scenario.

Imagine you are working in a setting for children under three.

How would you respond to a colleague who suggests that very young children do not need to have a close relationship with practitioners and that staff rotas in the area should enable staff to move around every week to get to know all the children and their routines and use all the resources available? The colleague suggests that it is 'good' for the young children to get to know all the staff in the setting, so that they will not become dependent on one person.

What might be your response to your colleague?

Whatever the setting, the key person approach is a way of working in which the entire focus and organisation enable and support close attachments between individual children and individual nursery staff or childminders. It is not about 'task management' or planning regimented routines for young babies (where the focus is on the activity or event rather than the care, play and learning needs of the young child). Rather it is about enabling young children to form a secure attachment to their key or primary carer and encouraging parents to become involved with that key person, developing a close professional relationship.

This might seem like a tall order, but looking after the emotional development and needs of children under three *is* a complex matter. Families bring a range of experiences and events with them when they choose out-of-home care for their children. It is up to the practitioner to ensure that families have time and space to be part of and contribute to their baby's daily routine in the setting. This can only be supported through the key person approach.

Goldschmied and Jackson (1994) tell us that 'The denial of close personal relationships is a serious flaw in most group day-care, which can partly be overcome by changes in organisation'. We already know that close relationships formed with adults are the key to a young child's play and learning. Babies begin by exploring the person closest to them, finding out who this person is, where they begin and end, what they smell of, what they taste of. Relationships need to be of a close, high-

Close, personal relationships between the young child and significant or key person are crucial.

quality responsive and responsible nature – the quality of the learning depends on the quality of the relationship. Having a secure attachment to their primary carers and to a key worker in a nursery setting appears to impact on a child's ability to cope with major life changes. This emphasises the importance of stable and sensitive care for very young children in an early years setting.

From the consistency (in terms of affection, behaviour, language and boundaries) of a young child's key person come other important constants – routines, which are responsive to changing and developing needs and behaviour, and sensitivity to changes in home circumstances, which can be traumatic (e.g. the breakdown in family relationships).

However, those of us who work with very young children know that it is the smaller events that can be just as significant – the change in the route to nursery, forgetting a precious toy or comforter, a sleepless night or a child beginning to feel under the weather (as demonstrated in *Key Times*, Manning-Morton and Thorp 2001) – and often only an adult close to the child can notice and respond to these. Then the planned walk to the postbox can be put off and the need for comfort, a nap and cuddles can be addressed when the child needs it and not 'after lunch when everyone has a sleep'.

Sensitive and responsive practitioners will ensure that materials, play experiences and opportunities are relevant and appropriate to the changing and developing needs of these young children.

REFLECTIVE ACTIVITY

Think about and discuss with a colleague:

What does a key person do?
How is the key person approach organised and managed in your setting?
How does the key person approach work within a key worker system?
What do families in your setting know and understand about the key person approach?
What do the national standards say about the key person?
Do you need to do some further reading before introducing the key person approach to your setting?
Is the relationship with the child similar or different in a small setting (compare a childminder and a large group)?
Can the key person approach be organised to work in a playgroup, a nursery and a childminder's setting alike?

In considering the rights and entitlements of babies and very young children, we have identified the need for close and constant relationships with the adults who care for them in out-of-home settings, promoting and supporting language development and communication by paying careful attention to the child and the environment.

PAUSE FOR THOUGHT

Observe the babies and young children in your setting and carry out an audit of the provision.

How is the practice respectful and responsive?

What entitlements do you think the children in your setting are receiving?

Are these the entitlements of all babies and very young children?

'A very young child in the nursery is often the only person in the nursery who cannot understand why he is there.' (Goldschmied and Jackson 1994)

PLAY, CARE AND LEARNING

Exploring, playing and learning

The most important element of a high-quality play and learning environment for babies and children up to three is the adult. In examining this critical role, we will be looking at the work of some of the 'grand theorists', such as Piaget, Bruner and Vygotsky, in relation to young children. We will explore how their work still influences our practice and provision today and how, through further research and practice, our views of babies and young children as 'competent learners' (DfES 2002) – as opposed to 'blank slates' – have developed.

Very early on, babies begin exploring through their own body what they can do and what effect their actions have on people and objects. They are very social beings (indeed it is crucial for their survival that they interact and engage with adults), wanting to engage adults and other children in 'proto-conversations' (Trevarthen 1998). These are the beginnings of conversations, where the baby and the adult talk to each other, listening, pausing, imitating and mirroring.

Play is a ubiquitous activity for young children, but what exactly do we mean by 'play'? We know that play is essential for healthy growth and development, and central to all young children's learning. However, there are many terms used to describe play, which mean many different things to different people.

Piaget saw play as the means by which the child's learning comes together and helps them make sense of the world. Vygotsky emphasised the importance of social interaction, of other people being involved in play. His theory focuses on children using play to act out and practice things before they manage them in real situations. He also described children's learning from a point he called the 'zone of proximal development to the zone of actual development' (see also p. 86). This is the basis of 'thinking theory', or social constructivism, which many early years settings use as a basis for their provision. Tina Bruce (1991) tells us that '…many things called play by those of us working with children are not so'.

By observing babies' and young children's play behaviour, practitioners can begin to think about providing an environment rich with opportunities, where babies and toddlers can choose where they want to be and make decisions about the resources available to them. This means practitioners will have to plan and manage an environment that is flexible to the changing and developing interests and needs of these young children. The very early years curriculum, then, will be based on the child's development, focusing on what they are able to do, either with some support or on their own. We can begin to think holistically – focusing on what the child is interested in, promoting and encouraging what they are able to do.

Practitioners will need to think about the following points:

- What is this baby/toddler like (e.g. noisy, quiet, shy, outgoing, inquisitive, beginning to crawl, just becoming stable when seated, showing preferences for particular people, particular areas of the home base, trying to pull themselves up on everything)?
- What is the child interested in (e.g. exploring noisy objects, being with a particular child, rolling objects, transporting objects, dropping objects into containers, watching older children in the garden)?
- With whom and where does the child prefer to be (with a particular child or group of children, a particular adult, at the role-play area, the book area, the block or workshop area)? How do they meet and greet other adults in the setting? How do you manage this? Have they settled in with their key person or significant adult?
- Providing opportunities for babies and young children to play by themselves and with other adults and children around them.
- Adding to the baby's and young child's play experiences (e.g. some new objects, using familiar objects in a different context).
- Supporting play with sensitive conversations and appropriate praise.

Emotional well-being is essential to play and learning

Babies and very young children need to develop healthy emotional attachments in order to feel secure. This feeling of being safe encourages them to feel safe enough to leave their key person and to explore, knowing that that person will still be available should they need them. The trusting relationship enables and supports risk taking (Bowlby 1988).

Daniel Goleman's (1996) writing on emotional well-being has led us to consider the need for love and security in a new context, helping early years practitioners to think more deeply about the 'how' and 'why' of their work, utilising systems such as the key person approach, and working closely with families and other agencies to promote emotional literacy and well-being. Considering young children's well-being has now become part of the curriculum in many settings.

This is not an entirely new approach, of course, with many practitioners having already offered young children opportunities to communicate their feelings through play experiences, puppets and special teddies, as well as telling and reading stories that illustrate difficult situations. New theories are helpful to practitioners, as Bruce (2001: 19) tells us: 'Theories help us to make sense of what we see... We may find our observations fit with theories. We may find that they do not. This will help us to think deeply'.

Encouraging practitioners to reflect

The work of Paley (1992) has also encouraged practitioners to talk and listen to the youngest children about what they believe and understand to be right and wrong, about their own feelings and those of other children. Listening to children, and supporting their ideas and thoughts to become part of policies and practice, are also vital, as demonstrated by Penny Lancaster (2003).

The Carnegie Foundation of New York (1994) identified six characteristics of competent three-year-olds:

- physically and mentally healthy
- empathic towards others
- intellectually inquisitive
- self-confident
- able to use language to communicate
- able to relate well to others.

Birth to Three Matters (DfES 2002) 'highlights the interrelationship between growth, learning, development and the environment in which they are cared for and educated'. The observations and responsive, reflective support of the growth, learning, development, environment and play opportunities of young children should form the framework for an appropriate 'curriculum'.

What does the play of babies and young children look like?

We need to be careful observers of young children in order to identify their play. Babies begin to play before they are born and scans show us how playful the developing foetus can be (Forbes 2004).

Finding out where you begin and end, reaching for a familiar face and hair.

Babies' play begins with the adult closest to them. For young babies it is the exploration of the adult's physical features, hair and jewellery, all within easy grasp.

This is how babies begin to find out about themselves and the people closest to them. Play offers them the opportunity to explore the following questions:

- Who am I, and where do I fit in with all these other people and things?
- What can I do?
- What effect do my actions have on other people and things?
- Who are you? Are you like me? How are we similar or different?

Play and other people

Babies and young children need adults with whom they have a close relationship to support their play. In out-of-home settings practitioners who are able to provide this are crucial. Sharing what happens in the setting and what goes on at home is essential. In settings where parents and families are involved by sharing their knowledge and observations of their child's play behaviour there is a good understanding of the benefits this brings to the practitioner, the parent and, most importantly, the child (Whalley and the Pen Green Centre Team 1997).

It is a very important part of your role to involve families in their young children's play, both in and out of the setting, and to support parents to understand and respond to it.

Think about how you might respond to young children's developing emotional, social and physical communication and cognition in play situations, based on the following principles:

- play should be supported and facilitated by the adult, through appropriate play opportunities
- play should not be directed
- babies and young children can and should be supported to be in charge of their play experiences, making and controlling the rules
- practitioners require the skills of observation and responsiveness in order to respond to the signals of babies and young children
- babies and toddlers need and enjoy the company of other children – opportunities for playing and being with peer groups and older children are important.

Vygotsky (1978) identified the zone of proximal development – the things children can do only with help – and the zone of actual development – what the child can do without any help (which shows the learning that has occurred). Vygotsky's theory recognises:

- the key role played by adults and other more knowledgeable or experienced children to support the baby's learning
- the gap between actual and potential is the zone of proximal development
- play leads to the enjoyment of games
- play helps children to make sense of what they learn.

PAUSE FOR THOUGHT

Think about opportunities you already give or might be able to plan to enable babies and young children to meet older children and play together.

For many children today the family experience has changed. Some children do not have siblings or lack opportunities to play with other children. Families are moving away, so we are losing the model of extended families, and parents often spend more time away from home in the workplace. There may be fewer opportunities for young children to play in informal group settings due to location (both rural and urban spaces can seem lonely, as well as being geographically challenging), environment or financial constraints. As a practitioner you will need to bear this in mind when planning settling-in or play experiences for young children. They may not have experienced being in noisy areas, where toys and people are 'shared', for example.

Gopnik *et al.* (1999) tell us that 'babies' minds are at least as rich, as abstract, as complex, as powerful as ours. Babies and young children think, reason, learn and know as well as act and feel. They consider evidence, draw conclusions, do experiments and solve problems and search for truth'.

Think about the very young children you know and how you see them every day trying to find out more about the exciting world they have become part of: exploring the sounds and actions they hear and see, watching people doing strange things and being part of new rituals and events. Then you can begin to think more coherently about the play and learning needs of these very young children.

WHAT DOES A CURRICULUM FOR YOUNG CHILDREN LOOK LIKE?

In this section we will examine the term 'curriculum' and its relevance to very young children. The term curriculum is defined as a course of learning or study, neither of which is particularly appropriate in relation to young children, especially those under three.

Selleck and Griffin (1996) remind us that it is important to differentiate between the training and learning of babies; they emphasise that 'it is the imaginative provision of materials, developmentally and culturally focused, with choreographed experiences that enrich a baby's emerging pattern of activity'.

'Choreographed experiences' would imply that some thought has gone into either creating an experience that is appropriate for a baby or toddler at a particular moment in time or building on a specific interest being demonstrated at a particular moment. For example, the practitioner who, following a conversation and time spent watching birds in the nursery garden with a young baby, lifts the chuckling baby up into the air and sings, 'Up up up baby flies, high in the sky, fly like a bird baby, fly like a bird…'.

This might be a kind of choreographed experience that is relevant and important for this young baby, not waiting until it is 'singing time' at a planned time later in the day or week (Forbes 2004).

Perhaps, then, we should think about a very early years curriculum for children not as a ready-made package or document with activities and 'learning outcomes or intentions' (possible or otherwise) already described and set up for practitioners to use, but in terms of their developing and changing needs, interests and innate curiosity. The expert practitioner will observe and then support and promote play and learning through respectful and responsive provision.

In the Reggio Emilia nurseries, visitors from all over the world are able to observe and share the learning experiences of the *pedagogiste*. The nurseries also employ artists, ceramic workers, potters and musicians to work with the children. Here the emphasis is on creative experiences.

A curriculum should be about everything a young child experiences during a day, everything they hear, see, smell, touch and taste. It should involve all the adults they come into contact with, whatever their role and responsibilities.

Dorothy Selleck (2001) observes that practitioners will use a range of theories and frameworks in their work with young children and that an absolute or definitive curriculum is not appropriate. She urges practitioners to debate, research, think about the families and communities these young children come from and are part of. She also identifies what she considers to be most important for babies and young children:

- following a child's inclinations, interests and schemas – enjoy their capacity for imagination and creativity

- being energetic and responsive – offering multi-sensory, aesthetically pleasing spaces, places and objects to engage with a child's power to think and express, represent, construct and reconstruct

- embracing each baby into a community – a social culture that may be modified and flexible in the interests of the people in it, including those under three years of age.

(Selleck 2001: 95)

REFLECTIVE ACTIVITY

What do you know about the treasure basket and heuristic play? Do some reading (Goldschmied and Jackson 1994; Forbes 2004).

The treasure basket and heuristic play respond to the needs of very young babies and toddlers to investigate, explore, mouth, collect, fill, empty and refill with a range of objects and containers. The treasure basket offers seated, non-mobile babies the opportunity to make choices from an array of safely selected objects, all from the real world and none made of plastic. All the objects offer rich sensory play.

Make a collection of objects for a treasure basket. (See Forbes 2004 to find out how to introduce a basket if the concept is new to babies, practitioners and parents.)

Observe a group of babies at the treasure basket. What are they doing? How can you extend their interest and exploration? Set up a heuristic play session for a group of toddlers. What do they do? How can you use the principle of heuristic play in other play experiences for these young children?

Curriculum planning

Practitioners working with very young children should be able to plan for the children's individual and changing needs, as identified in the National Standards (DfES 2001: 24). Annex A (babies/children under two) directs that 'there is clear planning of babies' activities' and that 'activities…are appropriate for the child's age and provide varied sensory opportunities and experiences both indoors and outdoors'. However, the Standards do not offer any guidance as to what is an appropriate 'activity' for children under three. Dorothy Selleck (1997: 18), reflecting on her visit to Reggio Emilia, offers food for thought on many of the 'art activities' she has observed in UK daycare settings, where babies in highchairs are made to 'paint' or glue 'pictures', when all they really want to do is explore the glue, watch it run down their fingers and hands, and smear it across a table.

As a practitioner you may need to share your planning with inspectors and other professionals in and out of the setting. Parents and carers should be involved in the planning and experiences for their young children. A daily dialogue between parents and practitioners can support planning, so that delivery is responsive to and reflective of the child's current interests and characteristics. Involving parents and young children in the planning and assessment cycle will encourage good practice in a setting and enable parents to have a better understanding of their child's play and learning, and so be better able to support and extend these opportunities at home.

Reflective practitioners will acknowledge that most parents have a better understanding of their child's interests and can be encouraged to share their knowledge and contribute to the planning and recording of their child's learning.

Observation has to be the starting point for all planning, ensuring that play opportunities and experiences are more meaningful and appropriate for the individual child or small group of children. However, it is not possible or practical to plan a developmentally appropriate curriculum six weeks in advance for a group of babies under one year, or indeed for a group of toddlers. Observation and evaluation of daily events and experiences can support short-term planning, and play opportunities can be rearranged or new elements introduced, based on the play and interests of the child. Daily discussion can enable practitioners to plan for individual children's changing and developing needs and interests.

As a practitioner you might find it more appropriate to use the headings from *Birth to Three Matters* (DfES 2002) or *Key Times* (Manning-Morton and Thorp 2001), using the key characteristics rather than transferring the headings from the *Curriculum Guidance for the Foundation Stage* (QCA 2000). Areas of the room or dispositions and schemas are also possible ways to record planning, as suggested by

Manning-Morton and Thorp in the *Key Times* framework (2001). PLOD – possible lines of direction – (Whalley 1994) is another helpful tool. Finding a system which works for your setting, implementing it and then revising it regularly, will ensure that your planning evolves as you learn more from the babies and children you are observing.

Key characteristics from *Key Times*	Schemas (not an exhaustive list: practitioners will observe and then identify the schemas displayed by the children in their care and use those)	Areas of the nursery	Dispositions (some suggestions)
Close relationships with key adults	Inside and outside	Home corner and dressing up	Curiosity
Physical and emotional dependency	Near and far	Outdoor area/garden	Persistence
Growing sense of self	Transporting	Workshop area, art, malleable materials	Cooperation
Social relationships with peers	Over and under	Water and sand play	Problem solving
Communication	Enclosures	Construction, block, small world	Reflection
Mobility, dexterity and independence	Heap and scatter	Discovery and exploration	
Curiosity, exploration and discovery	Connecting	Book corner	
Representation, creativity and imagination	Enveloping		

Table 2 Suggested headings for planning

REFLECTIVE ACTIVITY

Look up the work of Lilian Katz, Margaret Carr and Ferre Laevers to learn more about children's dispositions and attitudes to learning.

All the practitioners working with a group of very young children should get together to share their observations and knowledge of the young children in their care. Using information from families to support their discussions, they can begin to think about the child's inclinations, what they are interested in, any patterns that can be identified in their play behaviour and any schemas that are developing.

Adults who understand and have a high degree of knowledge of the needs of young children are an integral part of an early years setting and its curriculum. These adults must be able to make and sustain warm, close, positive relationships with both young children and their families, which are vital to the emotional well-being of the child.

The most important things for very young children are:

· the routines of daily life: feeding, sleeping and resting
· being with people
· developing close relationships
· interacting and being interacted with
· watching, exploring, investigating and examining a rich diversity of resources, materials and objects.

This would translate into an environment that offers babies and young children the following:

- space
  - to lie, sit, roll, shuffle, crawl, cruise and then walk
  - that is interesting – corners where mobiles hang and dance in the breeze, where mirrors and photographs reflect 'who I am' and 'what I look like'
  - inside and outside – where they can feel the breeze and watch other children playing, hear the birds, watch the seasons and the plants change and develop
  - that is not run or planned by the clock, but by the needs and interests of the children – flexible and responsive
  - empty or 'white space' – for contemplation and daydreaming
- resources, fabrics and furnishings that
  - reflect the diversity and culture of the children in the group and the community
  - are rich in texture, colour and sound
  - are a balance of natural and made objects – from the real world
  - promote and encourage young children's developing mobility – at heights where children can pull themselves up, lean on and use surfaces to explore objects
  - encourage children to reach into, choose and select resources themselves
- adults who
  - are interested in the 'minutiae' that fascinate and fill a young child's day
  - observe, listen and respond to the signals and signs from babies and very young children
  - are interesting and talk about everything that is going on
  - are confident to respond flexibly and spontaneously to the child's interests and needs.

For some settings, non-mobile babies, crawlers, cruisers and walkers will all be together in one home base; in other settings, non-mobile babies are together and move 'up' once they become mobile. Whatever the age range or mobility of the children, the core design of the home base may not be changeable; however, setting out the furniture and equipment is something you will be able to make decisions about. It is crucial that these are based on your knowledge of the children and adults who will be using the space – adults should be able to move freely through the area and noise has to be considered (background noise may distract or disturb young children – and the adults working in the area – especially if it is constant).

An appropriate environment is crucial, especially in group care, when more and more babies and young children are spending longer periods of time in out-of-home care settings.

In summary, an early years 'curriculum' must consider the experiences that are of most relevance to very young children themselves. The most important part of the curriculum is the adult, who must have the skills and knowledge to understand what very young children are entitled to and need. The adult must have a sound understanding of development and use this knowledge to respond to and plan for children's interests, play and learning.

BEYOND THE UK: COMPARING PROVISION

There has been an increase in the number of young children under three years of age attending formal (i.e. registered) settings in the UK. The expansion of programmes such as Sure Start, Neighbourhood Nurseries and Children's Centres means there has been an increase in publicly funded provision (Bennett 2003).

Britain has high numbers of adults with low levels of literacy and numeracy: 23% in Britain compared to 12% and 7% respectively in Germany. In practical terms this means that adults with functional illiteracy, about 1 in 5 of the population, would not be able to find a plumber in the Yellow Pages if they were given the alphabetical index. This has enormous implications as it affects the wealth and health of our society. 60% of people in prison have functional illiteracy and/or innumeracy (Moser, 1999).

We know from research such as Starting Strong and from practice in early years settings that adults make a big difference to the play and learning of young children, particularly in terms of supporting and extending young children's speech and language development. Some parents may not have experienced a rich language environment and so have little experience of nursery rhymes, songs and games that are essential in early language play. For many families, financial and environmental concerns are more relevant than the play and learning of their young children (Wells 2003).

In Sweden, Denmark and Finland, children start school at six years of age. The provision there for children under three is mostly subsidised and the emphasis is very much on the development of social skills and:

- the importance and need for close relationships with children and adults, and understanding and responding to children's signals
- self-confidence, self-esteem and self-respect
- awareness of children's learning through their senses
- children's rights to appropriate provision and nurture and care from adults.

(Jensen 1994; Griffin 1997)

PAUSE FOR THOUGHT

Think about the provision offered in your setting or a setting you know for children aged 0–3 years.

What opportunities for play are there, to ensure these young children have choices and can make decisions?

How is the environment planned and set out?

How do the adults respond to the changing and developing needs of these very young children?

Babies and young children in Western society are not always viewed as being equal or important. It would appear that much of early childhood is spent hurrying children along, moving them from one task to another, one stage to the next (Cousins 1999).

We do not always appreciate or give time to their efforts of exploring and finding out about the world. They spend much of their time surrounded by imitations of the real world, because the real thing is considered too risky or too challenging. It could be argued that we have become a society that tries to protect our children from the real world, from opportunities to play outside, having real experiences, thereby depriving them of many of the multi-sensory experiences of life. Even very small children spend long periods of time (passively) watching television and playing computer games, which can lead to delays in speech and language and, increasingly, to weight problems and even obesity.

In many other cultures babies and young children are part of the real world, of daily life. Children are viewed as equals in adult society and young children are encouraged and supported to try out and be part of 'adult activities', such as collecting firewood, making simple meals, collecting berries and making beads and jewellery and helping to care for babies and younger children. In New Guinea and Bali very young children are looked after by other children as young as four. And anthropologists have noted that midwives in other cultures do not treat the newborn baby with the kid-glove delicacy that is often seen in Western society: the head of the newborn is not supported especially and parents and families (because families are much more involved in childcare in non-Western societies) hold and carry the young baby around for much longer periods of time – in some societies, right up until the child is weaned at two. In some cultures this results in babies and children who appear to be a lot calmer and cry less. The babies appear to read the body language of their parents more closely, more instinctively, and adults seem to be much calmer and less anxious about handling and holding young children (Jackson 2002).

Many adults, including parents and practitioners, are unused to handling and holding young babies and can feel anxious about it (babies are incredibly attuned to the moods and feelings of the adult holding and handling them). Babies are not as fragile as is often supposed, but adults – especially those handling and holding other people's babies and young children – need to ensure that they are held and handled skilfully and comfortably.

In other parts of the world children as young as two are part of the family workforce. I saw this on a trip to Lima, Peru, where such children were collecting rubbish for recycling and selling sweets in the streets – no time for play or the experiences we associate with early childhood in the West. Out in the villages I also saw groups of children walking across the fields, smartly dressed in uniform as they headed for the nearest school, often over distances of many miles.

Comparing the provision and experiences in Reggio Emilia to the familiar provision in the UK, it is interesting to consider that the former settings do not have the familiar resources and equipment used in so many settings here in the UK. In Reggio Emilia it is about home-from-home comforts: the babies sleep in baskets and low beds; toddlers are able to choose when they want to sleep and to get themselves in and out of 'bed' (which included in one setting a mattress in a small alcove, curtained off from the rest of the space to allow some privacy and quiet time). Children as young as 18 months are involved in choosing when and where they want to rest.

Light and lots of space appear to be the key factors in the Italian nurseries. Many of the materials and resources are everyday objects, fabrics of all kinds for dressing up and wrapping themselves in, collections of pebbles, baskets containing shells, natural objects – cones, stones, wood, ceramics. Light tables and lighting generally are carefully considered and used for opportunities such as exploring shadows. Reflections and reflectors are used everywhere and mirrors of all different sizes and shapes are available for children. Mirrors are vital for the exploration of the self, but can be unnerving and disorientating – as I discovered when sitting inside the triangular mirror at The Hundred Languages of Children Exhibition during the UK tour in May 2000 and December 2004. The exhibition displayed young children's ideas, feelings and knowledge through a range of media, including paintings, sculpture, drawings and photographs. It inspired, stimulated and humbled. It also offered a challenge to the seemingly limiting opportunities and experiences sometimes offered to young children in the UK to explore and use the real world around them. The Italian children appear to play and learn in a culture where their abilities and potential are never underestimated – high-challenge, low-threat environments. Tables are laid out with objects from the real world, ceramic or glass jugs, no plastic plates and beakers. The youngest children are encouraged to carry, pour and fill at mealtimes.

In New Zealand the early years curriculum is called Te Whāriki, which means 'woven mat'. It describes a framework that is the guiding thread of the early years programme in each setting. It consists of four principles and five aims (Blatchford and Moriarty 1998). Each childcare centre creates a unique curriculum, responding to contexts which are relevant for the children of the centre.

The child has
A hundred languages
A hundred hands
A hundred thoughts

—Loris Malaguzzi

REFLECTIVE ACTIVITY

Look up Te Whāriki and identify the principles and aims.

Identify the differences and similarities between Te Whāriki and the framework provided by *Birth to Three Matters* (DfES 2002) and *Curriculum Guidance for the Foundation Stage* (QCA 2000).

Does the New Zealand document have learning outcomes and are they the same as those in our foundation stage?

Once you have begun to read around these topics you might like to organise some debates among your student group to discuss these and other questions and issues that you identify in your reading.

A child under three speaks in a hundred different ways. It is up to you as a practitioner to observe, listen, respond to and reflect on the thinking and communication of our youngest children, ensuring that their voices are not lost or misinterpreted.

KEY TEXTS AND RESOURCES

Abbot, L. and Moylett, H. 1997: *Working with the Under-3s: Responding to Children's Needs*. Buckingham: Open University Press.

Abbot, L. and Rodger, R. (eds) 1997: *Quality Education in the Early Years*. Buckingham: Open University Press.

Carr, M. 2001: *Assessment in Early Childhood Settings*. London: Paul Chapman Publishing.

Katz, L. 1997: 'A developmental approach to assessment of young children'. http://www.ceep.crc.uiuc.edu/ (accessed October 2004)

Laevers, F. *The Leuven Scale for Young Children*. Leuven, Belgium: Centre for Experiential Education.

Te Whāriki (New Zealand early years curriculum). www.minedu.govt.nz/web/downloadable/dl3567_v1/WHARIKI.pdf (accessed October 2004).

Videos:

Goldschmied, E. 1987: *Infants at Work. Babies of 6–9 Months Exploring Everyday Objects*. London: National Children's Bureau.

Goldschmied, E. and Hughes, A. 1992 (reprinted 2000): *Heuristic Play with Objects: Children of 12–20 Months Exploring Everyday Objects*. London: National Children's Bureau.

Goldschmied, E. and Selleck, D. 1996: *Communication Between Babies in their First Year*. London: National Children's Bureau.

THE FOUNDATION STAGE (3–5 YEARS)

IN THIS CHAPTER WE WILL CONSIDER THE FOLLOWING TOPICS:

* Historical roots of early childhood curricula
* Curriculum guidance or framework
* Principles underpinning the foundation stage
* Six areas of learning.

This chapter sets out to examine the influences that preceded the establishment of a foundation stage for three- to five-year-olds in England. We will reflect critically on both the principles which underpin it and the areas of learning which it aims to develop (QCA 2000).

HISTORICAL ROOTS OF EARLY CHILDHOOD CURRICULA

Until the publication of *Nursery Education: Desirable Outcomes for Children's Learning on Entering Compulsory Education* (SCAA 1996), early childhood education in this country was widely perceived as relying on an informal curriculum. In fact, nursery education has a strong tradition of practice (Blackstone 1971; Tizard 1974), sometimes referred to as the 'common law' of nursery education (Webb 1974) or, less flatteringly, by Bruner (1980: 53), as 'the nursery ideology of extreme dogmatism'.

These comments do not reflect the fact that early childhood education has a number of roots. The term 'nursery tradition' generally conjures up an image of progressive or child-centred education, in stark contrast to the elementary school tradition (Whitbread 1972), with its associated images of young Victorian children tied to desks to stop them roaming. These extremes have had echoes, albeit faint, in the negotiations over the Curriculum Guidance for the Foundation Stage (QCA 2000) – a headlong clash between those whose view of education is rooted in the elementary tradition and whose focus is on knowledge and skills, and those whose philosophy stems from the nursery tradition and whose focus is on the process of learning.

The second group, as Blackstone (1971) points out, has two distinct strands associated with the middle-class and working-class origins of nursery education. The middle-class strand emanated from the work of Froebel (1782–1852), which began to have influence in this country in 1851, when the first kindergarten was opened. Froebel is described as: 'the first person to formulate a comprehensive theory of pre-school education, with a detailed method of carrying it out and [whose] writings still provide the basis for many of the activities in pre-school agencies today' (Blackstone 1971: 12). Froebel has additional

Robert Owen (1771–1858)

significance in that it was his work which gave rise to the notion of a philosophy of education (Aspin 1983). This concept has influenced education as a whole, but particularly early childhood education.

The working-class strand developed in response to a more glaring need than the liberal education of middle-class children. Its aim was, in part, to save children surrounded by poverty 'from moral and religious debasement' (Blackstone 1971: 18). Robert Owen's school, founded in 1816 in New Lanark, for children from two years of age was an early attempt to provide group care and education for the very young children of working-class parents (see also Chapter 9, Early Years Policy in the 21st Century, p. 173). Without doubt he sought to improve production in his mill, but his admonishments to staff to show 'unceasing kindness, in tone, look, word and action, to all the children without exception' (Owen 1858, cited in Whitbread 1972: 14) also reflect his wish to engineer social change, replacing the 'competitive, class-structured' society with one which was more socialist in outlook.

By the beginning of the twentieth century the plight of the poor began to impact on the wealthier sections of society. The changes brought about by the Industrial Revolution were affecting the health and well-being of working-class families. The failure of many recruits to be deemed fit enough to fight in the Boer War (1899–1902) had highlighted the alarming health problems of poor families. Margaret and Rachel McMillan addressed these issues in practical ways by advocating the introduction of school meals, the school health service and the establishment of a night-camp for children. She believed that the major influences on the tradition of nursery education exerted by Pestalozzi (Green and Collie 1916) or Froebel paid insufficient

Margaret McMillan (1860–1931)

attention to the problems which faced working-class children and their families. (See Chapter 9, Early Years Policy, pp. 173–4, for more on the McMillan sisters.)

By the 1930s, certain basic maxims of nursery education had begun to emerge – an emphasis on fresh air, physicality and outdoor play, and a set of agreed practices. A government report on nursery education of 1936 (Board of Education), for example, declares that chairs should never be in rows and that no nursery teacher would even think of gathering children together as a group except at story time. The tone of this and other official publications of this period is surprisingly prescriptive in view of the fact that the message from both the middle-class strand and state nursery provision was that the education of young children should not be rigid. Isaacs (1929), who became the first head of the Child Development Department, now the Institute of Education in London, wrote of the importance of adults standing back from children and building on children's interests:

> The children are free to explore and experiment with the physical world, the way things are made, the fashion in which they break and burn, the properties of water and gas and electric light, the rain, sunshine, the mud and the frost. They are free to create either by fantasy in imaginative play or by real handling of clay and wood and bricks. The teacher is there to meet the free inquiry and activity by his [*sic*] skill in bringing together the material and the situations which may give children the means of answering their own questions about the world.
>
> (Isaacs, cited by van der Eyken and Turner 1969: 39)

Although her ideas had something in common with the views of Piaget, Isaacs challenged his theories. David (1998: 157) suggests that, had Isaacs lived longer, there might have been 'a more careful adoption of Piagetian assumptions during the 1950s and 1960s'.

The development of these learner-centred ideas about education coincided with concern about the social and emotional well-being of young children. The years following World War II saw the increased influence of Freud and other psychoanalysts, such as Erikson and Fromm; and the maternal deprivation theories of Bowlby (see Chapter 4, Working with Young Children (0–3 Years), pp. 77–9).

Despite favourable accounts of the benefits of nursery education in the 1960s, a decade later Tizard was calling into question both the reflectiveness of practitioners in seeking out and acting on research and the lack of holistic services, addressing both care and education (David 1998). As David (1998: 159) suggests, '[t]he persistence of these two themes…is an indictment of both policy-makers and those of us in the field'!

The 1980s saw an explosion of criticism of nursery education. Bruner (1980), for example, saw nursery teachers as overqualified for the work they carried out – implying, perhaps, that nursery education was insufficiently challenging for both adults and children. Tizard and Hughes (1984: 181) questioned the rigour of the early years curriculum when they wrote:

> Although clear about their educational aims, nursery school teachers are often puzzled if they are asked about their curriculum, in the sense of a specific body of knowledge or skills to be taught within a given period of time. Indeed, they see themselves less as teachers, and more as providing the children with a rich learning environment. On further thought therefore they will usually say that the selection of play materials constitutes the curriculum.

These and similar criticisms led to a plethora of curriculum documents. James (1981) defined a set of 'educational aims'; Curtis (1986) created a curriculum framework based on what she termed a body of skills; in its dying days the Inner London Education Authority (ILEA) – an organisation characterised by both the large quantity and high quality of its nursery education – produced a series of curriculum booklets (ILEA 1987, 1990); and interest developed in the self-styled, cognitively oriented High/Scope curriculum. One of the perceived benefits which High/Scope gave practitioners was the common language or agreed ways of communicating about curricula (Pound 1989). The informal, organic modes of curricula which largely prevailed in this country were often based on unspoken traditions or assumptions.

It is no accident that this trend also coincided with the development and publication of the National Curriculum (NC) in 1988. Although the Plowden Report (CACE 1967, cited by Cox 1996: 4) had suggested that 'for young children only the broadest divisions of the curriculum are suitable and even older primary school children should not be exposed to "rigidly defined subjects"', the NC included in children's entitlement a wide range of core and foundation subjects from the age of five.

CURRICULUM GUIDANCE OR FRAMEWORK

PAUSE FOR THOUGHT

Consider the statements below and try to come up with some clear ideas of your own about what a curriculum is:

- The Early Learning Goals (ELGs), like the Desirable Learning Outcomes (DLOs) which preceded them, 'are not a curriculum in themselves' (QCA 2000: 26).
- The *Curriculum Guidance for the Foundation Stage* (QCA 2000) identifies the six areas of learning as providing a framework for the curriculum.
- *Quality In Diversity* (ECEF 1998: 6) describes itself as a 'framework', 'not a tool that can be used to turn out identical copies of an original form; it is not a photocopier or a pastry cutter', not designed 'to specify an early years curriculum for all'.
- Te Whāriki (New Zealand Ministry of Education 1996: 13) describes itself as offering guidelines to provide the basis for programmes in early childhood settings. Curriculum is defined as including the sum total of the children's direct and indirect learning experiences, as well as planned and unplanned experiences.

PRINCIPLES UNDERPINNING THE FOUNDATION STAGE

The principles set out in the *Curriculum Guidance for the Foundation Stage* (QCA 2000) place particular emphasis on:

- the role of parents as partners
- inclusion, including issues of cultural and linguistic diversity and special educational needs
- play.

PAUSE FOR THOUGHT

Review your planning and
consider the following questions:

- Do you always include parents
  as partners, taking their views
  into account, giving them a
  chance to respond, contribute
  or initiate ideas?
- What indication is there that
  yours is an inclusive setting,
  taking into account children's
  individuality?
- In what ways do you plan for
  play?

These are all of paramount importance to high quality provision and
need to underpin the whole curriculum. The guidance frequently uses
the phrase 'well-planned play', but for many early years practitioners this
is uncomfortable. Play is by its nature dynamic, unplanned, free-flowing
(Bruce 2001). We can only plan *for* play. Once we plan play itself, it is
no longer play.

Observation is at the heart of assessment and planning at the
foundation stage and this is underlined within the principles. The
introduction of the 'foundation stage profile' (QCA 2003) has not been
without controversy (see Chapter 6, Educational Transitions (5–8
Years), p. 119); some of the concern has arisen from practitioners who
have been used to teaching in line with the elementary strand of early
childhood education, which stereotypically starts with what must be
taught, rather than with what children are driven to learn.

SIX AREAS OF LEARNING

The following sections address each of the six areas of learning (see also
Chapter 6, Educational Transitions (5–8 Years), p. 121 and Chapter 7,
Early Years and ILT, pp. 143–5). Their aim is not to repeat what is
already defined in the curriculum guidance but to raise thought-
provoking issues, encouraging you as a practitioner to develop critical
reflection on the foundation stage and to consider the range of
possibilities open to you in developing the curriculum.

Personal, social and emotional development

You might think that the paramount importance of young children's
personal, social and emotional development is beyond question.
However, although personal development was included in the DLOs
(SCAA 1996: 1), in the introduction to the outcomes it states that the
'desirable outcomes…emphasise early literacy, numeracy and the
development of personal and social skills'. This gave a dangerous
message that literacy and numeracy were more important than the
personal aspects of children's development. Following consultation and
the development of the early learning goals into the *Curriculum
Guidance for the Foundation Stage* (QCA 2000), this area of the
curriculum was changed to personal, social and *emotional* development
and was firmly listed first among aims for children.

This sequence of events probably owes much to the following factors:

- the roots of nursery education referred to earlier in this chapter, when, by the 1980s, emphasis of those aspects of development other than the overtly intellectual was viewed with suspicion

- the growing recognition of the importance of emotional intelligence (Goleman 1996) among the general public

- greater awareness of the work of Ferre Laevers on emotional well-being as part of the Effective Early Learning Project (Pascal and Bertram 1997)

- growing understanding of the role of attachment in cognitive development (Siegel 1999; Hobson 2002).

Communication, language and literacy

Within the DLOs (SCAA 1996) this area of the curriculum had simply been called 'language and literacy'. As with the area of learning examined above, in successive discussions and consultations it was renamed to include the vital aspect of *communication*. The introduction of the National Literacy Strategy (NLS) had preceded the introduction of the *Curriculum Guidance for the Foundation Stage*. The introduction of recommendations for reception classes had created particular tensions between the elementary (emphasising the importance of phonic knowledge and the formation of recognisable letters and the high-frequency words outlined in the NLS) and the traditional strand of nursery education (more concerned with the development of spoken language, oracy in a range of contexts, enjoyment of books and writing used expressively), but a compromise was finally arrived at.

In most European countries literacy is not seen as an appropriate part of the early years curriculum. However, in the English-speaking world this is a familiar debate. Carr (2001: 22, quoting Comber 2000) writes:

> I do not want to romanticise this at all, but it is interesting to think about the panic and anxiety that the demand for six year old, independent readers produces here in Australia, when in other countries children do not even begin formal schooling or literacy learning until later. We need to be careful about the effects of other important capabilities and explore ways that children's existing knowledge, capabilities and interests might be used in the design of school literacies.

Note here the reference to using 'children's existing knowledge, capabilities and interests' – one of the fundamental tenets of early childhood education – building on children's existing understandings. The same research which has enhanced the role of personal, social and emotional development in education also emphasises the importance of motivation, interest and enthusiasm for learning (Pound and Harrison

2003). The research of Moyles *et al.* (2002) underlines the skill that is required to plan for and evaluate children's progress in a process of observing, supporting and extending children's learning.

Some practitioners claim that they are driven to inappropriate practices such as colouring worksheets and teaching isolated skills (Braedekamp 1987) by pressure from senior management or Ofsted inspectors. There is some anecdotal evidence of inappropriately qualified or inexperienced Ofsted inspectors recommending such low-level approaches. NLS small group activities with young children can become times for very low-level activity. While young children can and do concentrate for significant periods of time on self-chosen activities, they may require a good deal of support and encouragement to focus on an activity that has been chosen for them.

There is some tension between NLS recommendations and the requirements of the curriculum guidance, a fact which impacts particularly on reception class staff. While both sides of the debate want good long-term outcomes for children, it is your professional responsibility, as an experienced and well-qualified early years practitioner, to ensure provision which meets the age and stage of the children you are teaching.

Mathematical development

In many early years curricular frameworks, mathematics is not seen as an area to be singled out. The table below gives some examples of where mathematics is located in such curricula:

Curriculum guidance or framework	Inclusion of mathematics
High/Scope (Hohmann and Weikart 1995)	The curriculum covers nine areas, only one of which (number) is specifically mathematical. However, the following are all important to the subject: • language • representation • classification • seriation • space • time. The remaining areas of key experiences for children from three to five, namely movement and social/emotional development, also have an impact on mathematical understanding.
Te Whāriki (New Zealand Ministry of Education 1996)	The five aims of this curriculum document are: • well-being • belonging • contribution • communication • exploration. Mathematics is not specifically included (although communication is), but the importance of mathematical ideas is obvious throughout the document.

THE FOUNDATION STAGE (3–5 YEARS)

Curriculum guidance or framework	Inclusion of mathematics
Developmentally Appropriate Practice (Bracdckamp 1987)	The areas considered for four- and five-year-olds are: • social and emotional development • motivation • language development and literacy • cognitive development • physical development • aesthetic development. Mathematical thinking and understanding would primarily be thought of as being placed within cognitive development, but also rely heavily on motivation, language and physical development.
Quality in Diversity in Early Learning (ECEF 1998)	Drawing on around 60 or 70 curriculum documents from around the UK, this framework identifies a set of foundations of learning which are entitled: • belonging and connecting • being and becoming • contributing and participating • being active and expressing • thinking, imagining and understanding. None specifically includes mathematics, but the goals which accompany them include such statements as: • 'being and becoming more aware of written languages…including those on a computer screen' (1998: 14) • 'discovering, investigating and practising their mental and physical powers' (1998: 15) • 'expressing their ideas…through a variety of forms…[and] symbolic systems' (1998: 15) • 'making sense of the world, as they meet it through their first-hand experiences and explore it through play' (1998: 16).

The fact that the National Numeracy Strategy (NNS 1999), like the NLS, preceded the development of the *Curriculum Guidance for the Foundation Stage*, and that the DLOs had prioritised early numeracy, made it impossible to countenance a curriculum framework which did not explicitly cite mathematics as one of its key areas. However, there were fewer points of conflict with the NNS than with the NLS since the timed structure was less rigidly adhered to. There were some clear points of agreement, which included the postponing of written approaches and the emphasis on explanation, promoting mathematical thinking.

Of course, numeracy is only a part of mathematics. Some very important areas have been omitted or undervalued in this area of learning. Pattern is an example of this. It is mentioned in a single early learning goal, suggesting that children should be able to 'talk about, recognise and recreate simple patterns' by the end of the reception year. This in no way signals to practitioners the fundamental importance of pattern. Mathematicians (Devlin 2000, citing Sawyer 1955, Steen 1988, Gleason 1984) describe mathematics as a science of patterns – or to use Devlin's (2000: 73) 'fuller definition', it is 'the science of order, patterns, structure and logical relationships'. Underplaying the importance of pattern takes us back to the two strands of belief about the nature of young children's learning. If you regard mathematics as a basic skill in the elementary schooling sense of that term, then it makes sense to deal with the simple – simple patterns included. On the other hand, if your beliefs lie within the traditional strand, then the focus of teaching will be on what most interests children – the belief that we must provide what will support children's growth, in body and mind. Neuroscience teaches us that pattern is something that we as humans are good at – that we are actually born with a strong sense of pattern, upon which much of our subsequent learning depends (Devlin 2000).

Another important aspect of early childhood education (of particular importance for the development of mathematical thinking) is imagination. This link is frequently overlooked. Mathematics is popularly thought of as a matter of logic, which has no place for imagination and playful pursuits. In fact, as Devlin (2000) highlights, mathematics is an area of learning which, in its advanced stages, requires the highest levels of abstract thought. Jenkinson (2001: 79, citing Chilton Pearce) echoes this view:

> Imagination means creating images that are not present to the senses... the whole crux of human intelligence hinges upon this ability of mind... nature has not programmed error into the genetic system... the child's preoccupation with fantasy and imagination is vital to development.

Devlin proposes four levels of abstraction:

- The first is simply thinking about things which can be seen (or heard, felt or smelt) in the immediate environment. The abstract part of this thinking is that it might be possible to think of another doll in the garden or another bone in the kitchen (since Devlin believes that many species of animal are capable of this level of abstraction).
- The second level (of which monkeys seem to be capable) involves known things that are not 'perceptually accessible' (Devlin 2000: 118).
- At the third level, humans (and probably only humans) can imagine things they have never actually seen or encountered in other ways. We can think about flying bicycles or unicorns, or visualise things that are not visible.
- The fourth level is mathematical thought. Mazur (2003) underlines Devlin's view. In his book, *Imagining Numbers*, Mazur writes of the importance of imagination, enabling us to deal with abstract ideas which not only do not exist but actually could not exist.

As an early childhood practitioner, you need to reclaim the concept of imagination and its importance not only to the development of mathematical thinking but to learning and development as a whole. The opportunity to play shops or buses offers untold mathematical experiences – but mathematical play can and must go beyond even this. The benefits of play outlined in the curriculum guidance – to explore and represent experiences in order to make sense of the world; practising and building up ideas and concepts; taking risks and making mistakes; thinking creatively and imaginatively (based on QCA 2000: 25) – must also be allowed to permeate the curriculum for mathematics.

Knowledge and understanding of the world

Because the national curriculum for key stage 1 was developed and introduced before any guidance or framework for the foundation stage, teachers have tended to think of and even plan for knowledge and understanding of the curriculum in terms of its constituent parts. This area of the curriculum encompasses:

- science (with goals for exploration and investigation)
- design technology (with goals for designing and making skills)
- information and communication technology (ICT)
- history (with goals for a sense of time)
- geography (with goals for a sense of place, cultures and beliefs).

In this area of learning we might also consider the idea that entitlement should not only be thought of in terms of learning goals or objectives, but for young children should also include an entitlement to certain kinds of experience. For example, should not all children have the opportunity to swim in the sea or a lake, to travel on a train or to visit a theatre?

There can be no doubt that all the subjects that make up this area of learning are important, but if we focus too much on each subject we may miss important opportunities genuinely to give children knowledge and understanding of their world. The underpinning principles remain of paramount importance.

ICT offers an interesting example of the ways in which an overly narrow focus on this whole area of learning can limit genuine knowledge and understanding of the world. The government has invested a lot of money in computers in schools and, over time, most early years settings have been acquiring computers and programmable toys. These resources have huge potential and can offer exciting challenges to children. John Siraj-Blatchford (2004: 3–9) writes about technology projects designed to develop in young children:

- creativity, curiosity and expression
- metacognition and learning to learn
- collaboration, participation and sharing.

> **PAUSE FOR THOUGHT**
>
> Geography was a part of the curriculum for children from two to six years of age in Robert Owen's nursery, opened in 1816 in New Lanark. However, books were excluded from this schoolroom (Whitbread 1972). Why do you think Owen made these decisions? Why were books excluded and why was geography seen as so important?

Young children have the advantage of coming to technology fresh, without the prejudices of older learners for whom computers are relatively new. They also have an advantage in that they have not yet become 'conditioned into the more traditional thinking and behavioural patterns of their elders' (Siraj-Blatchford 2004: 2). Children undoubtedly enjoy using computers and can learn to use scanners, photo-editing devices (Giudici *et al.* 2001) and programmable toys (see Chapter 7, Early Years and ILT).

Unfortunately they may also spend long periods of time preoccupied, staring at the screen. This can be a disadvantage, as Healy (1999: 222) indicates when she quotes a software reviewer as saying:

> I shudder when I think of teachers spending $2,000 on anything if they don't have blocks and paint. We must keep our priorities straight! One screensaver I previewed was so engaging that children tended to simply sit and watch it.

Healy (1999) points out three major disadvantages of an overemphasis on computer technology. First she draws attention to the fact that adults are easily impressed by children's technological achievements. She cites the results (1999: 20) of a survey undertaken among 'parents, teachers, leaders from various fields, and members of the general public'. Overall, computer skills were rated more highly than values such as honesty and integrity. Curiosity, love of learning and good citizenship came much

Technology: benefit or barrier to learning about the world?

lower down the list of stated priorities. Computer skills were ranked third in a list of 16 options, and were only considered less important than basic skills (literacy and numeracy) and good work habits.

Second, she points out the dangers of what she terms 'edutainment' and reminds us that 'just because children like something does not mean it is either good for them or educational' (Healy 1999: 53). Finally she highlights a more complex argument, but one which is highly relevant for early childhood practitioners to consider. She uses an emotive phrase to draw attention to the dangers of undervaluing the importance of human interaction when she writes of 'the social and emotional ramifications of interacting with minds that think but do not feel' (1999: 167). Developmental psychologists (including Murray and Andrews 2000; Siegel 1999) have drawn attention to the importance of social and emotional interaction and this term has been picked up and is frequently used in relation to software – namely that it is interactive. However, the interactivity required by babies, toddlers and young children is not that provided by computers. What is required for development is the interaction between minds that both think and feel (Siegel 1999).

It is undoubtedly true that computers can support aspects of creativity, may support children in learning to learn and may even – when used effectively and thoughtfully by practitioners – contribute to children's understanding of collaboration, participation and sharing (Siraj-Blatchford 2004). However, we should not overlook the fact that many of these things may be learnt more effectively in real situations. Healy (1999: 225) reminds us that 'no computer can teach what a walk through a pine forest feels like. Sensation has no substitute.' She points out that computers cannot take the place of opportunities for 'rubbing shoulders with the real world in the wild'; promoting 'the spontaneous joy of a child's learning experience' and 'building intelligent muscles'.

Physical development

Physical development is a high priority in most early childhood curricula and has been for centuries. Robert Owen emphasised the importance of physical action, including in the curriculum for two- to six-year-olds 'singing, dancing, marching to music' and three hours every day in the open playground (Whitbread 1972: 10), which was surrounded by beautiful countryside – river bank and woodland.

Physical well-being was considered by Margaret and Rachel McMillan to be of paramount importance. Lowndes (1960: 74) reports a conversation in 1913 which she claims led to the opening of the open-air school in Deptford in the following year: 'We must open outdoors to the toddlers... We must plan the right kind of environment for them and give them sunshine, fresh air and good food before they become rickety and diseased'.

New Lanark: the beautiful site of Robert Owen's mill and workplace nursery.

There are major current concerns about the physical well-being of young children. Diet and exercise are seen as being at the root of physical well-being, yet all too often there is an absence of fresh fruit and vegetables in school meals and children are influenced by advertisements for unhealthy foods – on hoardings, in newspapers and magazines, in cinemas and on television. For 20 years we have known that in the USA there is scarcely a child who can speak who does not recognise the McDonald's logo (Temple *et al.* 1982). Society as a whole is also less physically active than it used to be.

When the early learning goals were published, following extensive consultation, one of the goals in the personal and social area of learning required children to be able to sit still and listen. Many practitioners were concerned about this, suggesting that it was not an appropriate goal. They felt that unless what we were asking children to focus on was interesting and engrossing, achieving this goal could become a process of coercion rather than development and maturation. In the curriculum guidance this was changed by the addition of the phrase 'when appropriate'.

Physical activity and the brain

Recently, neuroscience has underlined the importance of physical development to all other aspects of development and learning. Mimetic representation (Trevarthen 1998) – the way in which babies copy the facial expressions and gestures of those around them – is now seen as important to cognitive growth, the beginning of thought. Vestibular activity (Eliot 1999) – the rocking, bouncing, hanging upside-down, skipping and hopping with which young children so often express their excitement and enthusiasm – stimulates the brain and has a role to play in its development. Odam (1995: 19) describes music and the rhythmic movement it stimulates as 'a unique schooling for the brain'.

Gross motor activity

Doherty and Bailey (2003: 101, citing Sharp 1991) remind us that children are not simply small adults and that provision for their physical development must take account of 'their different physical and physiological characteristics'. This means that young children should have opportunities for exercise which offer:

- daily physical activity
- low, moderate and vigorous activity, with rests in between, based on the needs of the individual child
- the accumulation of between half an hour and an hour of moderate activity each day
- physical domestic tasks (such as sweeping, pegging out clothes etc.) (Doherty and Bailey 2003: 25)
- physical play, which may include rough-and-tumble, chasing, climbing, walking, running, jumping, hopping, crawling, stretching, balancing, twisting, dancing, building, lifting, carrying, throwing, catching, kicking, finding out what it feels like to hang upside-down, learning to judge speed and distance (Maude 2001, citing Boorman 1998).

The exercise opportunities offered to many children, particularly those in reception classes, fall far short of this. The short period for a PE lesson, which is often offered only two or three times each week, cannot cater for this distinct range of needs. A policy in early years settings that allows children to choose whether to be inside or out, which does not demand long periods of vigorous activity at times when children do not feel ready for it or require them to be still for long periods when their bodies are demanding action is better suited to their physiological needs.

Fine motor activity

The *Curriculum Guidance for the Foundation Stage* (QCA 2000) identifies a range of 'stepping stones' related to the goals concerning fine motor development. These recommend that children should be able to 'use a range of small and large equipment' (2000: 112) and 'handle tools, objects, construction and malleable materials safely and with increasing control' (2000: 114). As in other areas of learning, play has an important contribution to make in ensuring that children have sufficient opportunities to practise fine motor movements. Just as a baby learning to walk does far more than could be imposed through required exercise regimes – spending hours falling over, standing up, taking faltering steps, stepping over obstacles and climbing over high hurdles that present themselves – so it is with young children learning a range of small motor movements.

Motivation is all-important. Doherty and Bailey (2003) suggest that we should not indicate to children that any one form of gross motor activity is more valuable than any other. In relation to small motor activity we need to be equally careful. Activities and experiences need to be enjoyable and relevant. Using pencil and paper for tracing or filling in a worksheet is no more effective in developing fine motor competence than using pencil and paper to keep a site record while playing at builders or answering the telephone and making appointments in the hospital corner. Tearing off and screwing up small pieces of tissue paper in order to fill in an outline drawn by an adult (or even another child) may have some potential for developing fine motor abilities. It may be enjoyable for a short period, but all but the most diligent of children will tire of it quickly – which means they will not get a great deal of practice. Its relevance is not easy to see and the task cannot be deserted until the whole outline is filled in – meaning that it is likely to be perceived as a chore!

Play can support learning across the curriculum.

Using blocks and construction materials, gardening, cooking, even playing with toy cars and dressing dolls all offer a range of relevant, interesting and stimulating opportunities for motor development. Playful situations encourage children to rehearse their skills on their own terms and in their own timescale. Musical instruments have a particular role to play in developing fine motor competence. Many instruments require children to use both hands – doing the same thing with both hands or, sometimes, doing different things with each hand. Similarly, songs with actions promote rhythmic physical activity.

Outdoor provision

Maintained nursery schools traditionally placed a strong emphasis on outdoor provision and usually had large gardens. As nursery classes were developed during the 1960s and 1970s, less attention was paid to the outdoor space and much higher priority given to finding appropriate indoor space. This resulted in less focus being given to the kind of activities which can only occur in large outdoor spaces – activities related to nature or weather, and opportunities to make a lot of noise or take up a lot of space. While many classes struggled to ensure a wide range of provision, in too many settings outdoor activity was limited to short periods when everyone had to go outside, instead of being able to exercise choice. By the time of the publication of the *Curriculum Guidance for the Foundation Stage* (QCA 2000) a high proportion of early years settings, including most reception classes, had no direct access to outdoor provision. Since that time, efforts have been made to increase outdoor access for all children.

The principles for practice underpinning the curriculum guidance include a number of recommendations about developing outdoor provision (QCA 2000):

Recommendation	Implication for practice
• Include the local community and environment as a source of learning (2000: 14).	In all settings, but particularly where there is no easily accessed outdoor space, staff should ensure that full use is made of such facilities as local open spaces, parks and soft play areas as well as markets, shops, museums and galleries.
• Make good use of outdoor space so that children are enabled to learn by working on a larger, more active scale than is possible in indoors learning (2000: 15).	The guidance for creative development emphasises the importance of ensuring adequate time and space for learning. Outdoor space can be used to supplement the available indoor space, but it also allows the development of large-scale projects such as large music installations (with which you can make some extra-loud sounds), large construction with washing-machine boxes, carpet rolls or other found materials, water channels constructed from drainpipes and hoses. For children who live in flats or other homes without gardens, the opportunity to play with wheeled toys, learning to steer, regulate speed, pedal, push or pull, building muscles and perseverance, is invaluable. However, all children benefit from playing in groups, negotiating their part in the game, exploring interesting spaces and finding quiet spaces to hide away. In society, children have relatively few opportunities to interact in these ways.

▶

Recommendation	Implication for practice
• Planning the indoor and outdoor environment carefully to provide a positive context for learning and teaching (2000: 23).	The need for planning for the outdoor environment is sometimes overlooked – staff may offer explanations such as the fact that rain makes it impossible to predict what will be done. However, even though it may have to be modified, or occasionally abandoned, careful planning is essential.
• Play, both indoors and outdoors, is a key way in which young children learn with enjoyment and challenge (2000: 25).	Children (like many adults) respond well to the outdoors. They have not yet lost their sense of wonder about puddles; the wind blowing a washing line of sari fabrics or paper ribbons flapping from a fence; the way in which balls roll down slopes and trickle away in different directions and at different speeds according to their weight, size and the material from which they are made. Challenge and enjoyment are important aspects of both physical development and learning in general.

Creative development

The arts have long been seen as an important part of early childhood education. The role of creative media has been developed and celebrated as the basis of the curriculum. This is most notable in the nurseries of Reggio Emilia in Northern Italy (see Chapter 4, Working with Young Children (0–3 Years), p. 76 and Chapter 9, Early Years Policy in the 21st Century, pp. 174–5), where *atelieriste* (who may be described loosely as artists), responsible for setting up and maintaining workshops within the nurseries, support children in describing and thinking about the world through the use of creative media. They describe the range of media used as the hundred languages of children (Edwards *et al.* 1993), allowing children to express or represent ideas and feelings in a range of media. Two- and three-dimensional works, dramatic play, music and dance are developed. The central metaphor of reflection and transparency, which underpins the philosophy of their work with children, is visible in the widespread use of mirrors, glass and light (Pound 2002). Children are encouraged to represent or translate their ideas into a variety of media.

When visiting the town square, for example, children are encouraged to mime (or mimetically represent) the positions taken up by the stone lions. They may sketch the lions; go back to nursery and stand in front of a mirror pulling fierce faces; wear a cardboard mane to see what that feels like; use a spotlight and zoo animals to create a life-size shadow of a lion on the wall; or paint and model lions. All of these activities will help to build the intelligent muscles that Healy (1999) wants for young children and to gain an emotional insight into 'lion-ness', creating a strong representation within the brain of concepts, allowing children to think about such ideas as ferocity and fear.

It is helpful that the creative development section of the curriculum guidance integrates thinking about dramatic and exploratory play, music, imagination and expressive and communicative modes of representation. However, few settings have developed these opportunities to the extent of Reggio Emilia. It is disappointing that guidance on planning in the foundation stage issued by QCA (2001) contains *no* reference to music in the section on creative development. If you are using this guidance, as a practitioner you need to take care not to fall into the same trap!

Creativity

Although creativity is included within the creative development section of the *Curriculum Guidance for the Foundation Stage* (QCA 2000), it is fundamental to all human learning, permeates the curriculum and has been described as 'an ineffable quality which brings us face to face with the very essence of what it is to be human' (Ramachandran and Blakeslee 1999: 197). However, it is true to say, as the example above from Reggio Emilia shows, that the creative arts have a particular role to play in supporting the development of creativity. The creative arts, in allowing children to represent their ideas and feelings, enable them to play with and develop ideas.

If children are to develop creativity, they need opportunities to:

- engage in abstract thought (Lewis-Williams 2002) – which requires the support of their imagination – in play and in discovering unusual connections (NACCCE 1999)
- plan and negotiate in groups, best developed in young children through play
- develop innovative or original ideas (Lewis-Williams 2002; NACCCE 1999) through play and exploration
- make use of symbolic behaviour (Lewis-Williams 2002) using the hundred languages of children (Edwards *et al.* 1993)
- see the purpose and relevance of what they are learning (NACCCE 1999)
- reflect, which will lead to critical evaluation (NACCCE 1999) – this is at the root of much that goes on in Reggio Emilia – but will be supported on a day-to-day basis by giving children tangible reasons when we praise them, rather than simply proclaiming that they have produced a beautiful picture, for example.

If as a practitioner you are to nurture and develop children's innate creativity, you need to ensure certain conditions. These include:

- freeing up time and space – an aspect which is clearly addressed in the curriculum guidance
- providing opportunities and encouragement

- helping children to feel safe enough to take risks
- encouraging children to make decisions, but also to tolerate ambiguity, not to mind not knowing or not making a decision
- bringing the perseverance associated with work and the exuberance associated with play to all their endeavours.

CONCLUSION

The introduction of the foundation stage has made it necessary for early childhood educators to examine the philosophies which have divided nurseries and other early years settings from reception classes. This is a vital part of successfully creating a cohesive stage of education. The REPEY project (Siraj-Blatchford *et al.* 2002) has emphasised the importance of a balance of adult-directed and child-initiated activities. The balance over the last 10 or 15 years has been very different. It remains to be seen whether this can be changed.

USEFUL WEBSITES (Accessed October 2004)

http://educationnow.gn.apc.org/n36houisaacs.htm

EDUCATIONAL TRANSITIONS (5–8 YEARS)

The Foundation Stage, as a discrete area of learning, has been widely welcomed. However, the transition to subject-based learning in Key Stage 1 can be problematic for teachers to plan for and children to adapt to. Some children have only been in school for little over a month when they move up to Year 1 and inevitably some pupils struggle. Parents too have expressed concern about the impact on their children of such a sudden change...

—David Bell, Her Majesty's Chief Inspector of Schools, *Ofsted News*, 19 May 2004

IN THIS CHAPTER WE WILL CONSIDER THE FOLLOWING TOPICS:

* **Differences in the structure and teaching of the foundation stage and key stage 1**
* **School management of educational transitions**
* **Supporting children's learning during transitions**
* **Pedagogies for smooth transitions.**

INTRODUCTION

From April 2004, all three-year-olds joined four-year-olds in an entitlement to free part-time nursery education and to receiving the foundation stage curriculum. This can be provided in a wide range of settings, including accredited childminder networks, early years centres, pre-schools and nursery schools. About half of three-year-olds are in the non-maintained sector, but nearly all four-year-olds are in maintained provision (DfES 2003). Regardless of the setting, children must be taught in accordance with the *Curriculum Guidance for the Foundation Stage* if the setting is in receipt of government funding to provide early education.

The foundation stage is a play-based curriculum that balances child-initiated and adult-directed learning according to the individual needs of the child. It became a statutory part of the national curriculum in 2002. The foundation stage is therefore the first stage of the national curriculum for children aged three to five (end of reception year). It is a distinct stage in the way it is structured, based on a curriculum of six areas of learning (see Chapter 5, The Foundation Stage (3–5 Years), pp. 102–16). A combination of teacher- and child-initiated play is central to the way it is taught. Children are expected to move from the foundation stage to the key stage 1 of the national curriculum, which is a subject-based curriculum, with prescribed programmes of study. During key stage 1, the style of teaching and learning moves from a play-based pedagogy to a more formal teaching style.

This chapter explores the current issues and concerns relating to the transitions that are experienced when children move from the foundation stage (pre-school education) to key stage 1 (primary school). In this context, the word 'transition' refers to the 'process of change' (adapted from Fabian and Dunlop 2002). We will look at the process of change for children who transfer from pre-school settings to the reception class (between the ages of approximately three and four), and those children who experience transition from the reception class to key stage 1 (between the ages of approximately four and five).

We will consider four main questions in this chapter. The questions have been selected because variations in curriculum structure, management, support for learning and pedagogy are all important factors that influence children's educational experiences when they progress from one educational setting to another (transference), or from one educational phase to another (transition). The four questions are:

1. How do variations between the ways in which the foundation stage and key stage 1 are structured and taught affect the process of transition between them?

2. What issues confront schools when managing successful transitions?

3. How can children's learning be supported to ensure smooth transitions?

4. What pedagogies successfully allow children to make a smooth transition from pre-school to primary school education?

The questions are addressed under four main headings, relating to the process of transition (and transference) from the foundation stage curriculum to key stage 1. Questions three and four differ in emphasis. In question three, which examines the idea of supporting children's learning during transition, we focus on adults who can support children's learning when adapting to new environments. In question four, which examines pedagogies for smooth transitions, we explore the continuity of teaching in different contexts, while also taking into account the child's perspective.

DIFFERENCES IN THE STRUCTURE AND TEACHING OF THE FOUNDATION STAGE AND KEY STAGE 1

External pressures on early years practice

Since the end of the 1980s there has been a range of working policies and practices concerned with the needs of children extending beyond education; for example, the 1989 Children Act, *Starting with Quality* (The Rumbold Report, DfES 1990, which recommended a curriculum based on eight areas of learning), the National Childcare Strategy (DfEE 1998) and, more recently, *Every Child Matters* (Green Paper 2003). Early years practice has been directly influenced by such external factors (Anning 1998). Additionally, reception class teachers have had the pressures of an overloaded primary curriculum, combined with increasing numbers of four-year-olds being admitted into their classes. This has meant that while reception class teachers have been trying to maintain good early years practice, they have also had the downward pressure of more formal programmes of study at key stage 1 of the national curriculum, alongside implementing literacy and numeracy strategies.

An appropriate early years curriculum

What constitutes an appropriate curriculum for the early years? This has been the subject of increasing debate between policy makers who emphasise *school effectiveness*, and early childhood specialists who focus on a *developmentally appropriate curriculum*. Policy developments tend to focus on preparing children for school. When children start school, they are thrown into an environment where the priorities are to raise educational standards. The 'standards' are measured by national tests that examine children's ability to achieve certain levels of attainment through a content-centred curriculum rather than a 'child-centred' curriculum. One example is the Foundation Stage Profile. It is a national assessment instrument to enable teachers to record observations and summarise children's achievements towards early learning goals. The 'goals' should be attained by the end of the foundation stage (and reception year). In this way, reception children are assessed in all 6 areas of learning for the Foundation Stage Profile. Teachers look at 9 achievements within 13 categories (assessment scales) as part of the assessment process. The 13 categories are subdivisions of the 6 areas of learning, as shown below:

Foundation Stage Profile
Summary assessments for each area of learning/scale as follows (13 in total):

1. Personal, social and emotional development
   - Dispositions and attitudes
   - Social development
   - Emotional development

2. Communication, language and literacy
   - Language for communication and thinking
   - Linking sounds and letters
   - Reading
   - Writing

3. Mathematical development
   - Numbers as labels and for counting
   - Calculating
   - Shape, space and measures

4. Knowledge and understanding of the world

5. Physical development

6. Creative development

Examples of the achievements within categories and case studies using the assessment in context can be found in *The Foundation Stage Profile Handbook* (QCA 2003). An early evaluation of this assessment system has indicated an unfavourable response (Ofsted 2004a). An evaluation by HMI (Her Majesty's Inspectors of Schools in England) revealed that teachers found it time-consuming, and schools without nurseries preferred to conduct assessments at the beginning of the reception year, rather than at the end, so that they would have a benchmark against which to judge the value added by their school at the end of key stage 1. The implications of the evaluation suggest that there needs to be a clear understanding of the purposes of the assessment system, alongside a careful review of whether it actually provides parents and teachers with the information they need to ensure smooth transitions.

Some early childhood specialists have expressed concern that government policies of raising standards can lead to an excessive concentration on formal teaching and on attaining learning goals (Drury, Millar and Campbell 2000; Anning 1998). This is an area of concern because the philosophy of many early years practitioners is rooted in the idea that education should cater for the needs of the individual child, rather than pre-specified levels of attainment. The philosophy assumes that the curriculum should be developmentally appropriate to the child's needs. Traditionally, children learn through an 'integrated curriculum', which is 'the blending of content areas into thematic or problem focused units of study and a child-centred approach to learning and instruction' (New 1992: 289); 'free play is regarded as the integrating mechanism that brings together everything that is learned' (Bruce 1987). Early years practitioners also have clear ideas about what 'good' practice is:

- practical, experiential learning
- one that takes account of the social context within which learning occurs
- recognises the important role of adults in supporting learning
- children taking responsibility for their own learning.

A range of research (see, for example, the EPPE project, Sylva *et al.* 1997–2003, 2003–8) also highlights the view that we need to understand learning in its context and that teaching and learning are dependent on each other. Links with Piaget's and Vygotsky's theories of child development are seen as part of an effective curriculum approach.

The value of play in the early years curriculum

There is a strong tradition in English early years education which regards play as essential to learning and development, and supports the provision of a play-based curriculum in nursery and infant schooling. However, the value of play has been subject to debate. In particular, questions have been raised about whether practices of free play are challenging enough for children's development (Sylva, Roy and McIntyre 1980; Meadows and Cashden 1988). Principles of play as central to learning are influenced by theorists such as Froebel, Montessori and Steiner. The introduction of the foundation stage curriculum and its guidance does, however, include a set of principles which reflect the philosophies of early theorists, and the importance of play.

Nonetheless, currently, the value of play is perhaps the biggest challenge facing teachers with the demands of the curriculum. Research has indicated that teachers' beliefs in the value of play are not always put into practice (Wood and Bennet 1997; Keating *et al.* 2002). One possible reason is that there is a lack of time for the teacher to observe or interact with children during play. Research in both pre-school and statutory school settings has indicated that play tends to be limited, lacking in cognitive challenge, poorly integrated into the curriculum and often lacking in adult support (Wood and Bennet 1997).

Structuring and teaching the foundation stage curriculum and key stage 1

There are some differences in the way in which the foundation stage and key stage 1 are structured and taught. The foundation stage is a flexible curriculum based around six areas of learning (see also Chapter 5, The Foundation Stage (3–5 Years), pp. 102–16 and Chapter 7, Early Years and ILT, pp. 143–5):

1. personal, social and emotional development

2. communication, language and literacy

3. mathematical development

4. knowledge and understanding of the world

5. physical development

6. creative development.

As a phase of education, the foundation stage has a distinct identity and contains explicit intended outcomes. By the end of the foundation stage, most children should achieve the early learning goals in the six areas of learning. Additionally, the foundation stage curriculum states that 'well

planned play, both indoors and outdoor, is a key way in which young children learn with enjoyment and challenge' (QCA 2000: 25).

In contrast, key stage 1 is a subject-based curriculum with prescribed programmes of study. During key stage 1, the style of teaching and learning generally changes, with children moving from learning, through play-based pedagogy, with opportunities for outdoor and self-initiated learning, to a more formal teaching style.

A survey of primary schools in England (conducted by Taylor Nelson Sofres with Aubrey 2002) examined how the foundation stage curriculum was implemented in reception classes. The researchers found that the way the curriculum was organised shifted over time. At the beginning of the year, the six areas of learning were integrated, but these gradually became more differentiated by the end of the year. National literacy and numeracy strategies were first delivered flexibly, across the classes. However, by the end of the year, the literacy hour and daily maths lesson were in place.

They also found that there were parallel shifts in the way the curriculum was taught (the pedagogy). There was a shift to more whole class teaching and ability grouping over the year, as recommended by the House of Commons Education and Employment Committee Report in Early Years (2000). Additionally, 25 per cent of reception teachers in the sample stated that the foundation stage curriculum did not address sufficiently the formal aspects of learning (for example, writing skills). The implication of this, according to the researchers, is that some teachers were concerned about the pedagogical approach being advocated by the foundation stage, where play 'should' be a key way of learning.

In terms of teachers' perceptions of what constitutes a smooth transition, Wood and Bennet's (2001) study of progression and continuity in pre-school and reception classes revealed similar findings. For the teachers in this study, continuity was about achieving smooth transitions between age phases and settings and in teaching approaches. These factors were influenced by national and local policies, rather than professional judgements grounded in early years philosophy.

Discontinuities in policy and teaching approaches

It is also important to understand the idea of discontinuity in transition. Discontinuity may mean that for some schools the 'transition' (the process of change) is too sudden, and may result in children's learning being put back. An over-abrupt transition into key stage 1 can undermine confidence, decrease motivation and so affect achievement. For example, Wood and Bennet's (2001) study revealed discontinuities in policy and teaching approaches. On the other hand, Hargreaves and

Galton (2002) found discontinuity to be a motivating factor. They found that children were 'excited' by the transition from primary to secondary schools and saw it as a progression, one which involved moving on to a more 'grown-up' context.

In Wood and Bennet's study (2001) all the teachers emphasised that personal and social education (PSE) was important in order to promote self-esteem, social skills and to establish a supportive ethos for children to feel safe and secure. However, in nursery, PSE was taught daily, but by reception and year 1 it was incidental. According to Bennet (2000), this suggests a discontinuity in the area of curriculum policy, because PSE is an area of the curriculum in pre-school, but not at key stage 1.

There were also discontinuities in teaching approaches (Wood and Bennet 2001). In nursery classes, teachers' planning was about free and structured play. However, there was limited time for play in reception classes and almost none by year 1. Bennet (2000) argued that the reduction of play can be seen as a discontinuity because there is no continuity in teaching approach.

The question, then, is should there be changes to the key stage 1 curriculum in order to incorporate the approaches and successes of the foundation stage? For example, should the foundation stage's emphasis on personal, social and emotional development be adopted in key stage 1 to support good behaviour and the motivation and development of 'the whole child'? On the other hand, does the foundation stage more effectively prepare pupils for some elements of the key stage 1 curriculum? Certainly, the survey evidence from Taylor Nelson Sofres with Aubrey (2002) suggests that it created a bridge between the nursery and key stage 1, giving structure to the reception year. The question remains as to how children are affected by such structures.

PAUSE FOR THOUGHT

Consider a reception class of 30 children, within an inner-city school, with a high degree of social and economic deprivation. Towards the end of the year, the children have been grouped by ability for literacy- and numeracy-related activities. What sorts of feelings might the children have about each other, or about themselves, as a result of being put in the red group (top), the blue group (middle) or the green group (bottom)? What effect do you think the groupings might have on how they see themselves as learners?

SCHOOL MANAGEMENT OF EDUCATIONAL TRANSITIONS

How schools manage educational transitions will depend on a number of factors. For example, how teachers interpret the demands of the curriculum in the light of their own professional knowledge, or the kinds of constraints schools and teachers experience, including:

- time
- the availability of human and physical resources
- the kind of commitment the school allocates to the value of outside 'play'.

Teachers' professional knowledge and curriculum management

Wood and Bennet's (2001) study of progression and continuity in pre-school and reception classes suggested that, although teachers agreed that children's learning does not take place in a linear manner, national policies were creating a linear structure that influenced how transition was achieved.

The teachers managed this mismatch through a cycle of planning, implementation, assessment and target-setting. However, there were inconsistencies across the three age groups (nursery, reception and year 1). There was a gradual shift from a 'learner-centred' model to a 'curriculum-centred' model of planning and teaching. This was influenced by the literacy and numeracy strategies. In particular, the teachers had to change their pace of working and how they ordered the content. Teachers' professional knowledge was crucial in this task. With their professional knowledge, they were able to adapt national curriculum policies, especially those areas that they considered inconsistent with how young children learn. Transition, and adapting to it, was also influenced by other factors – for example, whether children entered reception from nursery classes or local playgroups or with no pre-school experience outside the home.

The conflict that reception teachers experienced between supporting play and needing to support adult-initiated formal teaching, particularly the national literacy and numeracy strategies, was further indicated in research by Keating *et al.* (2002). However, the largest school in their survey, which had three reception classes, used a thematic approach. In the thematic approach, literacy and numeracy requirements were taught in 'chunks' of time over a period of weeks, instead of a daily activity. By managing the formal curriculum in this way, the teachers were able to integrate the literacy and numeracy requirements into play activities. For example, an 'office environment' was used to focus upon literacy activities, and a 'toy factory' environment was used for adult-initiated creative work and knowledge and understanding of the world (one of the areas of the foundation stage curriculum). In this way, formal teaching requirements were successfully reconciled with an early years teaching approach, through an integrated curriculum.

Constraints in managing child-initiated learning

Keating *et al.* (2002) examined how reception teachers were managing the foundation stage curriculum in their classrooms. Managing child-initiated learning with the role of the adult was a problematic area. Teachers interpreted child-initiated learning in their classroom practice in two ways. For teachers in some schools, child-initiated learning was about children being 'free' to choose an activity to engage with. For other schools, it was about children being free to choose from a given range of activities. The teachers in both interpretations, however, felt that their practice of child-initiated learning did not really reflect their own beliefs about quality child-initiated learning. There were management constraints to providing 'quality' child-initiated learning – notably time, physical and human resources and the organisation of the learning environment.

Managing time

Teachers may have little time to dedicate to child-initiated learning, despite knowing the value of play in children's learning. Their time is occupied by providing literacy and numeracy and other more formal experiences. Keating *et al.* (2002) argued that the over-emphasis on formal learning could have a negative effect on children's attitudes and motivation to learn. The EPPE project (Sylva *et al.* 2003) has indicated that providing opportunities for children to take responsibility for their own learning in a meaningful context is effective in children's learning. One way that teachers in Keating *et al.*'s (2002) study managed to make time for child-initiated learning (and therefore allow children to take responsibility for their own learning) was to allocate one or two afternoons a week for it. However, this still gives the impression that it is not as important for children's learning as the more formal experiences in the reception class.

Managing physical and human resources

If we are expecting children to become independent learners then we have to support them. One of the ways that teachers can support their pupils is by providing them with physical resources to choose from.

However, in the study by Keating *et al.* (2002), one of the constraints that teachers found in supporting child-initiated learning was that a wide range of physical resources was not always available for the children. This was sometimes because there was not enough storage space in the classroom, or because the school itself did not have a wide range of relevant resources. Therefore, one of the ways that they hoped to 'manage' the physical resource problem was to share resources with nursery teachers. This was possible because of the cohesion of the foundation stage curriculum. As Keating *et al.* (2002) pointed out, the introduction of the foundation stage had, in some cases, enabled reception and nursery teachers to work more closely together, share resources and develop a sense of 'early years unity'.

Managing to organise the learning environment

In order to facilitate child-initiated learning, teachers need to organise the learning environment so that children can initiate their own play-based learning. One of the teachers in Keating *et al.*'s (2002) research stated that children have to be 'trained' to access the learning environment on their own. According to the researchers, training children requires time. It requires finding the time to help children develop skills to be independent learners. This means more pressure on teachers to make that time.

Play for learning environments for young children does not only occur inside the classroom setting, but takes place outside the classroom too. In Keating *et al.*'s (2002) study, unless the schools were sharing nursery resources, there were few accessible outside play learning environments. The researchers argued that in order to invest in such resources, the schools would need to understand the value of outside learning environments. This would also require low adult:child ratios to meet health and safety requirements. Such requirements involve a commitment to the value of outside learning, as suggested in the foundation stage curriculum.

Management and training needs

Support for teachers through training can help to manage transitions effectively. The survey by Taylor Nelson Sofres with Aubrey (2002) highlighted the importance of training. Those schools with head teachers originally trained to work with the youngest children, who had received specific foundation stage training, and whose foundation stage and other staff had continued early years training, tended to have had positive experiences of implementing the foundation stage in reception classes. The survey also revealed that the majority of reception class teachers would welcome additional training in the foundation stage, and that there are large numbers of key stage 1 and key stage 2 teachers (and governors), who have not received specific training in the foundation stage. This leads us to ask whether practitioners within key stage 1 access professional development and advice that address curriculum support other than for the national strategies. If not, does this deter creative teaching and learning, which is advocated within the foundation stage?

Foundation stage training may also need to be extended to support staff:

> Understanding and commitment of all staff is necessary for the smooth implementation of a curriculum for 3- to 11-year-olds. Raising the general understanding and awareness of the teaching community as a whole through Foundation Stage training is likely to enhance whole school curriculum planning, teaching and assessment, as well as facilitate the transition between the Foundation Stage and Key Stage 1. Progression and continuity across the primary years is, thus, ensured.
>
> (Taylor Nelson Sofres with Aubrey 2002: 9)

Teachers in Keating *et al.*'s (2002) study felt that all practitioners needed to be given the opportunity to be involved and to evaluate curriculum and assessment materials. By 'all practitioners' they meant the range of people that teachers worked with within their classrooms. These included nursery nurses, classroom assistants and student trainees. However, there was a discrepancy in pay and conditions when such work took place outside the working day (Keating *et al.* 2002). Recent research into teaching assistants has revealed that their role as a support for teachers has changed (Lee 2002; Ofsted 2002). They now work more with teachers and are involved in supporting the implementation of the curriculum. More importantly, teaching and learning are more effective when teaching assistants support and collaborate with teachers. Joint training with teachers and teaching assistants, where they develop skills together, helps provide consistency in classroom approaches (Lee 2002). Teaching assistants have changed the way they provide support, from making and preparing materials to providing support for the formal curriculum, by playing an important part in implementing national literacy and numeracy strategies (Ofsted 2002).

The fact that a range of adults is now being trained to have the knowledge, skills and attitudes associated with the foundation stage curriculum (for example, through foundation degrees in early years and the option of a teaching assistant route) will hopefully lead to an improvement in pay and conditions within early years (see Penn 2000).

PAUSE FOR THOUGHT

Do nursery and reception children have the same teaching and learning needs?

How could resources (people/time/equipment) be used to provide them with quality child-initiated learning and a raising of standards?

SUPPORTING CHILDREN'S LEARNING DURING TRANSITIONS

Research suggests that the way children progress in their learning and the way curriculum content progresses do not work in parallel (Hughes 1995; Lindsey and Desforges 1998), and that they progress differently in areas such as literacy and mathematics (Munn 1995). Children's progress at different rates, at different times, can be influenced by a number of factors. For example, differences in children's development in social ability and behaviour when entering pre-school may be influenced by the child, parent and family factors (Melhuish *et al.* 1999). Such social influences have implications for children's transitions into pre-school and beyond.

> The child in educational transitions occupies three environments…their home world, the pre-school world and the school world. Although each contains the developing person, we need to look beyond the single settings to the relationships between them. These interconnections can be seen as important for the child as events taking place within any one of the single settings. Brofenbrenner (1979) calls them mesosystems.
>
> (Dunlop and Fabian 2002: 149)

Supporting children to adapt to the classroom environment

This view of how young children learn contrasts with curriculum policy at the foundation stage and key stage 1 in terms of what is taught, how much and how often (Munn and Schaffer 1996). Nutbrown (1997) argued that policy requirements divide between what we know about how literacy develops and how young children are taught in schools. Literacy does not develop in a neat upward line – there are peaks and plateaus. She asks whether children's literacy development may suffer as a result of over-prescriptive lessons, as required by the National Literacy Strategy. Therefore an understanding of children's transitions needs to consider how teachers teach the foundation stage and key stage 1 curriculum, their understanding of children's learning and the learning environments that children find themselves in.

Using knowledge from pre-school learning environments

In Scotland, Stephen and Cope's research (2003) found that the following factors influenced children's learning during their transitions from pre-school to primary:

- transition records
- children's adaptations to classroom environments
- teacher expectations.

The researchers found that transition arrangements paid more attention to informing parents and children about the new environment they were entering than to learning about children's pre-school experiences. Teachers lacked confidence in the information passed on from pre-school practitioners and made only limited use of the material available. Stephen and Cope (2003: 3) stated:

> Nevertheless, there were examples that indicated the value of paying attention to the information in pre-school records. For instance, reading a boy's pre-school record alerted his teacher to pre-reading skills that were masked by his immature behaviour and helped her to start him 'at about the right place'

The study also found that some teachers had information about a child from one setting but not the other settings that had been part of the child's all-day provision. This meant that, in some cases, a child's teacher was unaware that the child behaved differently when playroom circumstances varied.

Learning from parents

Informing parents about the new environment that children are entering needs to be accompanied by learning about a child's pre-school experiences from them. This is especially important when groups of children become disadvantaged because of poor understanding by early years staff (Siraj Blatchford 2001). All children have a right to a curriculum that supports and affirms their gender, cultural and linguistic identity and background. When children start school, they bring a wealth of cultural, linguistic and economic experiences that the school can call upon:

> It therefore becomes the responsibility of the teacher to localise the curriculum and to enlist the support of the local community and families in framing school policy and practice, and making the school and educational materials familiar and relevant to the children's experiences.
>
> (Sylva and Siraj-Blatchford in Siraj-Blatchford 2001: 107)

In England, Brooker's (2002) ethnographic study of four-year-old children starting school revealed that experiences of the reception class were not equally favoured for all the children. The school ethos and the classroom pedagogy stratified children in ways that reinforced inequalities they had displayed when starting school. Much of this was unintentional. For example, Brooker (2002) revealed that Bangladeshi parents' ignorance about school practices was matched by the school's ignorance of their home practices. Teachers 'blamed' poor progress on the fact that parents were unable to support children's learning. However, in the area of curriculum and pedagogy, Bangladeshi parents prepared children for school by instilling values of hard work, rather than play-orientated activities. In contrast, 'Anglo' (British-born) parents provided education through toys that children would encounter in the classroom. Similarly, Bangladeshi families were not anxious for their children to become 'independent' or 'to take initiative' as reception pedagogy requires. Anglo parents' views, on the other hand, were closer to those of the teachers, where starting school was the start of being a 'big boy' or a 'big girl'.

The school genuinely believed that effects of social disadvantage, of race and cultural discrimination or differences between home and school could be overcome by a 'good early years environment', where children follow their own interests and discover their own motivation. However, '[s]uch environments, though theoretically "inclusive" are founded on an exclusive view of childhood and specifically western views of learning, which for some children creates a barrier for learning' (Brooker 2002: 163).

This can slow down progress in learning and add to differentiated kinds of relationships:

> Children whose home and school experiences overlap to a significant extent, and where parents are present in the classroom, and engaged in continual exchanges with the staff, experience few setbacks in their developmental path. Those with wholly different experiences of home and school, where parents are not comfortable in the classroom and not able to engage the staff in dialogue, find many obstacles in the way of their continuous development.
>
> (Brooker 2002: 122)

A shift in the nature of adult–child relationships

In pre-school settings, children generally experience a greater adult:child ratio than in primary classrooms. This is a discontinuity. Some children will take time to adapt to the classroom environment and develop new relationships with adults. Stephen and Cope's (2003) study revealed that not all the children in their nursery class had experienced more formal relationships with adults; nor did all the children prefer that type of relationship. Cuddles and personal attention were issues that children raised as present in pre-school but not in school. In other words, there was a shift in the nature of adult–child relationships experienced on

---

PAUSE FOR THOUGHT

What are the advantages and disadvantages of the Bangladeshi pre-school experience and the Anglo experience? How can positive aspects be built on in the classroom?

transition to school – from the informal kind of relationship where the adult (or perhaps several adults) is not an authority figure to a relationship involving listening to one person who is a more authoritarian figure.

PAUSE FOR THOUGHT

What range of relationships with adults do children experience in pre-school settings? Does the mix of adults that children meet in the school classroom allow them to develop the kind of supportive relationships that some need or prefer? (Extract 1: cf. Stephen and Cope 2003)

How can the demands of the classroom be adjusted to accommodate those 'taking time to adjust' or 'having difficulty'? What kinds of experiences promote the development of personal characteristics that make adjusting to school easier?

Discontinuities in cultures of pre-school and school classrooms

Teachers hold expectations and children have experiences. Children are expected to learn and behave in certain ways when they move from pre-school to primary school. Mismatches can exist between what practitioners and managers in both sectors expect from the children. In those situations, staff from both sectors need to discuss their different educational cultures. They also need to consider ways the school can build on children's experience of learning in pre-school settings. Their nursery experience can prepare children for the adaptations necessary for transitions.

Stephen and Cope's (2003) study revealed discontinuities between the way that primary school teachers viewed pre-school and the actual perspectives of practitioners engaged in pre-school education (nursery nurses and nursery teachers in pre-school settings). Teachers expected pre-schools to ensure that children were 'ready' or prepared for effective learning in the classroom. 'Readiness' included characteristics such as being able to listen, being motivated and confident. Primary school teachers did not mention learning that children might have been expected to achieve as a result of the curriculum for three- to five-year-olds (aside from aspects of social, emotional and personal development). Practitioners in pre-school settings, however, believed that completing the requirements of the three- to five-year-olds' curriculum framework was highly necessary. They regarded pre-school education as a stage in its own right, not a preparation for school. Primary school teachers felt that nurseries provided better preparation for school than other pre-school provision – their preference was associated with their concern for discipline, and children being 'trained' for school so that they could behave appropriately in the classroom, rather than learning or attainment. Primary school teachers also referred to a 'negative legacy' from pre-schools if children experienced freedom from structure and time constraints, as this was not a way of working that always fitted in with the primary classroom.

> **REFLECTIVE ACTIVITY**
>
> Assume there are discontinuities between the 'culture' of the pre-school playroom and the school classroom. Find out what pre-school practitioners want to share with schoolteachers about their perspectives on the educational experiences they offer to children. How can school teachers and pre-school practitioners work together to offer children a gradual introduction to the demands of the primary classroom? (Adapted from Stephen and Cope 2003)

PEDAGOGIES FOR SMOOTH TRANSITIONS

This final section examines pedagogics that may help smooth transitions from pre-school to a school environment.

Successful pedagogic environments

In England, the Effective Provision of Pre-School Education, or EPPE project (Sylva *et al.* 2003), identified 'quality' as a characteristic of an effective pre-school environment, so that children are prepared for a good start in school in terms of their cognitive, social and behavioural development. Quality pre-schooling is important because it influences a child's outcomes. That is, if they have experienced high quality pre-schooling they are less likely to be anxious or antisocial when starting school. Among the findings of EPPE was the view that good quality was best found in integrated settings that combined both education and care, nursery school and nursery classes where staff were well qualified, and settings that saw education and social development as complementary.

'Researching Effective Pedagogy in the Early Years' (REPEY) (Siraj-Blatchford *et al.* 2002) was an allied project to EPPE. It investigated pedagogical strategies in the early years that were effective in supporting young children's development of knowledge, skills and attitudes. The case studies were based on a selection of effective pre-school settings, along with two reception classes. Therefore the context applied to the *Curriculum Guidance for the Foundation Stage*, with play as a central feature. The research reported that pedagogy was most effective in settings where practice was characterised by:

- cognitive interactions: cognitively challenging interactions impose demands on children that can be achieved only with structured support, fostering shared and explicit thinking
- sound teacher knowledge and understanding of the curriculum
- frequent use of questioning techniques by adults, especially in the context of children's play (for example, questions that provoke speculation and extend the imagination)
- disciplinary and behavioural policies which encourage children to be assertive and talk through conflicts
- pedagogic environments which encourage children's development: the most successful pedagogic environments were those that provided a combination of teacher-directed learning, children's play and a stimulating environment; the research suggested that where young children had freely chosen to play in a learning environment (for example, the 'home corner'), there was a greater opportunity for effective adult intervention – staff could therefore get directly involved in children's play to foster and sustain challenges
- home involvement in children's learning (through encouraging active involvement of parents in their children's learning at home).

In terms of the study's relationship to the *Curriculum Guidance for the Foundation Stage* (QCA/DfEE 2000), the guidance refers to principles for early years education in terms of parents and practitioners working together and opportunities for children to engage both in activities planned by adults and those they initiate themselves. It also advises practitioners to make effective use of unexpected and unforeseen opportunities for children's learning, to make systematic observations and assessments of children's interests and learning styles, and to use this information to plan motivating activities and learning priorities. So the guidance makes recommendations that the research identified as good practice. However, the REPEY study stressed the effectiveness of collaborative forms of adult–child intervention as a more effective pedagogy than modelling or direct teaching.

In terms of transitions from pre-school centres to reception classes, the REPEY study provided insights into how practitioners regarded transfers. The priorities of most early years practitioners lay in developing children's positive disposition to learning, self-confidence and independence. In most pre-school settings the practice of introducing children to more formal activities, such as carpet and circle time, were felt to be more important than specific curriculum work. Some settings provided visits to local primary schools and invited primary staff to visit the pre-school setting, and some settings provided special learning activities for pre-school children about to enter reception classes. In some cases, pre-school staff felt that the *Curriculum Guidance for the Foundation Stage* was helping to create stronger links between early years centres and reception classes. In other cases, pre-school staff were concerned about the lack of curriculum continuity between the two phases.

Pedagogical continuity

In terms of pedagogical continuity, Neuman (2002) has provided an international overview of transition issues and pedagogical approaches for smooth transitions. In her discussion of 12 countries, she highlighted strategies to facilitate transitions. Most European countries provide a national curriculum or framework of some sort for early childhood education and care. All of them make reference to ensuring collaboration with schools to help children's transitions. This is about providing continuity in children's learning experiences from early childhood education and care to primary school. For example, Sweden has developed three curricula for pre-school, compulsory school and upper secondary school. The three are linked by a coherent view of knowledge, development and learning. The goal is to develop an educational continuum and there are distinct values that are covered throughout the three curricula – for example, democracy and respect for the environment. The curricula have guidelines that require staff of each stage to cooperate with each other during periods of transition. Neuman argued that although such curricular structures may threaten to create downward pressure of overly formal schooling for the early years, the more that staff collaborate during transitions, the more they can develop new ways of understanding children's learning across a wide age span.

Professional continuity

The idea of communication and collaboration between staff in pre-schools and primary schools can help develop comparable philosophies and an understanding of what children have experienced and will experience. Neuman (2002) discussed the idea of joint pre-service and in-service training, to develop a common knowledge in order to build partnerships. She cited practice in Norway as an example. In 1997, Norway reduced the compulsory age for starting school, from seven to six. In order to ease transitions from one institution to another, the first four grades of primary school were based on integrating the traditions of kindergarten and the school. So school teachers and kindergarten teachers work with the six-year-olds in grade 1, and early childhood staff can qualify (with an additional year of training) to work with children in grades 2 to 4. As a result of this process, there has been a rethinking of the role of kindergartens and primary schools, and the way they teach. In practice, according to Neuman (2002), this has led to emphasising learning through play, age-mixed activities and organisation around themes rather than subjects.

In England, close collaboration between schools and allied services can also help to promote pedagogic continuity for children's development and learning, and may be particularly helpful for those children who are from less advantaged socio-economic backgrounds. Sure Start, Early Excellence Centres and, more recently, Children's Centres, offer a range of services for early years education and care. Using a partnership approach (part of their multi-agency philosophy) with local schools, they can help ensure pedagogic continuity for children's development and learning.

Certainly, if staff work together across settings then bridges can be built. For the children, this may allow them to adapt more easily to new ways of working while also retaining some familiar aspects of their pre-school learning routines.

Continuity in the home

Prior to and during the 1970s, a number of studies looked at the process of transition and transfer from primary to secondary school (see, for example, Hargreaves and Galton 2002). Such studies suggested that the children most at risk from the transfer process were those who were less confident, often from poorer socio-economic backgrounds. These children experienced such difficulties as coping with standards of work and pupil–teacher relationships. The most successful pupils were the academically able, who were self-confident, socially mature and received strong parental support (Spelman 1979).

The influence of the home background in periods of transition also transcends geographical boundaries. In most countries, both early childhood education and care services and schools stress the importance of cooperation with the family, and this applies especially during times of transition. Neuman (2002) suggested that staff need to create avenues for information sharing and discussion with parents so that there is a clear understanding of how to support children's transitions. For example, they can discuss strategies to help support children's development and learning in the home. In England, the EPPE project highlighted the importance of quality home learning, stressing that what parents 'do' with children before starting school can help with their cognitive, social and behavioural development. Additionally, Brooker's (2002) study revealed that the 'way' parents help support children's learning can help with their cognitive, social and behavioural development, particularly for the groups who are disadvantaged, and from poorer socio-economic backgrounds.

The child's perspective

Dunlop and Fabian (2002) draw our attention to the idea of being a 'transitional child', as new identities and roles are taken on. The process of becoming a school child from a pre-school child may have a hidden power to alter how a person is treated – how they act and what they do – and, thereby, even what they think or feel (Dunlop and Fabian 2002: 150).

PAUSE FOR THOUGHT

Consider two alternative perspectives:

a) **A child has difficulties making the transition from pre-school to school because the child has certain expectations and preferences, developed in their pre-school provision.**
b) **A child has difficulties making the transition from pre-school to school because the child has behavioural and personality problems.**

If we accept perspective (a), it implies that a more flexible approach should be adopted in the primary classroom. How would you try to make the transition easier for the child?

In Denmark, Brostrom (2002) examined the transition from kindergarten to school from the child's perspective. Interestingly, children lacked insight into what would happen at school. The issue of children's 'school readiness' is raised, so that the process of transition is a continuous rather than an abrupt phase. It suggests that the adults involved in such transitions, which may include pre-school teachers and teachers, alongside parents, should work hand in hand.

Fabian's (2002) research in England found that some children worry about the physical and social environment they will face. She discussed the idea of 'empowering' children with coping skills for the transition to school, giving them an understanding of what school is about and helping them to develop social and emotional resilience in dealing with new situations. In particular, she identified ways that teachers can help children to settle into school through stories that focus on critical incidents and experiences common to school. These are used to help children to think about new school situations and the kinds of solutions they might consider when faced with them.

CONCLUSIONS AND IMPLICATIONS

A number of issues may influence the process of transition as children move from the foundation stage to key stage 1. First, there may be variations in approaches to teaching these two stages. It would appear that one of the main 'structural' barriers to a smooth transition from the foundation stage curriculum to the key stage 1 curriculum is the difference in relation to play. Additionally, schools and pre-schools may be structured differently themselves. Structures can reinforce philosophical differences, reflecting different cultures. If the pre-school and school have developed independently of each other they may not have shared goals. The staff may have been trained differently. As a result they have different pedagogies and organisation. What appears to have happened, according to the research, is that for the majority of reception classes the foundation stage curriculum has provided a structure for the reception class, although evidence concerning 'play' is a cause of concern.

Given that play is central to the foundation stage curriculum, it could be argued that teachers now face strong pressures to ensure that play is a vital part of early years practice (Keating *et al.* 2002). In the past, teachers were required to show evidence of learning in the curriculum areas; now they need to show evidence of play-based learning. At the same time, the concern for raising standards in schools continues. The research by Keating *et al.* (2002) suggested that there were unreasonable demands being placed on reception teachers because head teachers and governors were not prioritising the importance of play, but rather the importance of adhering to the demands of the more formal curriculum. This obviously creates a conflict of priorities.

There may be variations in the *interpretation* of the foundation stage curriculum, along with variations in the learning environment and resources available. In trying to 'manage' educational transitions, it appears that teachers are having to adapt the curriculum using their professional knowledge, trying to reconcile formal teaching requirements with an early years approach that they have been using. Constraints of time, physical and human resources and, in some cases, a lack of commitment to the value of 'outside play' all make managing transitions from the foundation stage difficult for teachers. In response to such management constraints, and the desire to ensure smooth transitions for children, there are teachers who have shared resources (including outside resources), therefore creating a sense of early years unity.

In this chapter we have examined a number of issues which are vital to supporting children's learning during transitions. We can sum up these issues by considering the following questions:

- What information (including assessment details) is needed to support smooth transitions?
- How can we use our knowledge about the child's pre-school environment and/or assessment instruments in planning to support children's development?
- How is children's learning being supported by parents and family during transitions?
- How are children being supported to adapt to the classroom environment (especially those children who are disadvantaged socio-economically)?
- What can parents tell practitioners or teachers about their children?
- How can practitioners and/or teachers work with parents so that children feel valued and encouraged, alongside continuing to develop supportive adult child relationships in the new setting?
- What is the 'quality' of the pre-school setting like and what sort of pedagogy does it use? For example, does the setting:
  - employ teacher–child learning through play?
  - have qualified staff?
  - follow similar aims to the setting the child is going to (in terms of seeing both education and care as vital for the early years)?

Finally, hearing the child's voice is an essential instrument in the process of transition. If we can understand how children from different linguistic, cultural and socio-economic backgrounds feel and experience the process of becoming a 'schoolchild', then we as adults can improve our understanding of how best to encourage children's learning during the transition.

7 EARLY YEARS AND ILT

IN THIS CHAPTER WE WILL CONSIDER THE FOLLOWING TOPICS:

* ✳ The impact of computers and the digital age
* ✳ What is ILT?
* ✳ Embedding ILT in the curriculum
* ✳ Evaluating software
* ✳ Theoretical perspectives and computers
* ✳ Differentiation and equal opportunities
* ✳ Evaluating the use of ILT.

THE IMPACT OF COMPUTERS AND THE DIGITAL AGE

Computers have become an integral part of all our lives. We see them in our workplaces, libraries and more and more in our own homes. Indeed, figures from Ofcom show that 64 per cent of UK adults have a computer at home, and 53 per cent of adults have access to the Internet – approximately 13 million households (Ofcom 2004). But computers are there even when we cannot see them. When we take money out of the cashpoint, we are connecting to a computer; when we go shopping, the bar codes on the products we buy are read by a scanner connected to a computer; and when we travel on the railway, the time and position of the trains are relayed to a computer so that we can see when the next train is due. Everyday software – including word-processing, spreadsheet and database applications – has revolutionised our working lives.

More than that, the power of digital communication has changed the world of entertainment. We can interact with our televisions by 'pressing the red button'; we can use computers to email and chat online; and we can use our mobile phones to participate in television programmes like *Test the Nation* and *Pop Idol*.

Traditionally, items in the home like the telephone, the television and the camera had very separate functions. Nowadays, as these become digital, we are seeing a coming together or 'convergence' of use. We call this digital convergence. Put simply, this means that we can surf the Internet via a PlayStation™ instead of just playing games on it; we can take a photograph with a mobile phone and email it to anyone; or we can use a web camera to watch a grandchild on another continent via the Internet.

So, if the computer has changed so much of our lives both at work and at home, what has been the impact on learning and education?

WHAT IS ILT?

The 'L' in ILT stands for 'learning'. We use the term 'information technology' (IT) to refer to everything about computers, peripherals, software and infrastructure. When we are using IT for learning, we talk about ILT or sometimes just 'e-learning'. (You will also hear references to ICT – the 'C' stands for 'communication'.)

Peripherals

Peripherals are devices connected to a computer. Printers and scanners are examples of peripheral devices. They can be disconnected from the computer and the computer will still operate, but without the functions of the disconnected device.

Software

The computer and its peripherals are often called hardware. In terms of early years, hardware can also refer to equipment which does not attach to a computer but does respond to instructions, such as a tape recorder or a roamer (see below, and pp. 147–8).

The set of instructions that the computer needs to function is called software. There are two types of software:

- the operating system software
- the application software.

REFLECTIVE ACTIVITY

How many peripheral devices can you think of? Remember, they can be inside or outside the main computer 'box'. Common peripherals are used for inputting, outputting or storing information.

PAUSE FOR THOUGHT

Have you used any educational software?

Is the software child-friendly?

System software enables the computer to monitor events and controls the computer's memory and peripheral devices. It is responsible for the input, processing and output of information.

Application software is the extra software you buy to enable you to word-process, play games, edit videos or create a database.

Infrastructure

Computers do not usually work separately. They are part of networks and the infrastructure is the term for the cabling and services which join the machines together, especially in terms of Internet infrastructure. The Internet (with a capital 'I') is made up of thousands of smaller networks and is the infrastructure which allows the public to transmit data, for example; email and chat, or to surf the world wide web.

EMBEDDING ILT IN THE CURRICULUM

The education of three- and four-years-olds in England is covered by the Foundation Stage, which was introduced by the QCA (Qualifications and Curriculum Authority) in September 2000. The Foundation Stage covers a range of skills, which are detailed in six areas known as the early learning goals (see also Chapter 5, The Foundation Stage (3–5 Years), pp. 102–16 and Chapter 6, Educational Transitions (5–8 Years), p. 120).

These are:

- personal, social and emotional development
- communication, language and literature
- mathematical development
- knowledge and understanding of the world
- physical development
- creative development.

The early learning goals aim to make learning both challenging and fun, and they recognise the importance of play. Each of the learning goals is supported by stepping stones, which expand and clarify the goals. These detailed statutory requirements underpin the inspection system, as government inspectors will be looking for evidence that both practitioners and pupils use ILT in their daily lives.

There are many websites which provide information on how ILT can be used to support the early learning goals (all accessed October 2004):

http://www.ictadvice.org.uk/index.php

http://vtc.ngfl.gov.uk/docserver.php

http://www.ltscotland.org.uk/

http://www.ngfl-cymru.org.uk/

http://www.tlfe.org.uk/home.htm

http://www.bbc.co.uk/cbeebies/

We will look at each of the early learning goals in detail below.

Personal, social and emotional development

Turn-taking at a computer is an aspect of personal, social and emotional development. Working in groups at a computer offers children the chance to discuss and share. Computers can build confidence and motivate (for example, most applications allow children's work to be printed and displayed). Some computers are programmed to 'reward' correct responses with sound or animation. When children enjoy their computer time, they will have a longer concentration span.

As a practitioner, you can use the computer to create certificates and merit awards; these can be incorporated into children's work to build their self-esteem. Plenty of further useful resources and ideas can be found at http://www.ictadvice.org.uk (accessed October 2004).

Communication, language and literacy

Communication involves listening and speaking. Role-play with a range of IT hardware is a perfect opportunity to improve these skills (office equipment, kitchen equipment, tape recorders, digital cameras etc.). Talking books are widely available. On computers they have the added advantage of highlighting the words as they are spoken. Children can often click on the words to have them repeated.

Early literacy in the form of matching, rhyming and first letter recognition is the staple of many software word games. Writing can also be part of a young child's introduction to computers through early word-processing packages. Dedicated word-bank programmes (for example, Clicker from Cricksoft), allow the child to click on words to make captions and sentences. Moira Monteith's (2002) *Teaching Primary Literacy with ICT* looks at the current research in this area.

Mathematical development

It is relatively easy to see how computer counting games can be devised to add interest and variety to a child's learning. There are many excellent websites (including the BBC's) which offer variations on a theme. The children can be asked to click on correct answers to predict, estimate, calculate or simply count. You can also make PowerPoint® slides with, for example, one apple, two bananas etc. and ask the children to predict the next number.

Similarly, the computer can introduce children to shape and size. It is often easier for a child to sort the size of parcels on a screen than to have to create the parcels in the real world.

Knowledge and understanding of the world

Children have to find out about the uses of everyday technology as part of this early learning goal. Just as computers in our daily lives may be hidden (there are computer chips in videos, microwaves, washing machines etc.), so digital technology is becoming commonplace in children's toys and games.

This creates endless opportunities to introduce children to concepts like cause and effect and allows them to operate simple equipment. They can be encouraged to use and operate remote-controlled cars or programme a floor robot. They can complete simple computer tasks, such as drag and drop using a mouse, or they can input simple words using the keyboard.

They also have to explore and investigate their environment, and here digital cameras and tape recorders can be used to great advantage. Photographs can record sequences for science or capture the day's events at the zoo.

PAUSE FOR THOUGHT

Could you make any worksheets to help children improve their maths or literacy?

Do you use computers for record keeping, overheads, test items, school promotional material?

Can you think of other ways to use a computer?

Physical development

Using a keyboard and a mouse requires fine motor skills, which are a very important aspect of physical development. As computers become ever cheaper and faster, it will become commonplace to video activities and then replay them, just as world-class athletes do. This is a powerful form of learning as it is multi-sensory and combines many features, such as context, interest, memory and consolidation.

Physical development also includes health and bodily awareness. There are many website and software packages devoted to different topics like teeth and skeletons.

Creative development

Creativity is often the most undervalued aspect of teaching with computers. Nowadays music software is very interactive and does not simply turn the computer from a piano to a drum, but guides the child in rhythm, pitch, melody, tempo, harmony and composition. Paint programmes allow children to edit and retouch their artwork repeatedly before printing out the finished article, and singalong tapes or websites can be controlled easily by the child.

Again, the children's own singing and dancing can be captured on video or tape. (Always check your setting's policies on the use of recording equipment with the children.)

EVALUATING SOFTWARE

Unfortunately, there is no quick and easy method of evaluating software. As you use software, you will become more critical, however, these are some of the aspects you might like to consider:

- How easy is the software to install?
- How expensive is it (single user or site licence)?
- How easy is it to navigate and use the software?
- Are there help files or written instructions?
- Is the software accessible to all (e.g. visually impaired pupils)?
- Does the software have good equal opportunity role models (e.g. does it avoid stereotypes of race, gender, disability)?
- How good is the content (e.g. accurate, up to date)?
- Is it relevant to the curriculum?
- Is it pitched at the right age?
- Does the software offer depth and differentiation?

- How good is the presentation (e.g. graphics, sound)?
- Does the software add value to current teaching practices?
- Does the software offer scope for follow-on classroom activities?
- What is the underlying pedagogy?
- Are different learning styles catered for?
- Does the software offer interactivity?
- Could groups or pairs use the software?
- Does the software encourage thinking and problem solving?

There is an excellent website for teachers called TEEM (teachers evaluating educational multimedia), which you can find at http://www.teem.org.uk (accessed October 2004). The contributors have evaluated over 700 educational software titles and have recently added the evaluation of hardware to their remit.

THEORETICAL PERSPECTIVES AND COMPUTERS

Although computers are relatively new in early years settings, it is important to realise that everything you have learnt from the educational theorists (Piaget 1959, 1962) is just as relevant to computers as it is to any other form of teaching and learning. Applying what you know about educational theory will help you evaluate software.

Behaviourism relies on reinforcement and computers are particularly good at this. Keyboard skills, shape recognition and word recognition can all be taught by using a computer to reinforce the correct response. If the child sees the letter 'W' on the screen and then types the letter 'W' on the keyboard, the software can respond with appropriate feedback. This could be a voice saying 'well done' or an animated cartoon character doing a backflip.

Simple games can be devised. Imagine a game to grow sunflowers. You could have buttons to click for water and sunshine. Clicking on them alternately would make the plants grow, but too much sun or too much water and your sunflowers will wither and die.

Unfortunately, just using behaviourism to help children learn can result in a rather simplistic or repetitive pedagogy. The time on the computer becomes simple drill and practice and children can lose interest.

Computer programmes are often designed around Robert Gagne's conditions of learning (Gagne 1978). New knowledge is taught by having a clear starting point, maybe a clip of music or video to gain the child's attention. Then the objectives are stated and, if appropriate, reference is made to earlier learning. Computers are excellent at

providing new information, or 'content'. The content can be written, spoken or graphic, or a combination of these.

The child responds to the content by clicking on the navigation. The computer can then be programmed to ask questions to check learning and also to provide feedback.

Following these principles, the computer can take the child from prior knowledge to new knowledge, and, by using hyperlinks and friendly navigation, it can offer a less linear approach than a standard textbook. The computer allows the child to interact and explore while providing reinforcement and positive feedback.

Educational theorists tell us that it is easier for the child if the new learning is presented in a meaningful context (Smith 1996). Children have less experience and less knowledge to build on than adults, so context is very important for them. This means using children's prior knowledge, interests, skills and hobbies to engage them in the new learning. Many software titles are built around familiar television characters, such as Postman Pat® and Bob the Builder™.

Programmable toys (also known as roamers) are excellent examples of how to move from the known to the unknown. Children can press buttons, which allow the roamer to move up or down, left or right. The roamer can also remember sequences of buttons, which allows children to work out a route in advance (this is a simple form of computer programming). More sophisticated roamers can be programmed via a

Using programmable toys.

computer using a simple programming language like Logo. Roamers can play football, look for treasure, go shopping, dress up as pets, navigate mazes, draw shapes, even 'join in' small world play – the list is endless!

Constructivists (Dewey 1933) tell us that learning is work for the brain and, therefore, it is vital to make learning as much fun and as active as possible. It is also important that learning should not be stressful or the brain will not be able make good connections. Children must be allowed to make mistakes and learn from their mistakes without fear. Constructivism recognises the value of trial and error, allowing neural networks to be built up in the brain over time.

Undoubtedly computers can be great fun. They are also non-judgemental, so they can provide a stress-free environment for learning. A good computer programme will not give negative feedback; it will not call you useless or laugh at you. But it can provide support or scaffolding in the form of help or repetition. Software can be programmed to assess learning and then, if necessary, to reintroduce elements or reassess key areas of learning.

Games, music, animation, video, interactivity, sound, colour and communication can all be incorporated into software to make learning fun. Computers can appeal to different learning styles and, through the different senses, access different pathways to the brain. Using pictures and sound, they can access two brain channels simultaneously. Books on a computer often have pictures, text and the spoken word. Sometimes the word will be highlighted as it is spoken.

The example below is from a story called 'The Fish and the Shark'.

'Click on fish'

Here we see many aspects of good instructional design:

- it is colourful
- it is multi-sensory
- it has different pathways through the learning (the child can click on the fish or the yellow triangles) for trial and error
- it has animation
- it has limited use of text
- it has an easy interface
- it has a high level of interactivity to keep the child engaged.

You can take courses and degrees in HCI (human computer interaction) and there is detailed ongoing research into good design and constructivism in educational software.

One aspect of computing that is particularly interesting to educationalists is computer games. Playing games on computers can be highly compelling and if we could harness the power of games into learning then maybe we could transform education. Many people, especially children, enjoy computer games and will return to the same game again and again. Why is this?

- Do they enjoy the competitive aspect?
- Do they enjoy simulations?
- Do they enjoy familiar games and characters?
- Do they enjoy problem solving?

Using games in e-learning can be a very constructivist approach.

Other educationalists tell us that learning is inherently social (Vygotsky 1978, 1986). A computer, as we have seen, can be very successful in adopting different educational perspectives, but on its own it is not very sociable. To overcome this, it is important that a young child does not work alone on the computer for too long. Children working alone may get stuck and frustrated by not being able to move forward. Often they will stick to what they know and repeat behaviour without learning. If it is true that learning is essentially a product of social interaction, then children need to work together or with an adult for learning to take place. Conversations about what is on the screen and what they are doing allow the computer to be both interactive and social.

As the child gets older, the communication aspects of computing can allow other kinds of social learning to take place. Text emails or instant messages can be sent, voice emails can be sent and web cameras can be set up to allow for video conferencing. Children can communicate with other schools or with relatives around the world. Naturally, it is important that Internet safety procedures are in place if a child is to communicate safely with others. You should always check your setting's guidelines and procedures on the use of emails, web cams and all other forms of electronic communication.

DIFFERENTIATION AND EQUAL OPPORTUNITIES

Computers can make a major contribution to teaching and learning by allowing for differentiation and equality of opportunity.

Differentiation means accommodating the needs of each individual child. Software often has different levels so that all the children in a setting can use the same software at the appropriate level. As a practitioner, you can create lesson plans around the computer but alter them easily to reflect the individual needs of different children. It is important to remember that the software on a computer (for example, drawing or writing packages) is not an end in itself. It is a tool that should be brought into the theme of the lesson, to enrich and broaden each child's learning experiences.

Equal opportunities is another area where computers and assistive technology can bring down barriers. Most modern computers come

PAUSE FOR THOUGHT

Computers can be adapted for children with disabilities.

How many adaptations can you think of?

with a magnifier, a narrator, an on-screen keyboard and accessibility options. There is a whole host of other adaptive technology that you can buy to help children who would otherwise be unable to use the computer. Some examples of hardware include:

- touch screen
- foot-controlled mouse
- expanded keyboard
- mini keyboard
- remote controls
- switch access.

There is also an abundance of software for special needs. See http://www.ictadvice.org.uk and http://www.teem.org.uk/curriculum_focus/sen. Other useful sites include http://www.abilitynet.org.uk and (for the USA) http://www.cast.org (all accessed October 2004).

EVALUATING THE USE OF ILT

Computers cannot replace play and books and traditional teaching, but, with a little thought, they can play a positive role in all aspects of learning.

The computer is, of course, only a tool. Creativity may be possible with a computer, but it is also encouraged by paint, paper, egg cartons, fabric, and so on. Other functions of the computer are also available by other means – you can add up on your fingers or you can dress up and play-act to create a multi-sensory experience. The power of books cannot be underestimated, but technology will be a part of children's futures, so we need to help them feel confident and comfortable with computers.

There are restrictions, of course. For instance, young children should not be allowed to surf the Internet freely without adult supervision. There are also considerations for their health and safety, since most computers are not designed for small children. Standard computer hardware, such as the mouse and keyboard, is not the correct size for small hands, and monitors and chairs are often not correctly positioned. An adult should take regular breaks to relax muscles and eyes, and this is even more important for a growing child.

The use of computers in teaching and learning must always be supervised and led by adults. To blend computer learning into the work of a setting means that the hardware and software must be properly evaluated for suitability, quality and content.

> **REFLECTIVE ACTIVITY**
>
> Do you know the correct position for the child's:
>
> head
> eyes
> arms
> feet
> or for the keyboard and mouse
>
> when using a computer? Use a search engine to find Health and Safety recommendations.

Professional suites of software for word-processing and spreadsheets often have very similar interfaces so that once you have learnt one package, you are already halfway there with the second and third. For example, knowledge of Microsoft Word® will help greatly when learning to use Excel® spreadsheets. Unfortunately, each piece of children's software has a different look and feel, and the navigation is usually different. Therefore, you will need to evaluate the ease of use and look at the amount of available help. Are the menus written or pictorial? Does the software have sound? What is the underlying pedagogy? What is the learning objective? Is it an appropriate context?

It is up to adults and, more particularly, you as an early years practitioner to harness the power of computing for the benefit of young children.

USEFUL WEBSITES (All accessed October 2004)

http://www.2simple.com
http://www.becta.org.uk
http://www.bbc.co.uk
http://www.cricksoft.com
http://www.ictadvice.org.uk
http://www.qca.org.uk
http://www.teem.org.uk

MANAGEMENT, LEADERSHIP AND TEAMWORK

8

IN THIS CHAPTER WE WILL CONSIDER THE FOLLOWING TOPICS:

✳ Management or leadership?
✳ Leadership roles in early childhood settings
✳ Building and developing teams
✳ Managing change.

This chapter sets out to examine the place and function of management and leadership in early childhood care and education. It considers the leadership roles that need to be addressed in complex early years settings, highlighting two major issues that confront practitioners. The first is the need to foster teamwork. The second is the importance of managing the frequent and radical changes that confront teams, particularly those in multi-function or integrated centres.

MANAGEMENT OR LEADERSHIP?

These terms are often used interchangeably but in reality they cover very different roles and functions. Just about everyone working in an early years setting has a management role. The nature of the work means that all practitioners have to work 'with people to plan, organise and control activities in order to accomplish agreed goals'. This is a definition of management offered by Smith and Langston (1999: 10, citing Fayol, 1986). They go on to list the actions of a manager (drawing on the work of Shea, 1993) and their list includes controlling, organising, accepting current practice, administration and co-ordination.

In any early years setting, on every day of the week, practitioners are planning, organising and managing events and experiences. They are working with parents, children and colleagues to agreed goals; completing forms, making reports and co-ordinating their actions with other team members as well as those from other professions and agencies. This means that, although some early years practitioners may resist the label, every team member has a responsible management role.

Rodd (1998: 5) reminds us that management focuses on the present – getting things done, maintaining stability within an organisation. Leadership, she suggests, involves much more than 'routine management' and may be characterised as:

· an art rather than a science
· (being) focused on policy rather than on execution
· concerned with values rather than facts

- the use of broad strategies rather than specific tactics
- concerned with philosophy rather than action
- reflective rather than active
- concerned with human as opposed to material resources
- (being) focused on deliberation rather than detail.

(Rodd, 1998: 6, citing Hodgkinson, 1991)

Although these points may help us to differentiate between leaders and managers to some extent, they do not give the whole answer. Leaders, certainly in complex early years settings, have also to be managers – they have to deal with people and resources; they have to be concerned both with values and facts. Managers on the other hand have also to be involved in philosophy and action, people and resources, deliberation and detail. It's not enough when working with young children to know *what* to do – practitioners also need to understand *why* they do it.

The difficulty of untangling these overlapping roles is increased when considering the complexity of early childhood settings. Within any team, although there is usually a single leader, in reality leadership is often distributed amongst many people (Gronn, 2003). There is growing recognition of the need for *distributed leadership*. In practice this means that one person will, for example, take responsibility for community involvement, while another will take responsibility for links with local feeder schools. The complexity of current early childhood settings – children's centres, neighbourhood nurseries, extended schools and so on – makes it impossible for any one person to maintain the overview required to lead and manage all areas effectively.

In addition, leaders of one team may also be working as team members within another area. Harpreet, for example, leads a team of fifteen practitioners working with children up to the age of three in a children's centre. She is a member of the centre's management team and sometimes supports teachers who need help when working with parents who do not speak English.

Sandy is a special needs assistant in an early years unit in a primary school, in which the team is led by the class teacher. After school and during school holidays she also leads her own team of staff offering wrap-around care for children in the foundation stage and in year 1. In both cases the head of the school remains the leader, since it is essential for the unit and the out-of-school provision to have a shared ethos with the rest of the school. This ensures consistency and security for children. In her classroom role and on a day to day basis, Sandy contributes to the management of the classroom but the leadership rests with the class teacher. In her other role Sandy needs both to lead her team and with them manage the well-being of children, as well as the domestic and administrative tasks that form part of their work.

Think about the different roles that practitioners in your setting take on. The list you come up with will undoubtedly highlight the same kind of complexity that Sandy and Harpreet are faced with. Try to reflect on:

- those tasks or roles that relate to the day-to-day management of the centre or setting
- those that you think go beyond the present and require leadership qualities.

The remainder of this chapter will focus on a view of leadership as being about vision, motivation and teamwork. Even if you are not currently in a position where you have the opportunity or responsibility to motivate others, understanding the functions and processes of leadership will help you to manage more effectively. Rodd (1998: 13) considers this understanding to be vital. She writes:

> The work situation (of early childhood practitioners) is essentially autonomous; early childhood professionals have the greatest responsibility for the greatest number of working hours for the youngest and most vulnerable of children. Because there is substantial freedom from on-the-job supervision, *an understanding of leadership* and group processes, the possession of a range of organisational and management skills, as well as a high degree of technical expertise are required.

Leadership qualities

The three statements below explore a range of leadership qualities. As you read them, consider which of them fits your view of a leader, and why:

> Being a leader is something you do rather than something you are. It is the ability to bring out a number of talents and to operate effectively through other people making them gladly accept your goals while having the freedom to do things their way. A good leader therefore understands and meets other people's positive expectations of how they wish to be led. Becoming a leader is something you choose to do through a process of action and self-discovery.
>
> (van Maurik, 2004: 223)

...leaders create the sense that they truly want to hear employees' thoughts and concerns and that they are available to listen. They're also true collaborators, working as team members rather than top-down leaders. And they know how to create a sense of harmony – for instance, repairing rifts within the group.

(Goleman *et al.* 2002: 88)

Leaders are people who can influence the behaviour of others for the purpose of achieving a goal... Leaders are able to balance the concern for work, task, quality and productivity with concern for people, relationships, satisfaction and morale.

(Rodd 1998: 2)

These three definitions underline some important points about leadership. Firstly, van Maurik's definition highlights the dynamic role of a leader and the fact that leadership is something which has to be worked at – rather than something you are born to. However, its suggestion that the goals are those of the leader alone does not match with practice in early years settings. In effective settings, the goals are not set only by the leader, but by the whole team; time and energy are invested in coming to shared views and values, as a collective process. Obviously it is the leader's responsibility to ensure that there are goals and a vision, and that these are clearly communicated to all staff. It is not, however, his or her right to single-handedly dictate the aims.

Effective leaders need to motivate and encourage their team, as well as collaborating as team members themselves.

Moreover, there are now an increasing number of government initiatives (see also chapter 9) which must be satisfactorily incorporated into the centre's vision.

The second definition is from Daniel Goleman, the creator of the term *emotional intelligence*. He focuses on the emotional well-being of teams, an aspect which is important for early years settings where a lack of teamwork can impact very badly on children's well-being.

Finally Jillian Rodd's definition focuses on leadership in early years settings and reflects the complex roles which leaders in multi-function or integrated centres have to undertake.

LEADERSHIP ROLES IN EARLY CHILDHOOD SETTINGS

Although much has been written about leadership, not all of it is totally relevant to the field of early childhood. Leadership in the context of the early years involves some specific features not universally found in other areas requiring leadership. These differences have been acknowledged by the DfES in the setting up and funding of a specific early years leadership qualification. The *National Professional Qualification in Integrated Centre Leadership* is planned to run from September 2005. The main features of the qualification include creating 'an ethos of community partnership working... within multi-agency and multi-disciplinary environment(s)' (DfES/NCSL 2004: 2).

The role of a leader in early childhood settings is made more complex by the fact that he or she must address the following issues:

1. Working with young children

2. Involving parents and community

3. Female leaders

4. The wide range of staff in an early years setting.

1. Working with young children

The most important difference between early years settings and other sectors of work, of course, is that practitioners have a responsibility faced by few other groups of employees. Early childhood practitioners are dealing with young children who are at their most impressionable and most vulnerable. Staff who are treated with respect and empathy by their leaders will be much more likely to treat children in the same way. Moreover the way in which staff are treated, or led, will impact on the view that is held of them by children and parents. Practitioners, including leaders, are acting as role models for children and this can have a positive (or negative) impact on children's development and learning (QCA 2000). Everything that happens has an effect on young children, who are particularly conscious of relationships.

2. Involving parents and community

Secondly, leadership in early years settings requires communication with parents and community. The views of professional staff may not always coincide comfortably with the varied views and agendas of parents. This means that leaders need to work at developing shared understandings with parents, a task which requires considerable skills of negotiation, tact and respect. They must also liaise with a variety of other agencies and institutions who contribute to the support of children and families. This may include schools, clinics, playgroups, holiday clubs, voluntary organisations and charities, as well as health and social services.

3. Female leaders

A third difference between leadership in the early years and other sectors concerns gender. There is a growing view that since leaders in early childhood settings are mainly women, leadership styles may be markedly different. Rodd (1998: 11) suggests that 'the picture which is emerging is one of strong leadership within a collaborative framework' and that the work of effective leaders in early childhood settings is characterised by:

- vision behaviour – creating a vision and taking appropriate risks to bring about change
- people behaviour – providing care and respect for individual differences
- influence behaviour – acting collaboratively
- values behaviour – building trust and openness.

This is not to suggest that men in leadership roles in early childhood settings do not display these behaviours – nor even, of course, that all women in those roles do (Coleman 2002). However what is important about this list is that it reflects the ethos of effective early childhood care and education. Effective leaders interact with their teams, parents, visiting professionals and children themselves with the same respect, care, trust and spirit of collaboration that they intend should permeate their settings.

4. Wide range of staff in settings

A further difference concerns the variety of training, qualifications and experience that early childhood practitioners have. Different professionals working in multi-function or integrated centres may include:

- teachers (who may or may not have an early years specialism)
- practitioners holding NVQ2 or NVQ3 awards in nursery nursing or similar fields
- unqualified and inexperienced staff – new to the field but demonstrating an interest in young children
- volunteers
- students
- health practitioners
- psychologists
- therapists
- counsellors and advisers in debt, employment etc.
- staff with social work qualifications.

How do you think female leaders might run a setting differently?

Each of these groups (and the many other possibilities which have not been listed here) comes with different assumptions, expectations and practices. The leader of the centre has to work hard at melding these views – harnessing the strength that these different viewpoints bring and minimising any difficulties that might emerge.

Mark Fox (1998: 64, citing Doyle 1993) identifies four categories or levels of multi-professional work. He suggests that to get the full benefit of working with other professionals and agencies, it is necessary to achieve **transdisciplinary working** – with a sharing of knowledge, skills and collective decision-making. Early childhood practitioners (and other professional groups) usually work at one of three lower levels:

- **low-level cross-disciplinary** – where there is little collaboration
- **cross-disciplinary** – views are shared but not modified or developed in the light of meetings
- **interdisciplinary** – where there is some cross-fertilisation of ideas.

The functions of leaders in early childhood settings

A leader's most important function is to develop a shared vision amongst staff so that everyone is working to the same ends. Goleman *et al.* (2002: 209) describe this very persuasively. They suggest that a shared vision enables staff to:

> ...feel the heat of a collective excitement, of many people being enthusiastic about their work. A vision that 'tunes people in', that creates resonance – builds organizational harmony and people's capacity to act collectively.

> The invisible threads of a compelling vision weave a tapestry that binds people together more powerfully than any strategic plan... Success depends on what an organization's people care about, what they do, and how they work together.

Goleman *et al.* also emphasise the importance of the leader modelling the behaviour or skills they think are important. In the words '*be the change you want to see*', they suggest that leaders who want staff, for example, to be playful, or empathetic or reassuring should display these qualities themselves.

From that initial vision will flow everything that the team does. Vision creates a shared motivation – an excitement that enables everyone to move forward in a coherent way. The centre's improvement plan, team action plans and co-ordinators' development plans may then all draw on the central vision.

In order to turn such plans into something practical and tangible, settings need detailed targets which are SMART (adapted from Lindon and Lindon 1997), standing for:

- Specific
- Measurable
- Achievable
- Realistic, and
- Time-bound.

REFLECTIVE ACTIVITY

Imagine that you are asked to provide information for a story about your nursery in the local paper. The reporter tells you that you have 500 words to write about the factors that contribute to the success of your centre. What would you write? (Try doing this activity with a colleague who works with you, if possible, and then compare your answers. Are there any common threads in what you have written? Why do you think this might be?)

What are the tasks or projects that you have most enjoyed doing or being a part of? State your reasons. To what extent do you think that what you set out to achieve was SMART?

A collective vision will give staff a sense of being team members and enable them to have a shared purpose. It provides a framework for identifying, prioritising and achieving the necessary tasks. It can also assist in allocating funding, as it helps the leader to determine how and where money should be spent (Lyus 1998). Leaders must of course guard against allowing money to drive priorities, and must think creatively to ensure that vision is not controlled and modified more than absolutely necessary by funding. This is one of the differences between a leader and a manager, since managers must adhere to policy decisions once decided.

Promoting communication is another important function of a leader, and the leader should ideally be an effective communicator. Meetings are vital but can be overwhelming. In order to ensure that meeting time is used effectively, leaders should ask themselves whether:

- the purpose of the meeting is clear
- every part of the meeting is relevant to everyone, or whether some people can attend for part of the time
- some other people might make a useful contribution
- the items to be covered in the meeting could be better communicated in some other way.

(based on Hindle 1998)

Last but by no means least, leaders must promote staff development. Some training or courses will focus on the development of a member of staff as an individual. However, staff development must also have the good of the whole team at its heart. This may be achieved through on-going supervision and appraisals. Support of this kind is vital to all early years staff, and Elfer *et al.* (2003: 56), writing about those working with children under the age of three, remind us that:

> Boundaries between professional and parental roles may occasionally become confused. Mentoring and supervision is an essential tool for keeping these relationships under systematic review and is recognised as a complex but crucial element in all professional roles working in a caring or helping way with others.

Mentoring, appraisals and supervision are not usually taken on by the overall leader of a big centre but tend to be the responsibility of individual line managers. Nevertheless, leaders must pay attention to them, since the health and well-being of staff can impact heavily on the health and well-being of children.

The characteristics of leaders in early childhood settings

The previous sections identify a daunting list of tasks which seem likely to become ever more daunting! The complexity of the tasks to be managed in multi-function centres, such as children's centres and neighbourhood nurseries, has grown rapidly in the last five or six years. The level of demand looks certain to increase as the government's ten-year strategy indicates (H.M. Treasury 2004). All this requires leaders with a remarkable range of characteristics, as can be seen in the following lists:

Rodd (1998: 15, citing Bogue 1985) suggests that the following five characteristics are relevant for leaders in early childhood settings:

- Curiosity (an interest in learning)
- Candor (sic) (principles and action being open to public scrutiny and a willingness to speak the truth)
- Courtesy (treating others with respect and dignity)
- Courage (a willingness to risk and dare, and a willingness to make mistakes and learn from them)
- Compassion (creating trust, empathy, high expectations, hope and inspiration and providing opportunities for individual, group, personal and professional development).

Edgington (2004) suggests that in addition to the qualities considered essential for *all* early years specialists:

- warmth and empathy
- spontaneity and flexibility
- skills of reflection and analysis
- clear principles underpinning practice
- an ability to communicate with a wide range of people
- an ability to take the lead
- an ability to be playful and make learning fun
- imagination and creativity
- in-depth understanding of child development and effective learning
- conscientious record-keeping
- an optimistic disposition and 'can do' approach,

leaders in early childhood settings also require:

- commitment, enthusiasm and humour
- (an) ability to deal with others...
- consistency and a sense of fairness
- loyalty to the team...
- (and an) ability to earn respect by example.

(Edgington 2004: 25)

Some writers identify leadership styles. Bruce and Meggitt (2002) suggest four styles, namely *autocratic*, *democratic*, *laissez-faire* and *consultative*, and indicate that all four styles have drawbacks. Goleman *et al.* (2002: 55) identify a number of leadership styles and suggest that each one may be appropriate in particular situations. For example, they describe the visionary leader as being most useful when 'changes require a new vision, or when a clear direction is needed'. They also suggest that while a commanding leadership can be negative, in times of crisis, it can be very useful 'to kick-start a turnaround, or with worsen employees'.

Therefore, it seems that effective leaders, while having a preferred style, also need to be able to adapt their style to match the needs of their team. Rodd (1998: 68) suggests that a young and inexperienced team may need a more directive style than the leader might otherwise choose. Conversely, if the level of conflict seems high, they might opt for leadership which is 'more democratic and include(s) staff participation in making decisions about matters which affect the operation of the centre', rather than a more autocratic style which could worsen conflict.

REFLECTIVE ACTIVITY

You might find it helpful to do this activity with a partner, and then compare and discuss your answers.

1. Think about leaders in your setting or in other settings you may have worked in. It may be a team leader, it may be the inclusion manager or it may be the overall head of centre. It could even include you!

2. Reflect on the characteristics of effective leaders and the suggested leadership styles outlined above. How are these reflected in the leaders you are thinking about? What can you learn from them?

BUILDING AND DEVELOPING TEAMS

Early years settings are generally made up of a number of teams. In addition to the small team, common to all settings, who work together to support a particular group or class of children, there are now Sure Start teams, extended hours teams, community teams, teams supporting other settings, inclusion teams and so on. In some of the most complex centres these lists are endless! If such centres are to live up to the expectations placed upon them they must work, not simply as isolated teams, but as members of different teams, coming together as a single integrated team to ensure that the children's experience is consistent, stable and predictable.

Each of the teams will have its own leader and they will need to share many of the characteristics listed in the previous section. The notion of *distributed leadership* discussed earlier in this chapter means that many people in integrated centres have to display high levels of leadership. The major strength of both teamwork and distributed leadership is that it allows people to work to their strengths in certain areas and to rely on others more competent or confident to support them in other areas. It also means that practitioners at all levels of responsibility have the opportunity to observe at first-hand and learn from the leadership of others.

Whalley (1994: 171) reminds us that 'working as a team is a process not a technique', while Rodd (1998: 116) states that teamwork 'relies on open communication, democratic organisation and effective problem-solving skills'. The process involves a number of steps:

- achievable goals, agreed by team members. This will often be an iterative process since work with young children is dynamic and subject to change.
- clear roles and responsibilities, understood by all members of the team. There will sometimes be conflicts but if they are dealt with openly and constructively they can be a positive aspect of the process of team-building.
- supportive relationships which aid co-operation
- active participation, and
- a monitoring process which encourages everyone in the team to review and improve their work – as individuals and as a team.

(based on Rodd 1998, citing Neugebauer 1984).

REFLECTIVE ACTIVITY

Make a list of the teams operating within your centre. There will be a team for each class or group of children but there will be many others as well. Some people are likely to appear in more than one team. There may be teams working with one child in particular if he or she has complex learning needs – a speech therapist, learning support assistant, physiotherapist, peripatetic specialist, inclusion manager etc. There will be a management group – with representatives from other teams. Each of these teams will have specific goals but it is vital that they share a common vision.

While it is clear that the leader has a vital role to play in this process, it is sometimes forgotten that team members also have to take responsibility for making teamwork happen. Since many members of the team are themselves team leaders, it should not be difficult to see developments from both points of view. The following table explores the relationship between the two sets of responsibilities:

Responsibilities of designated leader	Responsibilities of team member
• overall co-ordination of centre	*responsibility for addressing individual responsibilities*
• provision of support and guidance	*acknowledging and valuing support and guidance*
• facilitation of open communication	• keeping the lines of communication open
• provision of feedback and encouragement	*recognising and responding positively to feedback and encouragement*
• identification of problems and sources of stress	• being co-operative and committed
• objectivity and consistency	*objectivity and consistency is as necessary in team members as it is in leaders*
• fairness	• accepting and acknowledging own and others' limitations
• flexibility	• being flexible, prepared to give and take
• knowing the difference between delegation and 'palming off'	• being reliable
• setting and communicating parameters that the team has to work within	• demonstrating respect for the ideology of the team and team effort
• sharing information	• sharing the workload and expertise
• acting as a resource	• ensuring confidentiality
• ensuring confidentiality	• being aware of the nature and scope of work relationships
• facilitating group cohesion	• developing strengths and working on overcoming limitations
• encouraging professional growth and development in all team members	• respecting and tolerating individual differences
• being aware of own limitations	• being available for others in the team
• facilitating the meeting of individual and group needs	• being aware of own responsibilities
• accepting final responsibility and taking control where necessary	*ensuring that those in the outside community know who is the designated leader;*
• liaising with the outside community	*and that your leader is aware of your contacts in the community.*

(based on Rodd, 1998: 102–103. Text in italics has been added)

MANAGING CHANGE

Any changes are likely to cause a certain level of anxiety and uncertainty to both individuals and organisations. As an early years practitioner you will be aware of the impact that change can have on children, and how change needs to be phased in gradually to allow children to settle and to understand new circumstances or routines. As indicated earlier, developments have been rapid in the field of early years care and education. Early years practitioners have become used to change – early years settings are constantly evolving new ideas, structures and systems.

Managing change should be about people, rather than just concepts and ideas. Organisations can only change at the speed at which the people in them are willing to change. It is important to consider that

Discussing any specific training needs with staff members can enable change to happen successfully.

fundamental changes, such as those affecting attitudes, take much longer than simple structural changes. Organisations tend to develop their own cultures and staff become comfortable within their familiar frameworks, so any change which disrupts this comfort can be disorientating. Early years leaders and managers should consider how planned changes will affect the most important people in early years settings – namely the children and their families.

Rodd (1998) reminds us that change is inevitable but also highlights the kinds of change that can occur in organisations. She suggests that change may be:

induced – involving a conscious decision, perhaps arising out of some training or new equipment

routine – designed to improve quality, perhaps arising out of monitoring processes

crisis – this usually happens as a result of an incident such as sickness or absence and typically does not involve consultation

transformational – occurs where an organisation must change in order to survive, for example, nursery schools threatened with closure. Rodd stresses that the personal costs to staff of transformational change can be very high and even cause emotional burnout

innovative – comes about through creative problem-solving in response to a recognised need.

When teams have successfully developed as a team, the inevitable changes which come about may throw up a range of responses. Edgington (2004) identifies three types of team:

1. the cosy team

2. the turbulent team (with undercurrents)

3. the rigorous and challenging team.

She suggests that the leaders of teams with these characteristics require different strategies to bring about change. The first type of team (cosy) may resist change because they feel that what they do works well, has worked well and will continue to work well for them. In the second (turbulent), change is difficult to accomplish because many team members do not express their views but go along – in public – with the views of a vocal minority. After the meeting there may be mumblings and grumblings but these are often left unsaid in any forum where they could be acted on. The third (rigorous) type of team:

> see themselves as professionals who want to do the very best for the children in their care... [who may need help to] recognize their strengths and... not just focus on weaknesses... prioritize developments... [and] relax and not work too hard.
>
> (Edgington 2004: 55)

Understanding a team's objectives and sense of identity helps leaders to analyse the difficulties they are likely to face in steering changes to practice and policy. This then makes it easier to select appropriate strategies to support the introduction of change.

Change is challenging for all of us but it can be particularly difficult for some people and in some circumstances, causing a range of emotions or anxieties. Practitioners may be afraid that their skills will be redundant or that they will be unable to learn the new ones required. They may panic and leap to negative conclusions about what will be involved and what it will mean for them. They may feel as though proposed changes carry an implicit criticism of what they have been doing for many years.

Other people's resistance may be based on practical considerations. *Will the room be big enough? Where will we put this? What will happen if...?* These objections are often based on emotional anxieties and need to be viewed by the leader in that light. Both groups require encouragement, reassurance and understanding. Despite the challenges, questions of this type can be very useful in helping the team to address the practical aspects of change.

The third aspect of resistance may be described as philosophical. What is being asked of a team may not fit comfortably with what they regard as their central vision or purpose.

The complex way in which these responses interact with one another may be best illustrated with an example: in common with many other early years settings the staff of a nursery school were asked to close one class for three- and four-year-olds and to replace it with provision for a group of children up to the age of three, including six children under one year of age. Most staff had worked in the school for many years and were resistant to change – perhaps it could be described overall, in Edgington's term, as a cosy team. Some staff opposed the change on emotional grounds, although this was not made explicit. Their fears were masked by saying that there wouldn't be a demand for places for young children or that parents wouldn't be able to afford them. Some staff voiced practical concerns: *where would all those buggies go? How could the other children be kept quiet enough to allow younger children to sleep? There isn't enough room in the staff room for a washing machine.* But often mingled with these concerns was the belief that such young children ought not to be placed in institutional settings.

REFLECTIVE ACTIVITY

What changes has your team faced recently? Try to list the concerns that were voiced. Do you think that they arose from emotional, practical or philosophical concerns? Can you think of any responses where these three elements appeared to overlap?

In the example just given, the head of centre, with the support of team members, had to:

- acknowledge the emotional anxieties which often remained unvoiced but which underpinned many people's responses. This might mean providing appropriate training and arranging visits, as well as finding ways to reassure staff about their expertise and to utilise it.
- discuss and, where appropriate, act on the physical constraints raised. This might mean talking to architects and the team most closely involved in order to come up with solutions.
- help the team to rationalise their philosophical anxieties, in particular by reviewing the relevant research and guides to good practice.

Integrated centres have many additional characteristics which can make managing change difficult:

- a rapid increase in team size
- communication is more difficult when staff work shifts and may miss meetings
- leaders may find it harder to retain an overview of the work of their team
- tension may develop between staff from different professional backgrounds.

(Edgington 2004: 58)

CONCLUSION

In this chapter we have considered the wide variety of leadership roles that exist at many different levels within complex early years settings. Most staff assume managerial responsibilities of some kind, and leaders often find themselves as team members in a range of contexts. Therefore early years practitioners need to reflect on the roles of managers, leaders and teams and the relationship between them.

EARLY YEARS POLICY IN THE 21st CENTURY

9

IN THIS CHAPTER WE WILL CONSIDER THE FOLLOWING TOPICS:

* Growth of early years policy and legislation
* Policy developments
* Planned policy or accidents of history?

This chapter sets out the context for the remarkable developments that have occurred in services for young children in less than ten years. We will consider these developments in the areas of care and education, choice and diversity, curriculum and assessment, and quality matters. We will also look at other factors that have influenced policy, such as historical accident, research, finance and social influences – reminders that policies rarely, if ever, emerge solely from political will.

GROWTH OF EARLY YEARS POLICY AND LEGISLATION

The opening years of the twenty-first century have seen a remarkable shift in early years policy. Services for the under-fives, viewed for decades as the poor relations of both the education and social care systems, have become the focus of government policy, receiving previously unimaginable sums of money.

The policy shift that occurred in 1997 marked a watershed and can, paradoxically, be traced back to both the Conservative government's decision to introduce vouchers and the New Labour government's decision to abolish them, following the 1997 general election. Both decisions were designed to ensure that all four-year-olds had a free nursery education place. Elements of the scheme, both before and after the election, attracted a great deal of controversy, mainly focused around the following issues.

First, free places for four-year-olds were to be offered in any group setting – in the private, voluntary or maintained sector – so long as that setting addressed the learning areas set out in six areas of learning in 'Nursery Education: Desirable Outcomes for Children's Learning on Entering Compulsory Education' (DLOs) (SCAA 1996) (see also Chapter 5, The Foundation Stage (3–5 Years), pp. 102–16, Chapter 6, Educational Transitions (5–8 Years), p. 120 and Chapter 7, Early Years and ILT, pp. 143–5) It quickly became a bone of contention between different providers that reception classes in primary schools could also accept vouchers. Following local decisions over many years to admit children to statutory schooling long before statutory school age, most four-year-olds were in reception classes, a process which was believed to be exacerbated by the free places scheme. Equally, many practitioners in maintained schools felt that the education of young children was being devalued, since a wide range of settings without qualified teaching staff were receiving grants for offering education places.

Second, the quality of provision in settings receiving vouchers or, following the election, those in receipt of grants from the government was to be scrutinised by Ofsted. Particular controversy arose out of the facts that:

- nursery (and reception) provision in the maintained sector was inspected under a more lengthy and rigorous framework than other settings
- there was a lack of clarity about whether children in reception classes should be inspected under the national curriculum framework or that offered by the DLOs
- the credibility of some inspectors was doubted (it was widely believed that many of those registered to inspect nursery provision lacked the necessary experience or qualifications)
- settings in the private and voluntary sectors were still subject to Children Act (DoH 1989) requirements, which meant that they were registered and inspected by social services inspectors in addition to the new Ofsted inspections.

The newly elected Labour government quickly made a decision to set up Early Years Development Partnerships (EYDPs) in every local authority. This decision was soon superseded by the creation of Early Years Development and Childcare Partnerships (EYDCPs) (DfEE 1999). These partnerships represented a new concept in local government and, to a certain extent, were able to bypass local authority policies, since funding for the government's agenda was directed to the partnerships themselves. A similar strategy was used for the Sure Start pilot initiatives.

The change in title reflected a growing range of responsibilities. As policy developed, so did the responsibilities of the EYDCPs. By 2004, the range of initiatives emerging from the National Childcare Strategy (launched in 1998, see www.surestart.gov.uk), designed to improve services for young children, included:

- free part-time education places for all three- and four-year-olds whose parents want them
- *Curriculum Guidance for the Foundation Stage* (QCA 2000, 2001, 2003) and related profiling; planning
- support for childminding
- tax credits to support increased employment among parents
- over 2000 Early Excellence Centres, aiming to improve coordination between services (Bertram and Pascal 2001)

- the development of 'wraparound' services, such as extended school initiatives, breakfast clubs and after-school centres (H.M. Treasury 2004)
- Sure Start programmes, supporting families with children aged three or under and targeting socio-economically deprived areas
- Children's Information Services
- Neighbourhood Nurseries (www.surestart.gov.uk – accessed October 2004)
- Children's Centres (www.surestart.gov.uk – accessed October 2004)
- healthy eating initiatives
- after-school support for children with special educational needs who require individual support
- the publication of *Birth to Three Matters* (DfES 2002)
- training to support these objectives.

POLICY DEVELOPMENTS

Change and development on this scale have inevitably produced issues and concerns. These can be categorised under four main headings:

- care and education
- choice and diversity
- curriculum and assessment
- quality matters.

Care and education

Provision in this country for young children and their families is notoriously diverse (DES 1990). This wide range of provision owes much to the lack of coordination of services. Services focusing on care or education have often been developed without a distinct policy. Historically this was not always the case.

Robert Owen, mill owner and philanthropist, established the first workplace nursery in the UK in New Lanark in 1816 (Whitbread 1972) (see also Chapter 5, The Foundation Stage (3–5 Years), p. 98). He regarded his school as offering education for children from one year of age, but it was established in a spirit of care for the whole community. Decent housing, humane working hours, nursery provision to match those hours and universal education for children and adults were all part of the Utopian dream Owen sought to establish in the mills of New Lanark.

Around a century later, Margaret and Rachel McMillan opened an open air nursery school in Deptford (again see Chapter 5, The Foundation Stage (3–5 Years), p. 99). They were also responsible for the development of the school meals service and the school health service. Their actions were based on their concern for the health of children in the community. But they also recognised the children's need for education, writing that 'they need experience now, just as they need food' (Lowndes 1960: 42, citing Margaret McMillan 1919).

During World War II, full day care and education developed in many parts of the country to support working mothers. At the end of the war, men returning from the war needed employment. This coincided with a fast-rising birth rate, creating an increased demand for nursery places. In most parts of the country the problem was solved by changing full-time nursery places to part-time. This doubled the number of places at little extra cost, but also made it more difficult for women to continue working. The shift in policy was given weight by the publication of Bowlby's (1951) theories of maternal deprivation, which appeared to justify the narrowing of choices in relation to nursery provision (Riley 1983). Daycare was no longer on the agenda. Nursery education was what was on offer. In turn, this led to a sharp divide between services for those requiring daycare and the part-time provision offered in nursery schools and classes.

The response in Reggio Emilia in Northern Italy was very different. Here the end of the war led parents to build new nurseries, 'created and run by parents... in a devastated town, rich only in mourning and poverty', funded from 'the sale of an abandoned war tank, a few trucks, and some horses left behind by the retreating Germans' (Malaguzzi

Wartime provision was to affect future policy.

1993: 42). By the last decade of the twentieth century, these schools, offering a rich blend of care and education, were being hailed as among the best schools in the world (see also Chapter 4, Working with Young Children (0–3 Years), p. 76 and Chapter 5, The Foundation Stage (3–5 Years), p. 115).

Choice and diversity

Although the Rumbold Report (DES 1990) suggested that diversity of provision could be healthy, it is clear that it has not led to choice for the parents of young children. The division of day care from education for young children has historical roots, as we have seen, but it is also the case that decades of underfunding led to the diversity which has characterised early childhood provision in this country for so long. The Preschool Playgroup movement, for example, was begun by parents who could not find nursery places for their young children and who therefore set up their own groups in order to offer developmentally appropriate group experiences. The movement arose from parents' frustration at their lack of choice, but has, over the years, added a distinctive form of provision which has increased the overall diversity. However, it could not offer greater choice to working parents.

Similarly, the Children Act's (DoH 1989) requirements to provide for 'children in need' led many social services departments to offer daycare only to carefully targeted groups of children and their families. This in turn also reduced the options of working parents, making it harder to access daycare. Childminders and private day nurseries filled some of the gaps, but no initiatives – full- or part-time – offered real solutions for parents.

The absence of choice has often meant that some children attend a bewildering range of services as parents struggle to cover their working day. Diversity and choice are not the same thing. However, choice is expensive. In order to offer genuine choice, large numbers of places would need to remain unfilled to ensure that all types of places and localities were available at all times.

PAUSE FOR THOUGHT

Why did the end of the war have such radically different consequences in nursery education here and in Italy?

What have been the long-term consequences for services for young children and their families in this country?

REFLECTIVE ACTIVITY

Try to find out how many children in the setting where you work attend more than one form of provision.

What are the reasons for this?

Even where the nursery or centre offers extended care, parents who work shifts or have commitments beyond the home may place children in a variety of settings. What difficulties might this create for children?

Curriculum and assessment

Many early childhood practitioners became alarmed at the downward pressures exerted on practice by the requirements of the national curriculum (NC) in key stage 1. While the nursery tradition had emphasised:

- play
- the social and emotional needs of the child
- physical development and active learning
- pleasure in living and learning,

the introduction of the NC, together with the absence of a clearly articulated early years curriculum, led many schools to believe that an earlier start to formal schooling would improve standards. This clash was in keeping with the legacy of the Plowden Report (CACE 1967). This report espoused the child-centred view of education which was derived from the philosophies of early childhood, and famously proclaimed that pupils of primary schools should 'learn to live first and foremost as children and not as future adults'. Paradoxically, children in nursery schools and classes were to learn to live and succeed as primary school pupils. If the priority was to prepare children for school, then literacy and numeracy were increasingly seen as vital to success. This is in marked contrast to policies in most other European countries, where young children have generally been protected from an overly formal curriculum and there has been much greater value placed on the development of communication, social and emotional well-being and physical competence.

The DLOs further exacerbated the situation because there was widespread misunderstanding about the age of statutory schooling. The tendency of the vast majority of schools to admit children at the age of four meant that many policy makers, practitioners and parents forgot that children are not actually required to attend school until the term after their fifth birthday.

The introduction of Ofsted inspections led many settings – such as playgroups and day nurseries that had hitherto not been involved in NC requirements – to attempt to teach reading and sums. Since the DLOs appeared to prioritise early literacy and numeracy, many anxious or underqualified practitioners came to rely on worksheets and formal sessions, believing that they were doing what Ofsted wanted. The literacy and numeracy strategies further increased perceived pressure to develop formal literacy and numeracy sessions.

The Early Learning Goals (ELGs) were published in 1999, following consultation on the DLOs. Many early childhood practitioners were disappointed in the results and working groups were established to create clarification in the form of the *Curriculum Guidance for the Foundation Stage* (QCA 2000). In offering more detailed guidance, many misunderstandings were addressed and, once more, play and personal and social development were given greater focus. Most importantly, the introduction of the foundation stage reduced confusion, making the position of reception classes clearer. Although it is not wholly free from ambiguity, the document has reduced pressure on many young children.

More recently, *Birth to Three Matters* (DfES 2002) has been published, providing a framework for the care and education of children under three years of age. While it has managed to avoid the danger of being made to fit in with the ELGs, there remains some concern about the extent to which downward pressure may be brought to bear. Demands to make links between the NC and ELGs have often led to downward pressure driven by subject knowledge. Demands for links between ELGs and *Birth to Three Matters* must take warning from this and be careful not to be driven by top-down initiatives.

Children in the UK are tested more frequently and from an earlier age than in many other countries. Practitioners and parents hold strong views – some wanting to end the pressure on young children and others wanting to ensure that achievements are measured and compared. Although there have been major shifts in thinking, pressures on children and staff remain. Clearly there is a need for formative assessment, which informs planning, highlights progress and identifies areas for development. However, the argument centres on summative assessments and those used for value-added procedures.

Baseline assessment has given way to profiling (QCA 2003). This has many benefits, yet the controversy over the effectiveness of the scheme remains. Those who are opposed to it point to the high number of statements, the temptation to use the form as a checklist and the fragmentation of understandings of children's learning. There are widespread demands to end testing at the end of key stage 1. An end to testing need not lead to a lowering of standards. Staff at Reggio Emilia articulate this by suggesting that testing is only necessary if you believe that learning is not visible (Giudici *et al.* 2001). Their approach to assessment involves documentation – records involving transcripts of talk, photos and samples of children's work – demonstrating steps or stages in children's learning.

Quality matters

The link between quality and visions of curricula has been clear throughout these policy shifts. By setting up the DLOs and Ofsted at the same time, policy makers were clearly acknowledging this link. The early years of the twenty-first century have raised a number of important questions about the nature of quality and how to assess it. Three important strands are identified – inspection, training, and quality and equality.

Inspection

The major problem facing the inspection regimes is that the care and education agendas have not yet been 'joined up'. It has still not proved possible to find an appropriate inspection framework against which to evaluate such a diverse range of provision. The major questions which have not been addressed through policy include:

- Can different modes of inspection for different types of provision be justified?
- Does the separation of inspection from support and advice really lead to higher quality?

Training

The diversity of provision is reflected in the diversity of qualifications. Research funded by the DfES (Siraj-Blatchford *et al.* 2002) suggests that settings employing trained teachers produce higher standards of achievement than those where staff are not similarly qualified. Interestingly, these findings have not been reflected in policy – children's centres are not required to employ qualified teachers (although they will have some support from teachers.)

Moreover the REPEY (Researching Effective Pedagogy in the Early Years) project did not include in its study other graduate practitioners. As more practitioners gain foundation degrees or honours degrees in early childhood studies it will be interesting to review research findings and policy in the light of their contribution to practice.

Quality and equality

The childcare agenda owed much to two North American initiatives. Follow-up studies of High/Scope (Sylva 1999) made political play of the notion that for every dollar spent on early childhood education, seven dollars could be saved through the children's improved work habits, health and social awareness. The Carnegie Foundation (1994) claimed that early intervention was likely to be the most effective way of improving the life chances of families locked into poverty and unemployment.

Issues of equality are at the heart of current policies in seeking to eradicate poverty, providing an entitlement curriculum for all children in an effort to raise achievement.

PLANNED POLICY OR ACCIDENTS OF HISTORY?

Early years policies, like all other areas of policy and decision making, are subject to all sorts of influences. Finance shapes policy in very obvious ways. The voucher scheme was built around the redistribution of funds drawn from local authorities, in a policy move designed to make parents feel that they had financial control. Subsequent policies about both care and education have cost a great deal of money. The hope here is that (as promised by High/Scope) money can be saved as a result of investment in the early years – an example of policy, advocacy and research coming together.

There are many examples of historical accidents influencing or shaping policy. For example, it is claimed that children in the UK start school earlier than those in other European countries because politicians wanted to outdo their French counterparts. Was the fact that different decisions were taken at the end of World War II due to the fact that Bowlby's research was in English, or were the policy decisions based on the need to limit the workforce? We can see that these social, cultural and research issues have all combined to shape policy.

Sometimes policies are driven by political vision, such as in the setting up of the EYDCPs, or the bold vision of the childcare agenda; but even in these cases, we cannot ignore the impact of previous policies and actions. Taking advantage of a new organisation created by the voucher scheme required creativity; battling with the diverse patterns of provision in order to create a cohesive whole has proved more difficult. As all those within the early years sector know, this will take time and patience.

USEFUL WEBSITES (Accessed October 2004)

www.surestart.gov.uk

10 SPECIAL EDUCATIONAL NEEDS, DISABILITY AND INCLUSION

> **IN THIS CHAPTER WE WILL CONSIDER THE FOLLOWING TOPICS:**
>
> ✳ Definitions of special educational needs (SEN) and disability
> ✳ The prevalence of children with special educational needs
> ✳ The historical perspective
> ✳ Theoretical models used to explain special educational needs and disability
> ✳ The parental perspective
> ✳ Working with the *Special Educational Needs Code of Practice*
> ✳ The professionals involved.

INTRODUCTION

At some time in their school careers approximately 20 per cent of children will require extra support to access fully all aspects of the curriculum. This may be because they have a physical disability, such as blindness or deafness, or perhaps because they have a behavioural or learning difficulty that prevents them from progressing at the same rate as their peers. In the past many of these children would have been educated away from other children, either in separate establishments (special schools) or in specialist units within mainstream schools.

Children who are deaf may need extra support at school.

Nowadays it is recognised that educating children with special educational needs apart from their peers is a form of discrimination, denying them the opportunities that other children take for granted.

As an early years practitioner you are required to have a good understanding of the legislation surrounding provision for children with special educational needs. You also need to have strong professional skills in planning appropriate provision and working in partnership with the children's parents and relevant agencies. You may be concerned that you do not have the specialist skills necessary to work with children with special needs. However, you are actually in a very good position to offer inclusive provision – the principles of providing for the needs of children with SEN are the same principles that we apply to all children. Recent research has shown that young children showing early signs of special educational needs show marked improvements if they attend good quality early years provision and that pre-school education is a very effective intervention for children at risk (Sylva *et al.* 2003).

In this chapter we will be looking at how we define special educational needs and the number of children requiring specialist provision within the education system. We will investigate how children with special educational needs or disabilities were viewed throughout history and the models which influence our perceptions today. As an early years practitioner you will need to implement government guidelines for children with special educational needs; these are explained clearly below.

DEFINITIONS OF SPECIAL EDUCATIONAL NEEDS AND DISABILITY

Before we look at the subject in detail it is necessary to clarify certain terms. The terminology we use to describe children has to be carefully thought through; words that were once considered appropriate to use are now thought to be stereotypical or to have negative connotations. As an early years practitioner you need to be sensitive in the terminology you use and be aware of words that may be offensive. What is considered appropriate or inappropriate is liable to change over time and it is always best to check with parents the terminology they prefer you to use.

The definitions that will be used in this chapter are explained below and come from the 2001 *Special Educational Needs Code of Practice* (DfES 2001; also available online at http://www.teachernet.gov.uk/_doc/3724/SENCodeOfPractice.pdf – accessed October 2004).

There are four main areas of special educational needs:

- communication and interaction
- cognition and learning
- behavioural, emotional and social development
- sensory and physical needs.

Children have special educational needs if they have a *learning difficulty* which calls for *special educational provision* to be made for them.

Children have a learning difficulty if they:

a) have a significantly greater difficulty in learning than the majority of children of the same age; or

b) have a disability, which prevents or hinders them from making use of educational facilities of a kind generally provided for children of the same age in schools within the area of the local education authority

c) are under compulsory school age and fall within the definition at (a) or (b) above or would so do if special educational provision was not made for them.

Children must not be regarded as having a learning difficulty solely because the language or form of language of their home is different from the language in which they will be taught.

(DfES 2001: 6)

Likewise children who have a disability that does not affect their ability to learn or access educational provision are not classified as having special educational needs. For example, a child who only has one leg and is proficient using a prosthesis would be classified as having a disability, but this is unlikely to affect their education.

A child is disabled if he is blind, deaf or dumb or suffers from a mental disorder of any kind or is substantially and permanently handicapped by illness, injury or congenital deformity or such other disability as may be prescribed.

(Section 17 (11) Children Act 1989)

THE PREVALENCE OF CHILDREN WITH SPECIAL EDUCATIONAL NEEDS

It is not always easy to be exact about how many children in our schools and nurseries have special educational needs. Later on in the chapter you will discover that there are set procedures to follow if a child is thought to have special educational needs. It takes different lengths of time for children to be identified and assessed. Some children will be helped by activities and learning programmes set up within schools and nurseries. Other children will go on to have a formal written 'statement' of their needs and a plan drawn up detailing how these needs will be met. It follows, therefore, that the number of children with a formal statement fails to represent *all* the children with special educational needs. Every year the British government publishes a document called *Statistics for Education*. The following statistics are from 2003 (DfES) and cover schools and nurseries in England:

- 3 per cent of all pupils in schools had statements of SEN in 2003
- 60 per cent of pupils with statements were placed in mainstream schools (nursery, primary and secondary), 37 per cent in either special schools or pupil referral units and 3 per cent in independent schools
- primary schools had 17.5 per cent of pupils with special educational needs, secondary schools had 15.4 per cent
- the number of boys with statements is double the number of girls
- when figures are broken down by ethnic group, in primary schools the figures of children with a statement and awaiting statements are as follows:

Ethnic group	Percentage of children with a statement	Percentage of children classed as SEN without a statement
White British	1.9	18.1
Black Caribbean	2.1	26.0
Chinese	1.3	11.5
Pakistani	2.0	Figures not available
Travellers (Irish Heritage)	2.6	52.6
Travellers (Gypsy/Roma)	3.0	46.6
Indian	1.2	Figures not available

Table 1 The prevalence of children with SEN in England, 2003 (adapted from DfES 2003)

PAUSE FOR THOUGHT

Can you think of reasons why more boys than girls have special educational needs?

Why do you think that travelling families have a much higher percentage of children who have SEN but do not have a statement?

Types of special educational needs

Some conditions are genetic, that is, children are born with a condition that leads to them having difficulties in learning, such as Down's syndrome. Other conditions are acquired at birth, such as cerebral palsy, which may be the result of a birth injury. Conditions may be acquired later as the result of illness or injury or other adverse life events. Often there is no single cause that can be identified – some conditions are a complex interaction of environmental and genetic factors.

In February 2004 the government launched a new strategy for SEN. In *Removing Barriers to Achievement* (DfES 2004) it was noted that certain types of special educational needs are placing growing demands on schools. These are:

* autistic spectrum disorder
* behavioural, emotional and social difficulties
* speech, language and communication difficulties
* moderate learning difficulties.

Below is a brief outline of the types of conditions that may lead to a child having special educational needs in different forms (adapted from Dare and O'Donovan 2003).

Physical conditions:

* cerebral palsy
* spina bifida
* cystic fibrosis
* sickle cell disorder
* arthritis
* muscular dystrophy
* epilepsy, asthma, eczema.

Speech, language and sensory impairment:

* stammering
* poor pronunciation
* difficulty in understanding the meaning and structure of language
* vision and hearing impairment.

Learning difficulties:

* Down's syndrome
* Fragile X syndrome
* autism
* dyslexia
* dyspraxia.

SPECIAL EDUCATIONAL NEEDS, DISABILITY AND INCLUSION

Emotional and behavioural difficulties:

- attention deficit hyperactivity disorder
- poor impulse control
- aggression
- withdrawal.

THE HISTORICAL PERSPECTIVE

The question of how to provide for children with special educational needs is one that has been addressed differently in different cultures at different times.

In the eighteenth century, before the Industrial Revolution, Britain's was a rural economy and individuals with disabilities were accommodated within their communities. In the nineteenth century, large sections of the rural community moved into the cities and there was little work that disabled people could undertake. Education became more universally provided and the difficulties of children not able to make full use of such provision began to be recognised. At this time it was not seen as a function of government to provide for the needs of children with disabilities or special educational needs. Any such provision that existed was organised by charitable institutions and the Church. Gradually it has been recognised that all children have a right to an appropriate education and the government has a responsibility to arrange for this provision.

Alan Dyson (2001) considers that there are three ways of viewing the history of special educational needs provision:

- the optimistic view – where there is uninterrupted progress made in the practice and policy of special needs education
- the pessimistic view – where any attempts at progress have been hindered by vested interests in the educational system
- the 'dilemmas' view – where changes in policies and procedures can be seen as the result of trying to reach a compromise between the need to give all children equal access to education, while making provision for children's very individual needs.

Prior to the 1980s, children with special educational needs or disabilities were educated in special schools. In 1978 the Warnock Report (DES 1978) recognised that educating children apart from their peers was denying them their rights to equal access. The report recommended that:

> ## REFLECTIVE ACTIVITY
>
> If you work with staff and parents who have lived in different countries, ask them how children's special educational needs were met in that country.
>
> Ask an elderly friend or relative if they can remember what happened to children with special educational needs when they were young.
>
> You may be surprised with some of the information you receive.

- children should be integrated into mainstream schooling as far as possible
- parents should be more involved in consultation and decision making
- a multi-professional assessment of children's needs should be undertaken as soon as possible and reviewed annually
- families of children under five should be given a named person to support them, such as a health visitor or a social worker.

Baroness Warnock

The Warnock Report was universally accepted and the main recommendations have been the basis for subsequent legislation.

The 1981 Education Act

This act was a direct result of the Warnock Report. The main points are as follows:

- children were no longer to be labelled according to their disability/condition – the focus was to be on the child's needs
- local education authorities (LEAs) were to have a statutory responsibility to meet children's learning needs by special provision
- wherever possible, children with special educational needs should be educated within mainstream provision

- the process of 'statementing' was introduced, whereby children would be assessed by a multi-disciplinary team and a statement outlining the child's special needs would be drawn up; the statement would include details of how the LEA was to meet the child's needs and was to be a legally binding agreement
- parental views and wishes had to be taken into account when deciding on provision for a child; parents were given a right of appeal.

There was a gradual move, first to integrate children into mainstream schools and, later, to provide fully inclusive education.

The 1993 Education Act

This act can be seen as a continuation of the 1981 Education Act and refined the provision for children with special educational needs. The main points were:

- a code of practice was to be published, giving schools and LEAs further guidance on assessment procedures and provision
- the need for LEAs and parents to work closely together was reiterated and parental rights were strengthened
- an official definition of 'Special Educational Needs' was drawn up
- inter-agency cooperation was strengthened
- parents of children under two years were given the right to ask for their child to be assessed.

The Special Educational Needs and Disability Act (SENDA) 2001

This is the legislation that outlines the regulations that we use today for the assessment and statementing of children with special educational needs (these regulations are described later in this chapter). The act also extends the Disability Discrimination Act (1995) to schools, colleges and universities.

Integration or inclusion?

The Warnock Report took evidence from children, young people and parents about how educational provision for children with special educational needs should be organised. At the time there was a growing opinion that educating children separately from their peers was denying them the right to be treated on equal terms. Many young people felt that although they needed specialist provision, this should be made available for them at the school their friends and siblings were attending.

PAUSE FOR THOUGHT

Although the process of integration meant that many more children with special needs were being educated within mainstream provision, do you think that children were being treated with equality?

The first initiatives involved integrating children with special needs into a mainstream school. 'Integration' was interpreted very differently in different settings. In some schools children were educated in separate units, rarely coming together with the main school body. In other schools children were taught alongside their peers for parts of the day, but were taught in specialist classes at other times.

Since the 2001 Code of Practice, schools and early years establishments have been working towards a more inclusive form of provision. The principles are as follows:

- inclusive education enables all students to participate fully in any mainstream early years provision, school, college or university
- inclusive education has training and resources aimed at fostering every student's equality and participation in all aspects of the life of the learning community
- inclusive education aims to equip all people with the skills needed to build inclusive communities.

(Tassoni 2003: 12)

The Alliance for Inclusive Education outlines nine principles of inclusive education (cited in Tassoni 2003):

1. a person's worth is independent of their abilities or achievements

2. every human being is able to feel and think

3. every human being has the right to communicate and be heard

4. all human beings need each other

5. real education can happen only in the context of real relationships

6. all people need support and friendship from people of their own age

7. progress for all learners is achieved by building on things people can do rather than what they cannot do

8. diversity brings strength to all living systems

9. collaboration is more important than competition.

The social constructivist approach to early childhood care and education emphasises the importance of the social context of learning. Looking at

PAUSE FOR THOUGHT

Can you think of any theoretical approaches commonly used to underpin early childhood practice that are reflected in these principles?

these principles, you can see that as an early years practitioner you are in an ideal situation to deliver inclusive care and education, based on meeting individual need.

The backlash to inclusion

Although it can be seen that early years practitioners are ideally placed to deliver inclusive education, adequate training and resources are vital in order to do this properly. In the UK and the USA there is a growing 'inclusion backlash'. Dyson (2001) points out the contradictions between trying to give all children the opportunity to participate in common learning experiences, and the practical and resource implications. The 'inclusive movement' emphasises what learners have in common, but there is growing concern that the *differences* between learners are being neglected. This may lead to all children's needs being neglected in the effort to provide an adequate experience for children with special educational needs within the classroom.

There is also concern that with the closure of 'special schools' and the inclusion of children, wherever possible, into mainstream provision, some excellent provision and specialist knowledge was lost. Indeed, inadequate provision within mainstream schools can lead to children being less prepared to take up a role in society than when they were educated separately. Ultimately, this can lead to social exclusion.

It is clear that we are in a period of transition with dilemmas to reconcile. As an early years practitioner your expert knowledge and opinions may well help move this debate forward.

THEORETICAL MODELS USED TO EXPLAIN SPECIAL EDUCATIONAL NEEDS AND DISABILITY

In the section exploring the historical perspective (above) we saw that opinions on the best ways to meet children's needs changed over time, and are still changing. One of the influences on how we think derives from the model of disability that we hold and, clearly, those models are a product of the society in which we live. There have been three main models which have influenced people's thinking about disability and special educational needs:

- the religious model
- the medical model
- the social model.

> ### REFLECTIVE ACTIVITY
>
> If you work in under-fives provision that comes under the National Standards for Day Care, investigate the guidelines for Standard 10. Discuss with your colleagues how far your provision meets these guidelines. What other standards will you have to consider when planning to meet the needs of children and their parents?

The religious model

This model was widely held before the causes of disability were understood. If a child was born with a special need or a disability (or became disabled because of illness or accident), the explanation given was that this was a result of God's intervention. Sometimes a parent would feel that it was retribution for a sin that they had committed. Conversely, conditions such as epilepsy were considered to be a blessing from God because some people who have epilepsy report intense religious experiences. One negative consequence of this view was that, in some cultures, very little was done to help the family or the children – because this was God's will.

Religious explanations are still used today, sometimes expressed openly, other times believed but not expressed. It may be tempting to dismiss such beliefs, but many parents, who do not profess a faith, may nevertheless blame themselves for their child's disability. As an early years practitioner you need to listen carefully to what parents tell you, because many parents of children with difficulties feel a great sense of guilt.

The medical model

Historically, the medical model has been the most pervasive and views the person with the disability as being imperfect and needing to be 'cured'. As its name suggests, the focus is on the ability of the medical profession and science to offer treatments. Although no one would deny the positive influences of medicine and science, the medical model tends to label individuals – blind, deaf, wheelchair-bound etc. The danger of this is that people with a disability are not accepted for what they are or valued for the contribution they can make. Many people with disabilities reject this model because it leads to discrimination and lack of opportunity. The disability movement has put forward the social model of disability as an alternative.

The social model of disability

In this model the emphasis is not on trying to help the person with a disability fit into society, but on how society can be changed to allow equal opportunities for people with disabilities. For instance, a person who uses a wheelchair is only 'handicapped' because society is not organised to allow ease of access into buildings and on public transport systems. While not rejecting the contributions made by science and medicine, the social model of disability calls for social and structural changes to ensure equality for those with special educational needs and disabilities.

There needs to be social and structural change to ensure equality for this child.

THE PARENTAL PERSPECTIVE

The birth of a child with a disability or the realisation that a child has special educational needs very often has a profound affect on a family. Parents may experience a range of feelings, including grief, anger and a sense of loss of control. Suddenly they are drawn into an orbit of professionals, agencies and a system that can be difficult to comprehend. As an early years practitioner you should have an understanding of some of the issues facing parents as these will have an impact on the way that parents relate with the early years team.

Attwood and Thomson (cited in Wall 2003) outline the features that distinguish parents of children with special educational needs:

- they are long-term players
- they tend to become isolated
- their emotional involvement is heightened
- they know that the welfare of their children is much more dependent on the continued effectiveness of the family.

The diagnosis

When parents discover their child has a disability, either at birth or later on in life, they often experience many conflicting emotions. These emotions are similar to those experienced after a bereavement, as parents may feel a profound sense of loss for the child they might have had. Initial feelings include:

- anger
- denial
- self-pity
- frustration
- guilt.

If it is obvious at birth that a child has a profound disability, parents may feel that others on the maternity ward are embarrassed to talk to them, or may be discussing the situation behind their backs. Parents may continue to feel, throughout the child's life, that everyone is watching their child.

After the initial shock has died down, most parents enter a period of adjustment where they start looking towards the future and planning to meet the needs of their child. It is only in a few cases where parents do not come to love and enjoy their children for what they are and the joy they can bring.

PAUSE FOR THOUGHT

Ann had a child with a disability. One day she was walking in the park with her son and feeling depressed when she saw another mother with a pram. Her first feeling was how different this mother's life was and that she probably had no idea of the traumas that Ann was going through. As the pram came closer she realised that this baby also had a disability. Ann realised that she was not alone.

Parents often find that meeting with others who have similar challenges to face is very helpful. If possible, discuss this with a parent or carer of a child with a disability or special educational needs who belongs to a support group.

Impact on the father

Fathers can find this period of understanding and adjustment difficult. If the mother is the primary caregiver, they may feel that all the support is centred on her and that they are expected to be strong to support their partner. Professionals sometimes forget that fathers need support too. Research conducted by Herbert and Carpenter (1994, cited in Wall 2003) identified how 'out of place' fathers felt as they desperately tried to find a semblance of normality in their lives.

Impact on the grandparents

Grandparents can play a vital supporting role in the lives of children with disabilities or special educational needs. However, they may also feel grief similar to that experienced by the parents. They too are faced with a situation which they had not anticipated and may go through moments of pain in the early stages of diagnosis and subsequent adjustment. For many families, the support that grandparents can give, both practically and emotionally, is vital.

Impact on the siblings

The arrival of a newborn creates many changes for other siblings in the family. Jealousy, attention-seeking behaviour and regression to more infantile ways of behaving are all seen as normal behaviour at such a time. However, having a brother or sister with special needs can sometimes create deep-rooted problems. If the mother is in hospital for a long time and the other child (or children) is cared for by the father (who is anxious and preoccupied) or by other relatives, the child might feel some insecurity. It is important to handle this period carefully. Carpenter (1997, cited in Wall 2003) highlighted points which are specific to siblings:

- The sibling must be given age-appropriate information. This can be very difficult as parents might not understand it fully themselves. Cultural interpretations should be taken into account. Sometimes there are no exact words to describe 'a syndrome', for example, especially to young children.
- The child may end up feeling that they are in some way responsible for their brother or sister having a special need. They are usually unable to articulate this and the guilt can lead to negative consequences. Feelings of resentment towards the new sibling may result in difficult behaviour, bed-wetting or feelings of isolation. Siblings may feel cut off from their parents or close relatives and this can affect behaviour and performance at school.

However, this experience does not need to be a negative one. Children do not see disability in the same way as adults. For them it is simply their brother or sister and they usually have no problems adjusting to their particular needs. One parent brought home a child whose head was shaped like an egg and was oversized compared to the size of the body. The father coined the phrase, 'to see is to kiss' – this meant that every time they saw their little brother the other children had to pick him up and kiss him. The older children soon learnt to hold him so that his head was supported, and the baby learnt to respond to his older siblings.

It was a long time before the older children realised that their brother's head was different and by then it was of little consequence to them.

> ### PAUSE FOR THOUGHT
>
> **You are the key worker of a three-year-old boy whose mother has given birth to a baby who has spina bifida. The baby and the mother are staying in hospital. The three-year-old is being looked after by his father. The boy has a full-time place in the nursery. What can you do to meet this child's needs?**

Social and economic consequences

Having a child with a profound disability will not only affect the family emotionally; there are also wide-ranging social and economic effects:

- there is a high incidence of relationship breakdown, leaving one parent to care for the children
- if parents stay together, income may be reduced as one parent has to stay at home to look after the needs of the child
- there are increased costs in bringing up a child with a disability (transport, heating and laundry can all cost more)
- some families get little opportunity to go out or go on holiday together
- many live in poor or inappropriate housing.

A study undertaken by the University of York for the Rowntree Foundation (Beresford and Oldham 2002) revealed that 90 per cent of families with a child with a severe disability reported significant difficulties with their homes. The report also showed that only a minority of families received help with their housing needs from statutory agencies.

WORKING WITH THE *SPECIAL EDUCATIONAL NEEDS CODE OF PRACTICE*

Children may arrive at your setting already identified as having a disability or a special educational need, or it may be that the early years team is the first to realise that the child is not progressing as expected. When this happens, the procedures outlined in the 2001 *Special Educational Needs Code of Practice* are triggered if your setting is in receipt of government funding. In early education settings the procedures set up for the child are called 'Early Years Action and Early Years Action Plus' (DfES 2001: S.4.11).

The Code of Practice 2001

The Code of Practice (CoP) is a guide for educators and local education authorities on the practical help they can give to children with special educational needs. It recommends that educators should identify children's needs and take action to meet these needs as early as possible, working with parents/carers. The law states that all settings must have regard to the Code of Practice.

The code recommends that settings should deal with children's needs in stages, matching the level of help to the needs of the child. The setting's staff will meet with parents/carers and together decide which stage is best for the child, what it involves and what should be done to help the child progress...

(Lewisham Early Years Special Needs Team 2003)

The 2001 CoP, which evolved out of the 1994 CoP, is based on the principles that:

- every child with special educational needs should have their needs met
- children with special educational needs should be provided with a broad, balanced and relevant curriculum, as far as possible in a mainstream setting
- parental views should be sought and taken into account.

The CoP specifically requires that early years settings:

- produce an SEN policy, the production of which should involve the whole team
- appoint a Special Educational Needs Coordinator (SENCO), who is responsible for the day-to-day operation of the SEN policy.

The Special Educational Needs and Disability Act (SENDA 2001)

It has been illegal for childcare settings to discriminate against disabled children since 1996 when the Disability Discrimination Act came into force. SENDA has extended disability legislation to education so that from September 2002 it has been illegal for any service to discriminate against children with a disability. This means that early years settings must make 'reasonable adjustments' to their existing policies, practices and procedures so that children with a disability can have access to the setting.

Lewisham Early Years Special Needs Team (2003) gives the following examples:

- providing auxiliary aids and services
- making physical alterations to buildings to accommodate children with disabilities (this could include providing ramps to allow access, making sure wheelchairs can access all parts of the building and providing toilet facilities for wheelchair users)
- using colour to provide visual cues in corridors, around doors and steps
- implementing PECS (Picture Exchange Communication Systems) for children who have communication difficulties
- adjusting table heights for children who have mobility difficulties
- providing a distraction-free work station for children who are on the autistic spectrum
- providing a calm area for children suffering from anxiety or sensory overload.

PAUSE FOR THOUGHT

Do you know who your SENCO is? Have you read the SEN policy?

Make sure that you are familiar with your workplace procedures.

All local authorities run training courses for early years practitioners on fulfilling the requirements of the CoP. If you are at all unsure about this, try to arrange to go on an INSET course.

What measures has your setting implemented to fulfil the requirements of the Special Educational Needs and Disability Act 2001? Are they adequate?

A graduated response

As an early years practitioner you are in a good position to recognise when children are experiencing a difficulty that is preventing them from making the progress you would expect. If you have concerns you need to share these with other members of the nursery team to see if they share those concerns. Sometimes the child's parents/carers may express their worries to you and ask you what you think. Whatever happens, you will need to observe the child carefully and record your observations in the usual way for your workplace. From your observations you will be able to plan to meet the specific needs of the child using the resources that are available in the setting. For instance, if a child appears to be exhibiting challenging behaviour to the extent that their learning is affected, you may check that the setting's behaviour management policy is implemented consistently. This is called a differentiated response because you are planning to meet the individual needs of the child.

If your concerns persist then it is time to talk to the child's parent/carer and refer to the Early Years Action Decision Checklist (DfES 2001: 35, 4:21). If the nursery team feel that all other options have been fully explored, the child will then be put on the setting's SEN register and Early Years Action evoked. At this stage the SENCO will be involved and an individual education plan for the child will be drawn up.

The individual education plan (IEP)

The individual education plan is a document that outlines two or three targets that relate directly to the child's abilities. It is set by the child's key worker in conjunction with the parent/carer and the SENCO. Each setting is likely to have a standard format to follow, often one that has been worked out in conjunction with the local authority early years inclusion team. The IEP should outline the targets the child will be working towards, details of how these targets are to be achieved, who will be involved and a date for review. All those involved in the care and education of the child should be involved in the review process, especially the parent/carer.

At review, if the child has made progress, it may be decided that no further action is needed. If progress is limited it may be decided to keep the child on Early Years Action and extend the IEP, or to seek the help of professionals from outside the setting. In this case the child is moved on to Early Years Action Plus.

If it is felt that a child is not making sufficient progress at this stage, a request will be made for the child to undergo a statutory assessment of their needs.

Statutory assessment

The local education authority will look at evidence supplied by the setting and other professionals (such as an educational psychologist) to decide whether or not the child should undergo a statutory assessment. If it is decided that this would be in the child's best interests, a full assessment of the child's needs will be made using information from the parents, the setting and all the other professionals involved.

A statement of special educational needs

If a child is given a statement of educational needs, money is assigned to support the child. This can be used by the setting to buy specialist equipment and/or employ a support worker to ensure that the child's needs are addressed. The statement will identify the educational provision that is best suited to the child's needs. This may be in mainstream provision or in a specialist school.

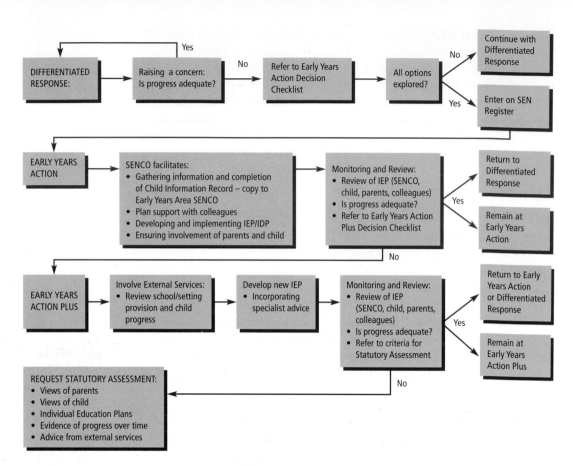

Revised Code of Practice – Graduated Response: Quick Guide (Early Years Settings/Schools). [Based on a chart produced by the Isle of Wight Local Education Authority.]

Working in partnership with parents

In a report by the Rathbone Society it was revealed that parents often feel frustrated by the way in which their children's school treats them. The report concluded that: 'The overall picture is one of frustrated and anxious parents wanting to help and contribute as fully as possible to their children's education, but all too frequently feeling at best confused and at worst ignored' (Rathbone). It was because of findings such as this that the 2001 Code of Practice made parental partnership a key feature. The Code of Practice recognises that:

> Parents hold key information and have a critical role to play in their children's education. They have unique strengths, knowledge and experience to contribute to the shared view of a child's needs and the best ways of supporting them. It is therefore essential that all professionals … actively seek to work with parents and value the contribution they make.
>
> (DfES 2001: 16, 2:2)

Barriers for parents

The procedures around meeting the needs of children with disabilities or special educational needs are complex and many parents feel that negotiating the system is an almost impossible task. Parents may face the following barriers:

- terminology and procedures that are difficult to understand; also, some parents may have special educational needs or disabilities themselves
- lack of translations/translators if parents do not speak English well
- many different professionals to liaise with from a variety of settings
- being asked to attend many meetings and appointments in working hours.

Parental partnership service

Each local education authority is required to set up a parental partnership service to provide advice, information and support for parents. The service can allocate an independent parental supporter to accompany parents to meetings and explain proceedings to them.

Working with parents/carers in early years settings

A good relationship with parents/carers starts before the child joins the setting. The parents may have approached you about the possibility of a place or your setting may have been identified as being the most appropriate provision for the child. Much of the information that follows is good practice for working with all parents/carers, not just those with children who have a disability or special educational needs:

- parents/carers should be shown round the setting and introduced to staff members; if a child has a disability it is an opportunity to discuss issues such as access and what changes may need to be made to the setting (at this stage you need to be realistic about what can be provided in the time available)
- at the first meeting parents/carers will want to be reassured that the staff are able to meet the needs of their child (a pre-admission plan that identifies the specific needs of the child and how these will be met within the setting will help to reassure parents); at this stage specific training needs for staff can be identified (e.g. if a child wears a hearing aid staff will be required to know how to adjust it and change batteries; staff may need to go on a lifting and handling course and learn how to use equipment such as hoists)

> **REFLECTIVE ACTIVITY**
>
> Contact your local authority's parental partnership service. Investigate the services they supply and the information they make available to parents. If you look on the Internet you will find that many local authorities have websites for their parental partnership service.

- other professionals, such as occupational therapists or physiotherapists, can talk to the staff team about aspects of care for the child
- the parents/carers should be fully informed about the setting's SEN policy and they should be introduced to the SENCO
- the settling-in process should be worked out with the parents/carers, and everyone involved should be clear as to exactly how this process is to be handled
- once the child has settled in, the key worker should arrange a regular time to meet with the parents/carers (this may be fitted into the normal day-to-day routine of bringing and collecting the child, but if parents are working and the child is brought in by another carer it may be necessary to think of alternative methods – such as a home/nursery book, telephone conferences or meetings at other times)
- it is important that the principle of inclusion extends to outings; as part of the normal risk assessment process the number of adults needed to accompany the child should be realistically assessed (parents/carers should always be invited to accompany the child, but if they are unable to attend alternative arrangements must be made).

THE PROFESSIONALS INVOLVED

The following table gives a brief description of all the professionals who may be involved in planning for the care and education of a child with a disability or special educational needs.

Professional	Role
Health visitor	A trained nurse who has undergone an extended period of additional training. Health visitors give advice and monitor the development of children from one month old until school age. They can give advice and support for parents of children with SEN and are often a parent's first port of call if they are worried. Health visitors may contribute to the statementing or assessment process.
Social workers	Social workers have a university qualification in social work. They offer support to families and are often involved in the assessment process.
General practitioners	GPs are qualified doctors who have undergone a considerable period of extra training to become a GP. They look after the health of children on a day-to-day basis and are often the first person a parent or health visitor consults if there are concerns about a child's development. GPs may contribute to the statutory assessment process.
Hospital consultants	Consultants are qualified doctors who have undergone many years of training in a particular speciality. Paediatric consultants are experts in the care of children with disabilities, although other consultants will also be involved, depending on the child's condition.
Psychiatrist	A qualified doctor who has undertaken additional training in mental illness. There are paediatric psychiatrists especially for children.
Clinical psychologist	A psychologist who specialises in the developmental assessment of children and the treatment of behavioural difficulties.

Professional	Role
Educational psychologist	A psychologist who is also a trained and experienced teacher. Educational psychologists have received extra training to help them diagnose, assess and plan for the special educational needs of children. They are involved in the assessment and statementing process.
Physiotherapist	A qualified practitioner who supervises exercise programmes and other physical support for children with disabilities.
Occupational therapist	A practitioner who helps children and their families with everyday skills. The occupational therapist will identify the aids that are needed, such as ramps and hoists, to enable children to live as independent a life as possible.
Speech therapist	A practitioner who is trained to help children who have delayed speech or other communication problems.
Special educational needs coordinator (SENCO)	An early years practitioner or teacher who is responsible within the setting for coordinating SEN provision.
Learning support teachers	Specially trained teachers who work with children either individually or in groups. Learning support teachers can also advise teachers and early years practitioners on ways to support children with SEN.

CONCLUSION

As an early years practitioner you are in an ideal position to support children with disabilities and special educational needs. Your observation and assessment skills should ensure that children with difficulties do not go unnoticed, and the strong tradition of working closely with parents helps ensure that the children's needs can be fully understood. The principles of early childhood care and education that emphasise the meeting of children's individual needs ensure that appropriate care and learning experiences are provided for children in an atmosphere that encourages inclusion, yet values diversity. Early years provision, by its very nature, can support children in ways that may not be possible as a child enters into 'formal education'.

GLOSSARY

Disability 'A child is disabled if he is blind, deaf or dumb or suffers from a mental disorder of any kind or is substantially and permanently handicapped by illness, injury or congenital deformity or such other disability as may be prescribed.' (Children Act 1989, Section 17 (11))

Early education setting All pre-school provision, such as nursery classes and schools, day nurseries and playgroups.

Independent parental supporter Someone who can support parents, for example, going to meetings, encouraging parents to get involved and helping parents understand the SEN framework.

Learning difficulty 'Children have a learning difficulty if they:
a) have a significantly greater difficulty in learning than the majority of children of the same age; or
b) have a disability, which prevents or hinders them from making use of educational facilities of a kind generally provided for children of the same age in schools within the area of the local education authority
c) are under compulsory school age and fall within the definition at (a) or (b) above or would so do if special educational provision was not made for them.' (DfES 2001: 6)

Mainstream school An ordinary school which is for all children, not just those with SEN. This will normally be a state school, although it could also be an independent school.

SEN Code of Practice A guide for education settings and LEAs on the help they should give to children with special educational needs.

Special educational needs 'Children have special educational needs if they have a learning difficulty, which calls for special educational provision to be made for them.' (DfES 2001: 6)

Special educational needs tribunal An independent body that hears appeals against decisions made by LEAs on statutory assessments and statements.

Statement of special educational needs A document that sets out a child's needs and the extra help they should get.

Statutory assessment A very detailed examination of a child's special educational needs. It may lead to a statement.

KEY TEXTS

Dare, A. and O'Donovan, M. 2002: *Good Practice in Caring for Young Children with Special Needs* (2nd edn). Cheltenham: Nelson Thornes.
Wall, K. 2003: *Special Needs and Early Years: A Practitioner's Guide*. London: Sage Publications.
Wolfendale, S. 2000: *Special Needs in the Early Years*. London: Routledge Falmer.

USEFUL WEBSITES (Accessed October 2004)

http://www.dfes.gov.uk/sen
http://eduwight.iow.gov.uk/the_lea/spec_needs/images/COPFlowchartQuickGuideEarlyYears.pdf

CHILD PROTECTION

Somebody may abuse or neglect a child by inflicting harm, or by failing to act to prevent harm. Children may be abused in a family or in an institutional or community setting: by those known to them or, more rarely, by a stranger.

—DoH, 1999, p. 5

IN THIS CHAPTER WE WILL CONSIDER THE FOLLOWING TOPICS:

* Definitions of abuse
* Identifying abuse
* Good practice: working together
* Responding to disclosure
* Working with families
* Child protection within a child-centred curriculum
* Abuse and disability, race and gender: challenges and issues for practitioners.

In this chapter we will examine child protection in relation to children and their families in a range of early years settings, as well as the practitioners and other adults who may come into contact with children. Child protection is an issue with the potential to cause considerable conflict. For you as a practitioner it may involve a fear of making 'wrong' judgements, upsetting relationships which have taken a long time to build with children and their families, or simply a sense of disbelief. So taking the essential step of passing on concerns or worries about a child or a family can involve conflicting emotions and may even trigger unknown or deeply buried experiences or attitudes.

However, the health, safety and welfare of every child must come first in all early years settings. It is essential that families understand this, and also that they are aware of the legal requirements of those working with other people's children and the role they have in child protection. As a practitioner, you have a responsibility to ensure that all the policies and procedures in place for child protection in your setting are complied with, and that families are made aware of these. The need to keep up to date with legislation and guidance adds to the already considerable amount of information you are required to manage, analyse and use to inform your own practice and that of other practitioners.

DEFINITIONS OF ABUSE

The definitions of abuse and neglect used in this chapter are taken from *Working Together to Safeguard Children* (DoH 1999) and *What To Do if You're Worried a Child Is Being Abused* (DoH 2003).

We will begin by identifying abuse and neglect and some of the indicators or symptoms which young children may present. It is important to understand the legal framework for child protection and to know which documents to access. The requirements are all laid down in the National Standards (Ofsted 2001, 2003, 2004). Standard 13 addresses child protection legislation and requirements. Standard 11 refers to behaviour and how adults in the setting must manage and respond to children's behaviour without 'physical punishments' or 'physical intervention'. It also requires that there be a named person in the setting, with responsibility for behaviour, who can support other staff.

The Children Act 1989 states that 'it shall be the general duty of every local authority to safeguard and promote the welfare of children within their area who are in need' (DoH 2003). Those practitioners providing full and sessional care and education (family centres, children's centres, day nurseries, including workplace nurseries, childminders, pre-schools) are well placed to identify and signpost families to agencies for support across a range of issues. Many settings support families who may be under stress or dealing with complex personal and social issues. Early intervention and support may prevent future abuse and neglect.

REFLECTIVE ACTIVITY

How current is your knowledge of child protection practice? How long is it since you attended a training day?

Are you familiar with your setting's policy?

Familiarise yourself with the requirements of the National Standards (Ofsted) in relation to child protection.

Look at the document *What To Do if You're Worried a Child Is Being Abused* (DoH 2003).

Look up the legislation that underpins child protection and children in need.

What section of the Children Act 1989 is the basis in law for the provision of local services to children in need?

Which key principles of the Children Act safeguard vulnerable children?

Look up the guidance document *Working Together To Safeguard Children* (DoH 1999).

There are three areas of abuse identified by the DoH documents:

- physical abuse
- emotional abuse
- sexual abuse.

Somebody may abuse or neglect a child by inflicting harm, or by failing to act to prevent harm. Children may be abused in a family or in an institutional or community setting; by those known to them or, more rarely, by a stranger.

Neglect is the persistent failure to meet a child's basic physical and /or psychological needs, likely to result in the serious impairment of the child's health or development. It may involve a parent or carer failing to provide adequate food, shelter and clothing, failing to protect a child from physical harm or danger, or the failure to ensure access to appropriate medical care or treatment. It may also include neglect of, or unresponsiveness to, a child's basic emotional needs.

(DoH 1999: 5–6)

The Children Act 1989 identifies children in need as those who are so vulnerable 'that they are unlikely to reach or maintain a satisfactory level of health or development, or their health and development will be significantly impaired, without the provision of services' (DoH 2003: 2).

Neglect, then, is when a child's most basic and fundamental needs for food, safety, security and shelter are not being met. Examples of neglect include:

- never giving children boundaries
- allowing children to watch unsuitable adult films and look at inappropriate magazines and books
- not meeting children's most fundamental needs (e.g. not changing nappies or leaving a baby to become so sore that nappy rash becomes a severe infection).

Neglect also covers the failure to respond to children's needs for love, support, encouragement and respect. It could include failure to provide medical care, physical neglect in hygiene, or the lack of adequate nutrition that results in a 'failure to thrive'.

The Children Act 1989 introduced the concept of 'significant harm' 'as the threshold that justifies compulsory intervention in family life in the best interests of children' (DoH 2003: 3).

It is the responsibility of the local authority to find out whether a child is actually suffering from, or is likely to suffer from, significant harm.

Under the Children Act 1989 (Section 31(9)):

'harm' means ill-treatment or impairment of health and development

'development' means physical, intellectual, emotional, social or behavioural development

'health' means physical or mental health

'ill-treatment' includes sexual abuse and forms of ill-treatment which are not physical.

A 'core assessment' will be carried out to find out whether any harm has occurred or is likely to occur.

The DoH (1999: 7–8, 2.17) guidance states that there 'are no absolute criteria' when judging what constitutes significant harm. Professionals involved in assessment have to consider 'the degree and extent of physical harm', how long the abuse has been going on and how frequently it occurs. Professionals need to consider the whole context of the family, whether the harm was a single episode or whether it is part of a long-term or ongoing chain of events. One single acute event can be as significant as ongoing or sustained events, and either kind can 'damage the child's physical and psychological development'.

An assessment will consider:

- the family context
- the child's development within the context of their family and wider social and cultural environment
- any special needs, such as a medical condition, communication difficulty or disability that may affect the child's development and care within the family
- the nature of harm, in terms of ill-treatment or failure to provide adequate care
- the impact on the child's health and development; and
- the adequacy of parental care.

(DoH 1999: 8, 2.18)

IDENTIFYING ABUSE

Recording changes in behaviour and sharing observations with colleagues and managers will help to build up a pattern of children's normal behaviour, play and development. Identifying significant clusters of changes or symptoms should alert us to the possibility that the welfare of the child is at risk. However, it is important to remember that children's behaviour changes as they grow, and they go through many stages in their development. Some children have complex family and social issues to deal with as part of their daily life. This does not necessarily mean that they are being abused or neglected.

Physical abuse

…may involve hitting, shaking, throwing, poisoning, burning or scalding, drowning, suffocating, or otherwise causing physical harm to a child, including by fabricating the symptoms of, or deliberately causing, ill health to a child.

(DoH 2003: 3)

It is important to remember that as part of everyday life – growing up and trying out new skills – children will have accidents that may result in both minor and major injuries (e.g. falling off bicycles, climbing frames or out of trees). Many injuries will be treated at home or at local accident and emergency departments.

However, children who have been physically abused may present with a range of injuries which are unexplained. Where the explanation does not match the injury, or where it becomes frequent, practitioners need to be alert. Injuries which could indicate abuse include: black eyes, bruises, cuts, scratches, fractures, pinch marks, scalds and burns, imprints of objects used (e.g. cigarette burns, belt/buckle marks).

Practitioners also need to be aware of other signs that could indicate physical neglect and abuse. These include:

- being hungry, tired and listless, not interested, withdrawn
- being underweight, failure to thrive
- not being cared for, not being bathed or having their hair washed
- having a poor complexion
- unlaundered clothes, ill-fitting, inappropriate for the season/weather
- low self-esteem
- being aggressive to peers
- inappropriate behaviour towards adults
- attempting to be independent, brushing off help and support
- always being on edge, watching what is going on around them
- eating problems, bed-wetting, nightmares
- lacking concentration, not able to become 'involved' in their play
- the child who does not want to be undressed or to undress in front of others
- the child who may be reluctant to leave the setting with their parents/carers

- the child who is absent from school and has faded or fading injury signs
- the child who does not want to answer questions about an injury – appears frightened or has a 'ready-made story' (a parrot-fashion account of 'events')
- there is delay in getting medical attention for an injury
- information about an injury being inconsistent
- the injury may not match the account of the accident
- the parent/carer may have an abnormal attitude, or be more concerned with themselves than the child; they may become hostile to questions and the account of how the injury came about alters as they tell concerned professionals
- parents may give unrealistic or inconsistent explanations or deny all knowledge of the injuries; their stories may change during the telling or include conflicting detail

(adapted from Bruce and Meggitt 2002; Taylor and Woods 1998; Becket 2003)

There may be other circumstances that the practitioner needs to take into account. These include families where there is already a history of violence, abuse or neglect. Alternatively, families might be experiencing a particularly stressful period, such as working out visiting orders or parental responsibilities when families are separating, or there may be a new adult in the family relationship. Children in these difficult circumstances may display abnormal behaviour. When with their parent/carer, they may be:

- withdrawn
- overly compliant
- frightened or fearful
- sad or unhappy.

Clearly, the whole family context must be considered as well as the child's development within the context of their wider social and cultural environment.

Children may present with specific injuries as already described. However, as an early years practitioner you have a responsibility to share concerns where there is suspicion of abuse or neglect, but it is not for you to make judgements or decisions. As a practitioner you need to be skilful in your listening and reporting, but it is the role of a medical practitioner to ascertain how injuries have been caused. This is why it is crucial for settings to have procedures in place for recording, reporting and disclosing injuries, as any subsequent investigation will require clear evidence and thorough records.

Smacking and children's rights: equal rights for children – they are people too

Goldschmied and Jackson's book, *People Under Three*, begins by stating that 'a society can be judged by its attitude to its youngest children' (1994: 1). Since 1994 there have been many changes to policy relating to children and families and considerable investment in the early years, through changes to tax credits for working families, free nursery education for three-year-olds, support and early intervention through Sure Start programmes and the introduction of Children's Centres, to address the issue of poverty in the UK.

Goldschmied and Jackson called for more accessible services, joined-up thinking and recognised support for parents and the well-being of families, 'because in our view no distinction can be drawn between the well-being of parents and that of their young children' (1994: 2). Sure Start programmes and, more recently, Children's Centres have promoted activities to improve families' health, education and employment and to offer further training opportunities and improve the well-being (economic and physical) of all children and their families.

There are 4.3 million children in Britain living in poverty (Daycare Trust 2004). The links between abuse, poverty and stress in families are unquestionable – very often, poor parenting skills, complex family relationships and dynamics go hand in hand with low-income, low-achieving families. (Although this does not mean that abuse occurs only in families from lower socio-economic groups – abuse occurs across all families and all social groups.)

Early evidence (from Sure Start and other early intervention programmes) is recognising that the impact of working with parents and children together – learning to play together, cook together and having a better understanding of how children develop and learn – is making real and meaningful changes to children's lives. It may be that this will lead to changes in attitudes in society towards children, which, in turn, may influence policy makers.

In 1986 corporal punishment was made illegal in state schools, followed by the 1989 Children Act, which banned physical punishment in daycare settings. It was not until 1998 that corporal punishment was made illegal in all schools, including those in the independent sector. When the draft National Standards were first introduced in 2000, and subsequently published in 2001, childminders were able to smack children in their care, with parents' permission (although this was not the case for childminders in Wales, where it had already been outlawed in the National Minimum Standards for Childminders in Wales).

In September 2003, after a long campaign, childminders won the fight to have smacking banned for children in their care, as stated in the revised wording to the Childminding Standards (Ofsted 2004: Standard

11, Behaviour: Physical punishments and interventions, 11.4–11.6): 'Physical punishments, or the threat of them, must not be used. This includes smacking. You must not smack children in your care. Also you must never shake children in your care. It can cause damage to the brain'.

The debate on banning smacking continues in the UK. A vote in the House of Commons on 5 July 2004 to ban smacking was defeated. The House voted for an amendment that legitimises certain levels of physical punishment, but outlaws bruising, scratching and reddening of the skin, caning and causing psychological distress.

The defence of 'reasonable chastisement' (dating from 1860), which allows physical punishment of children by their parents, was not outlawed and peers rejected the proposal of a total ban on smacking. Many organisations, such as the NSPCC, the Children are Unbeatable! Alliance and The Children's Society, view this as failing to give children equal protection from assault under the law.

In September 2004 the Parliamentary Joint Committee on Human Rights (JCHR) published a report (19th report) urging complete abolition of the outdated nineteenth-century law. The report summary on Clause 49 concludes '…that, although the continuing availability of the defence of reasonable chastisement does not give rise to any present incompatibility with Convention [United Nations Convention on the Rights of the Child] rights, there is a risk that it will in future be held to be incompatible with the ECHR [European Committee for Human Rights]'. The key Articles from the Convention on the Rights of the Child discussed in the JCHR report are Articles 19 and 37a (see http://www.publications.parliament.uk – accessed October 2004).

Article 19 To protect children from all forms of physical or mental violence while in the care of parents or others.

Article 37a No child shall be subjected to torture or other cruel inhuman or degrading treatment or punishment.

(United Nations 1990)

State parties shall take all appropriate legislative administration, social and educational measures to protect the child from all forms of physical or mental violence, injury or abuse, neglect or negligent treatment, maltreatment or exploitation including sexual abuse whilst in the care of parent(s), legal guardians or any other person who has care of the child…

(JCHR Report No.19, Paragraph 148)

The Parliamentary Assembly of the Council of Europe adopted the following recommendation in 2004:

The Assembly considers that any corporal punishment of children is in breach of their fundamental right to human dignity and physical integrity. The fact that such corporal punishment is still lawful in certain member states violates their equally fundamental right to the same legal protection as adults. Striking a human being is prohibited in European society and children are human beings. The social and legal acceptance of corporal punishment must be ended.

The Assembly proposes a 'co-ordinated and concerted campaign in all member states for the total abolition of corporal punishment of children. The Assembly notes the success of the Council of Europe in abolishing the death penalty and the Assembly now calls on it to make Europe, as soon as possible, a corporal punishment-free zone for children' (cited in 'Green light to abolish "reasonable chastisement"', available at www.childrenareunbeatable.org.uk – accessed October 2004).

Clause 49, allowing parents to continue to justify what some perceive as common assault as 'reasonable punishment', which was added to the Children Bill (the Green Paper, Every Child Matters) does not meet human rights obligations under three international treaties. The JCHR report recommends 'replacing this clause with equal protection for children under the law on assault'.

Smacking, then, is still legal in the UK within the family. Between one and two children die every week from child abuse and neglect in the UK. In Sweden between 1979 and 2000 the total number of children who died due to physical abuse was just four. A large-scale government commissioned research study in the 1990s found very high rates of corporal punishment in the home – 91 per cent of children had been hit. Of these:

- half the children were hit weekly or more often
- 1 in 5 had been hit with an implement
- 35 per cent had been punished 'severely'
- 75 per cent of mothers had already 'smacked' their babies before they reached one year old
- 14 per cent of one-year-olds had been hit with 'moderate' severity
- 38 per cent of four-year-olds had been smacked more than once a week.

(Source: Children are Unbeatable! 2004)

A report for the National Children's Bureau and Save the Children (Willow and Hyder 1998), entitled *It Hurts You Inside. Children Talking About Smacking*, talked to very young children, aged between four and seven, about what smacking was and how it might feel. The children explained 'smacking' to an alien from another world. The children described smacking as: 'hitting', 'wrong', 'hurting', something that happened when they had been naughty, broken something or failed to listen to their parents. The report consulted 76 children; 50 per cent of these said they will not 'smack' children when they are adults.

However, many other European countries have already passed legislation prohibiting all such corporal punishment. Sweden has banned smacking since 1979 and research (Children Are Unbeatable! 2004) shows that, subsequently, there has been no increase in prosecutions for parental assaults and even a decline in relation to parents in their twenties who were brought up without smacking. There has been a decrease in the number of children taken into care and also of compulsory social work intervention. The levels of convictions for theft and drug-related crimes have declined, as have measures of young people's drug and alcohol intake and suicides: drug use among young Swedes is 'negligible' and the youth suicide rate has dropped between 1970 and 1996.

Injuries from abuse

Children may have some bruising due to everyday occurrences, simply as a result of accidents; these tend to be on bony parts of the body, as a result of walking into or falling over something. Such bruises are part and parcel of their growing independence as they practise and develop gross motor skills – running, riding bikes, skipping and climbing. However, as a practitioner you need to be alert to signs of possible non-accidental injury, and when children and adults are unable or unwilling to disclose how the injury occurred, you should be on the alert. Consulting with colleagues to confirm information in a sensitive and confidential way can support those initial concerns, unless, of course, a child is considered to be in immediate danger, in which case a report should be made to the duty officer in the Child Protection Unit.

Bruises may also occur as a result of being held in a tight grip, being slapped or being hit with an object. Sometimes objects (and even hands) will leave an imprint on the child. Bruises to the face and other soft tissue areas should always give cause for concern, as should bruising to the buttocks.

Burns may present as cigarette stub marks or scalds from hot water. Cigarette burns may present in a cluster or pattern and be on 'hidden' areas of the body, such as the soles of the feet. Standing in a hot bath also results in these kinds of burns.

Fractures tend to be accidental injuries; however, any fracture sustained by a child under three or with limited mobility needs to be investigated.

Shaking can cause fitting, severe brain damage and fractured ribs, and we now know that babies presenting with these signs should be carefully examined.

Victoria Climbié was eight when she died in February 2000. A range of agencies had been involved in her care. The inquiry and subsequent report by Lord Laming highlighted the need for improved inter-agency work and further training for practitioners involved with children. The Laming report made 108 recommendations and set out a course for action. *Every Child Matters* (Green Paper 2003) was also published, setting out, among other things, revised policies to protect children and support inter-agency working and the sharing of information. Victoria was known to several agencies and had been taken to hospital on several occasions, when non-accidental injury was suspected but not identified.

Victoria had been beaten, burned with cigarettes, tied up and made to sleep in the bath in a bin liner – this because Carl Manning and Marie Therese Kouao, who were charged with murder, said she wet the bed. When Victoria died she had 128 separate injuries on her body. She died of malnutrition and hypothermia. Victoria had also missed a lot of schooling. Her lack of attendance was raised during the inquiry. Missing school can be an early indication of physical abuse, as children are kept at home for marks or cuts to heal. Manning and Kauao's assaults on Victoria had begun with chastising and smacking for disciplinary action and developed into acts of torture, when she was beaten with a bicycle chain. (See http:// www.victoria-climbie-inquiry.org.uk and http://news.bbc.co.uk/1/hi/in_depth/uk/2002/victoria_climbie_inquiry/default/stm – both accessed October 2004)

Munchausen's syndrome by proxy

This is a rare condition, where the adult claims that the child is suffering from a particular illness, or invents false symptoms for the child. If not discovered, this may lead to unnecessary surgical and medical intervention, subjecting the child to trauma. Although rare, medical practitioners have to be alert to the possibility of Munchausen's. Adults with Munchausen's often have a substantial medical history, and vigilance on the part of the medical staff can help bring this to light. Obviously, they need to consider the family context, and any unusual history of attending emergency departments and the GP.

Emotional abuse

> ...the persistent emotional ill-treatment of a child such as to cause severe and persistent adverse effects on the child's emotional development...conveying to children that they are worthless or unloved, inadequate...age or developmentally inappropriate expectations being imposed on children, causing children frequently to feel frightened, or the exploitation or corruption of children.
>
> (DoH 2003: 3)

Emotional abuse is the most underestimated form of abuse (Evans 2002a), as well as being the least recorded or reported. With an increasing awareness of emotional development and well-being as an essential part of holistic development, practitioners are becoming more skilled at supporting and promoting emotional well-being in young children. They are also becoming more skilled at identifying and referring those who are showing signs of emotional abuse or neglect.

Emotional abuse includes:

- not giving love and attention, approval and acceptance (e.g. the child is never good enough, everyone else is better than they are)
- insulting remarks, behaviour or treatment (including swearing)
- constant shouting and screaming
- constant criticism, threats and sarcasm
- degrading punishment
- undermining a child's sense of self and worth.

The behaviour that results from this sort of ill-treatment is sometimes quite difficult to identify. Some children may become withdrawn (this is quite different to simply being quiet or shy), while others may become aggressive.

It is important to have a good understanding of child development in order to distinguish behaviour which is normal from that which may be a cause for concern. Practitioners who are good observers of children and settings where observation underpins planning and learning will be alert to changes in individual children. This should lead to discussions if there are concerns over a child's behaviour, followed by further observation; talking and listening are required to check out that 'all is not well'. Since emotional abuse has none of the immediate signs of physical abuse, close observation and discussion are where most practitioners start.

As a practitioner you may observe emotional abuse during daily exchanges with families. Persistent sarcasm or insults about the child's abilities or efforts can result in a child who:

- has a very low sense of self-esteem and self-worth
- becomes very passive, depressed, withdrawn or aggressive
- is very worried when faced with new places/situations
- underachieves
- is reluctant to go home with parent/carer
- is over-anxious to please
- overreacts to mistakes
- shows developmental delay in numerous areas
- displays neurotic or obsessive behaviour.

We know that emotional abuse can cause lasting damage. Brain research has shown that very young children exposed to continual violence or violent behaviour (shouting, arguing and emotional neglect) can suffer distortion or damage to the neural pathways. These children often have a predisposition to flight or fight, the adrenaline response, which should occur only when real danger is apparent. Steele (2001) identified these children as having raised levels of cortisol, the hormone produced by the brain in response to stress.

It is essential, then, that practitioners are alert to the possibility of emotional abuse when a child displays subtle changes in behaviour. Children living in households where there is domestic violence or an adult with mental health problems will be under enormous stress and may be on the receiving end of damaging adult behaviour, such as being rejected. Evans (2002b) cites the work of Hart *et al.*, who identified the following damaging adult behaviours:

- rejection – when the child feels 'abandoned' by the adult either physically or emotionally
- isolating – stopping children from joining in outings, trips and normal social activities
- ignoring – not responding, either physically or psychologically (where the adult is 'unavailable' to the child), not hugging or touching a child, not responding to normal conversations and behaviours
- corrupting – encouraging the child to behave unacceptably or antisocially and promoting this as normal or okay.

For many families there will be moments when an adult behaviour has, due to an incident of stress or crisis, been inappropriate, without harming the child – a cross word, a refusal to listen to a request or ignoring the constant plea for a toy or treat! Parents are human and we have all had difficult days or experiences. But children cannot live with continuous psychological and physical neglect without their emotional health being damaged. Children need to be emotionally healthy and to have a sense of well-being in order to develop and learn. Without this, children may show other signs – failing to thrive, not growing or developing physically. In the English *Birth to Three Matters* (DfES 2002) emotional well-being is recognised as an essential part of a young child's right to be 'a healthy child'. Emotional well-being is about feeling special and having someone who is special to the child, and gradually becoming independent. This can only happen if a child has a healthy dependent relationship or attachment. Children who are emotionally starved may not be able to express their own feelings or understand how other people feel.

Sexual abuse

> ...forcing or enticing a child or young person to take part in sexual activities, whether or not the child is aware of what is happening. The activities may involve physical contact, including penetrative (e.g. rape or buggery) or non-penetrative acts. They may include involving children in looking at, or in the production of, pornographic material, or encouraging children to behave in sexually inappropriate ways.
>
> (DoH 2003: 3)

Sexual abuse is when an adult forces a child to take part in acts of a sexual nature. These acts range from masturbation (including fondling and oral sex) to sexual intercourse (vaginal and/or anal). Children may be forced to watch or take part in pornographic activities.

Beckett (2003: 77) points out that some children whose behaviour might appear to indicate sexual abuse might be being emotionally abused, and the child is looking for the love and comfort not being provided by the key adults in their life.

Apart from the disclosure from a child of inappropriate behaviour by an adult or older child, other early indications of sexual abuse can be physical (e.g. vaginal or anal tears or redness). Bed-wetting or daytime wetting may also be indicators, particularly if this is a change from the child's normal behaviour.

Other indicators of sexual abuse may include the child who:

- is withdrawn, anxious, has poor concentration
- has low self-esteem and lacks confidence
- displays inappropriate sexual behaviour, either in play situations with toys or when playing with other children
- displays sexually abusive behaviour towards other children
- displays inappropriate sexualised knowledge, uses sexual language
- is a reluctant sleeper – may have fears of going to bed or the bedroom, nightmares
- is a poor eater
- displays inappropriate sexual behaviour with adults (e.g. inappropriate touching, 'flirting')
- is inappropriately interested in sexual behaviour
- has frequent urinary tract infections.

A study by the NSPCC (2000) found that:

- 1 per cent of respondents had been sexually abused by a parent or carer
- 3 per cent of respondents had been sexually abused by another relative

- just over a quarter of respondents had reported incidences of sexual abuse when it occurred
- one in three had not told anyone.

The study was part of the Full Stop Campaign; young people between the ages of 18 and 24 were interviewed to find out about the scale of abuse and maltreatment in the UK.

It is crucial that early years settings and practitioners are confident about responding to disclosure of any sort of possible abuse and are alert to possible signs and symptoms when children are not confident to disclose. The NSPCC survey suggests that many children never speak out.

Protecting children and staff

All early years settings registered by Ofsted must comply with the national standards for their provision. Standard 13 on child protection states:

> The registered person complies with local child protection procedures approved by the Area Child Protection Committee (ACPC) and ensures all adults working and looking after children in the provision are able to put the procedures into practice.

The focus of Standard 13 is the welfare, safety and protection of the child. All staff, students and volunteers in a provision must be aware of and understand their responsibilities if they suspect abuse or neglect.

Daycare providers should identify a designated member of staff with responsibility for child protection in the setting. Schools will have a named teacher with child protection responsibilities.

GOOD PRACTICE: WORKING TOGETHER

It is essential that all agencies involved in working with children have an integrated approach to their safety and welfare. Practitioners with responsibility for child protection in a setting must have an understanding of the legal and ethical rulings and restrictions for the sharing of information.

Information must be shared to enable informed analysis and decisions to be made, ensuring that good outcomes are achieved for all children. Providers must understand and implement the protocols and procedures for sharing information across professional boundaries and ensure that all legal requirements are fully complied with. These include the Human Rights Act 1998 and the Data Protection Act 1998 (DoH 2003: 43–45).

Practitioners working with children and families should follow the guidance from the Department of Health (DoH 2003), their local Sure Start and the Area Child Protection Committee (ACPC). Here is a useful checklist (adapted from DoH 2003; Ofsted 2003, 2004):

- all providers must have a child protection policy statement and internal procedures as a requirement of registration
- families using the provision must see a copy of the policy and procedures and understand the responsibilities of the provider and all the adults working in the setting for children's welfare and safety
- day care providers must have a policy for addressing allegations of abuse by a member of staff/volunteer/student (this must include what action will be taken while an investigation is started; who should be informed, e.g. local area child protection unit, Ofsted; how any investigation will be conducted and by whom), without interfering in any investigation by the Child Protection Authorities/police
- childminders will have a similar policy for action and investigation of allegations against themselves or anyone living in the house
- who is the named person in your setting and is their child protection knowledge up to date?
- does everyone (including volunteers) working in the setting understand their responsibilities for child protection and are they able to implement the policies and procedures?
- is the contact number for Social Services correct and do you have the emergency out-of-hours duty numbers?

Having an understanding of the Framework for Assessment of Children in Need and their Families

This Assessment Framework underpins the assessment process. Early years settings are well placed to share appropriate information on aspects of the child and family, such as:

- all aspects of the child's development: physical, cognitive, emotional
- social skills and behaviour
- relationships
- health
- education
- how the family and child interact.

The framework is used as the tool for initial assessment of the child's immediate needs. Information is gathered from other agencies involved

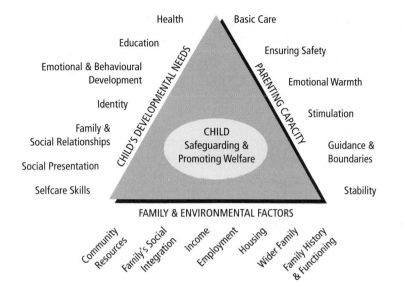

The Framework for the Assessment of Children in Need and their Families (DoH 2003: 6) underpins the processes of assessing needs. This in turn will affect plans, services and the monitoring and reviewing of how effective these services are.

with the child, such as the school or nursery, the health visitor, school nurse and GP. This is all recorded by social services and a decision is made as to whether there is a risk of actual or likely significant harm to the child.

The Area Child Protection Committee (ACPC) is responsible for ensuring all agencies work together for the protection of children. It is made up of senior managers from health, the police, social services and the LEA.

Following the murder of the schoolgirls Jessica Chapman and Holly Wells in Soham in August 2002, Sir Michael Bichard's inquiry and subsequent report made 31 recommendations affecting all adults who work with children and social services. He recommended a clear national code of practice to ensure that revised procedures for the recording and sharing of information are used by all agencies working with families and children, including the police. Improved information sharing across agencies and joint working has also been called for as a result of the (2003) inquiry into the death of Victoria Climbié in 2000.

The Green Paper *Every Child Matters* called for:

- improving the sharing of information between agencies
- a common assessment framework to be established to enable core information to follow the child (see figure above)
- a lead professional to be identified in cases when children are known to several agencies

- services tailored to meet the needs of families
- multi-disciplinary team working and integration of professionals
- co-locating services in Sure Start Children's Centres
- effective child protection procedures in place across all organisations (Green Paper 2003: 51).

RESPONDING TO DISCLOSURE

As a practitioner, a disclosure, allegation or even suspicion of abuse or neglect (which may come from your close observation and detailed knowledge of a child's development and behaviour) can be difficult. You will often play a special role in the lives of children and their families, developing secure and trusting relationships with both the child and adults. Many practitioners will be privy to personal information about the daily lives of the children in their care. With the extensive national media coverage of child abuse cases and subsequent investigations of agencies, you may feel unsure about sharing information.

You may feel initially that you are being disloyal to the family, or you might be unsure of the formal procedures. You may be concerned that your actions will result in the removal of a child from the home and worry that the situation will develop into a complex or even distressing event. However, it is vital that you recognise your responsibilities as a practitioner and the requirements placed on you by the legislation of the Children Act 1989 and the Protection of Children Act 1999.

Therefore, continued support and current training for all early years practitioners on child protection procedure and legal responsibilities and requirements are vital. During training sessions you can discuss any personal fears, share concerns with colleagues and consider all aspects of your own setting and local procedures.

Here are some key points to keep in mind when responding to disclosure from a child:

- take all allegations seriously
- try not to show disbelief or shock; keep calm
- listen carefully and do not ask any leading questions
- reassure the child that you believe them; use appropriate language to make them feel secure in the situation they are now in
- reassure the child that what has happened is not their fault
- explain, using age/stage-appropriate language, that you may have to tell someone else (if you are not the person in charge), to ensure that the child is protected from any further harm

Time for discussion and sharing information, knowledge and concerns is essential in all early years settings.

- report the disclosure to your line manager and make a written record of your conversation with the child as soon as possible
- if, after discussion with your line manager or other senior colleagues, you still have concerns for the child's welfare, then refer the matter to Social Services
- you should also contact your local support worker at the EYDCP/Sure Start Unit.

The child may experience a range of emotions after talking to an adult about abuse or neglect. They may feel guilty or afraid and have thoughts about whether they will suffer further abuse or 'get someone into trouble' because they have disclosed.

It is also important to consider that the adult dealing with a possible disclosure or allegation may need to talk through their own feelings. There are agencies that can support early years practitioners with this.

Recording and sharing information

- Recording information accurately is crucial.
- Note the date, time and place in which the allegation was made (e.g. Anyplace Nursery, Sunbeams Room, 11 am 7 January 2004).

- If there was anyone else present, make a note of this.
- Record the child's allegation verbatim (word for word), recording the exact language they used, if possible.
- Keep the information objective and factual and avoid any opinions or expressions of your own feelings.
- Records should be made within 24 hours of an incident or conversation if they are to be legally admissible.

Once you have made a referral, an investigation will be made to decide the level of risk and whether any further action is needed. (See figure, below, for the procedure following referral.)

There are procedures for events after initial assessment, when urgent action is required to safeguard children and when strategy discussion and Section 47 inquiries are initiated. Full and further details of these procedures can be found in *What To Do if You're Worried a Child Is Being Abused* (DoH 2003).

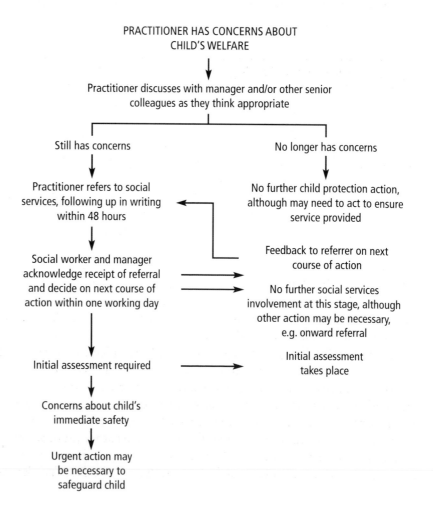

Case conferences

If there is to be further action, a case conference will be held. This is where information is shared and decisions are made about how best to look after the welfare and safety of the child. Reports or records from the early years setting may be required, detailing the child's general development and behaviour, and how they play and interact with other children and adults. These observations and assessments can be used to inform other agencies on the overall behaviour and experiences of the child.

Child protection conferences are not about finding people to blame. Their intention is to determine the level of risk and make decisions for the benefit of the child. The conference may also discuss the need for family support, parenting skills and whether the child should be placed on the Child Protection Register. The family will be invited to attend the conference, as will relevant agencies. Some practitioners may find attending these conferences daunting. There should be support available from local development workers or the education department to support you in preparing for and attending a conference, and dealing with child protection allegations.

WORKING WITH FAMILIES

Working with children and their families where abuse has occurred is an important part of the child protection process. It is important that practitioners acknowledge their own feelings about the abuse or the adults responsible for the abuse. They may need extra support for themselves as they support the child.

For most of us, it is very difficult to think about adults hurting young children or abusing them for their own pleasure. As a practitioner you also need to be aware that the abuser may be another child – children can be abusers.

Children need consistency and it is important that they remain in a setting where they have already made positive relationships with other adults and children. Children may also be placed in an early years setting by the local authority as a result of specific issues in the family or because they have been abused.

Family support groups, run by experienced practitioners, offer support to adults who need help with their parenting skills, advice on how to respond to difficult or challenging behaviour or opportunities to play alongside their children. Interacting and supporting children's play and learning may not come easily to families whose own experience of parenting may not have been a positive one. Alternative appropriate behaviour and responses can be 'modelled' by the practitioner in an environment where the child's safety and welfare come first. We know that abuse and poor parenting behaviour are cyclical. Integrated early years settings, working across multi-agency disciplines such as Sure Start programmes and Children's Centres, will offer opportunities for early intervention and family support for both the child and the adult, together, in groups or in one-to-one sessions.

Children who have been abused will need support to express their feelings through a variety of ways. They will need help to build relationships, as they may have difficulty trusting adults or other children. As a practitioner you will need to have a sound knowledge of child development and how abuse and neglect can affect this. Children may need support with language skills to begin to express themselves. They may benefit from access to a range of other materials in order to express their feelings – paint, collage materials or role-play resources, and a play therapist may become involved. They may need a one-to-one relationship in the setting; a key person can be vital for both the child and the parents.

REFLECTIVE ACTIVITY

- How do you think a child who has been abused might feel? Make a list of possible feelings.
- How might you begin to support a child who has been abused?
- Think about how the situation might make you feel and where you could go for support.
- Make a list of the agencies involved in child protection and collect some contact numbers and leaflets.
- How would you go about maintaining a positive relationship with the family of a child who has been abused? Think about all the issues. Remember that abusers in families are not necessarily the child's parents – they might be other relatives, older siblings or close adults.

CHILD PROTECTION WITHIN A CHILD-CENTRED CURRICULUM

A genuinely child-centred curriculum, based on supporting and encouraging the emotional and social development of young children, is essential. The emphasis is to promote self-esteem and enable young children to participate in decision making and to address potential conflicts. Providing an appropriate environment and routine gives security and responds to children's need for consistency. A significant adult or key person for the very youngest children also contributes to a curriculum focused on social and emotional development. Providing children with a framework in which they can participate, take responsibility and make decisions is a good starting point for early years settings (see the suggestions in Miller 1997; Finch 1998). Offering support to young children to be able to negotiate, become articulate at communicating their needs and rights and not use force or physical actions such as hitting or smacking other children, is vital.

ABUSE AND DISABILITY, RACE AND GENDER: CHALLENGES AND ISSUES FOR PRACTITIONERS

The UN Convention on the Rights of the Child (1990) applies to all children under the age of 18, without discrimination. This includes disabled children and children from other cultures and races. As a practitioner you must ensure you understand the way in which different families and communities may function; however, the safety of the child is always paramount and should supersede any concerns over accusations of racist practice (DoH 1999: 79). Article 3 is about the best interests of the child and the responsibilities the state must have for providing adequate care when the child's parents are unable to.

The report *Working Together To Safeguard Children* (DoH 1999) suggests that children with disabilities are at increased risk from abuse. However, Miller (2002) observes that there is a lack of research and statistical data in the UK relating to child protection and abuse of children with disabilities. There are many reasons why children with disabilities or special needs may be at increased risk of abuse. However, communication may be an issue; for example, when children's signals and behaviour are misunderstood or misinterpreted, resulting in a lack of understanding of and attention to their fears and concerns about abuse.

Miller (2002) suggests that disbelief across the sector that disabled children would be the subjects of abuse could result in a failure to report and, consequently, the denial of incidence. When we consider the specific needs of many disabled children for more intimate care, being cared for by more than one person (e.g. in a residential setting) and reliance on other people for medication and feeding, we can begin to identify the increased vulnerability of these children.

In identifying the abuse of disabled children, Miller (2002) cites the study of over 40,000 children in the USA by Sullivan and Knutson, which found that disabled children were 3.4 times more likely to be abused or neglected. Incidence of sexual, physical and emotional abuse was also three times higher and 31 per cent of the total number of disabled children in the research had been abused. Families, too, may feel less confident about reporting suspected neglect or abuse, especially if the services and provision for children with specific needs are limited.

Miller (2002) calls for a national safeguarding strategy for disabled children. It is crucial that in the twenty-first century the rights of all disabled children are met and that all practitioners working with disabled children and their families are appropriately trained and supervised.

> **REFLECTIVE ACTIVITY**
>
> If you are unfamiliar with the Articles of the UN Convention, look them up. What does the Convention say about sexual abuse, drugs, torture and the protection of children without families?
>
> Which other countries have banned smacking since Sweden in 1979?

CONCLUSION

Supporting young children to talk about and confront abusive or bullying behaviour appropriately is an essential part of the early years curriculum. Being assertive and able to identify and discuss appropriate and inappropriate behaviour in the nursery can and should start very early on (Paley 1981: 92).

We know that young children are affected by violence, and for many children living with abuse, domestic violence is part of daily life. We must ensure that even our very youngest children are given opportunities to make choices and decisions about the behaviour of adults and other children towards them.

The NSPCC and Triangle (an organisation that works with children with disabilities and their families) have developed an image vocabulary called How It Is, to support and enable better communication for children about a range of important issues. It uses pictures and symbols and may be useful to practitioners working with distressed or very young children. It will give many children a voice about their rights and safety, where they have previously gone unheard.

Adults working with children and families across a range of settings and contexts can and do make a difference to children's lives. Early intervention and programmes planned to support families in the early stages of anxiety or crisis have begun to show positive changes to the lives of children and families. Initiatives such as Sure Start and Children's Centres are beginning to show the benefits of inter-agency working, with positive outcomes for all children's health, education and welfare.

Listening is essential to early years practice, it is essential for young children's 'voices' to be heard, understood and responded to.

KEY TEXTS

Beckett, C. 2003: *Child Protection: An Introduction*. London: Sage

DoH 1999: *Working Together to Safeguard Children: A Guide to Inter-Agency Working to Safeguard and Promote the Welfare of Children*. London: The Stationery Office.

DoH 2000: *Framework for the Assessment of Children in Need and their Families*. London: The Stationery Office.

DoH 2003: *What To Do if You're Worried a Child Is Being Abused*. London: The Stationery Office.

Every Child Matters 2003. London: The Stationery Office.

Gillham, B. (1994) *The Facts about Child Physical Abuse*. London: Cassell.

Leach, P. 1997: *Getting Positive about Discipline: A Guide for Today's Parents*. Ilford: Barnardo's.

Leach, P. 1997: *Why Speak Out Against Smacking: Questions and Answers from the Physical Punishment Debate*. Ilford: Barnardo's.

OFSTED 2001: *Guidance to the National Standards Full Day Care, Sessional Care and Childminding*. London: The Stationery Office.

OFSTED 2003: *Guidance to the National Standards Childminding Revised*. London: The Stationery Office.

OFSTED 2003: *Day Care: Guidance to the National Standards*. Revisions to Certain Criteria: Version 2. London: The Stationery Office.

OFSTED 2004: *Childminding: Guidance to the National Standards. Revisions to Certain Criteria: Version 2*. London: The Stationery Office.

Renvoize, J. 1993: *Innocence Destroyed: A Study of Child Sexual Abuse*. London: Routledge.

Taylor, J. and Woods, M. (eds) 1997 (2nd edition 2005): *Early Childhood Studies: An Holistic Introduction*. London: Hodder Arnold.

RESOURCES

The following organisations (by no means an exhaustive list) hold a wealth of material for research purposes, statistics, support packs for children, families and practitioners, and training resources (all websites accessed October 2004):

Barnardo's http://www.barnardos.org.uk
Childline http://www.childline.org.uk
Children 1st http://www.children1st.org.uk
Children Are Unbeatable http://www.childrenareunbeatable.org.uk
Daycare Trust http://www.daycaretrust.org.uk
Department of Health Publications
 http://www.dh.gov.uk/PublicationsAndStatistics/Publications/fs/en
Kidscape http://www.kidscape.org.uk

National Early Years Network (NEYN)
  77 Holloway Road, London N7 8JZ
  020 7607 9573
NCH http://www.nch.org.uk
NSPCC http://www.nspcc.org.uk
Save the Children (SCF) http://www.savethechildren.org.uk
UNICEF http://www.unicef.org.uk/tz/resources/assets/pdf/
  what_rights_flyer_2002.pdf – summary of the UN Convention on the
  Rights of the Child
Young Minds http://www.youngminds.org.uk

Study Skills

Over ten years ago, I made a career move from being an early years teacher to lecturing adults. I quickly realised that while I needed to be well prepared for lectures, supporting students' individual learning was equally important. I have studied part-time as a mature student myself and know what it is like to return to learning after a long break, and to juggle personal and study needs alongside a career. What follows are some of my recommendations for successful study.

GETTING STARTED

Study habits

Successful study requires organisation – of resources, time and energy. Finding a place to store your materials and a space to sit and work are very important. Some people are able to work in a noisy environment (at one time, my husband particularly liked Euston Station food court, where he wrote a number of books amid the hustle and bustle of the central London railway station), while others (like myself) prefer a very quiet room. You will quickly find out which suits your academic personality best.

   Storage and work areas do not have to be stylish. You need to organise your materials so that you can find them quickly, but this does not require expensive filing systems or shelving. Someone I knew studied very successfully by keeping all the materials for her Open University degree in a cardboard box under the kitchen table. What is very important is that you keep things together; much time can be lost searching for a missing book or an elusive quote on a single sheet of paper. Invest in a number of ring-binders and box files to store loose papers; write on the labels in pencil so that you can change them to reflect the topics/modules you are currently studying. Careful storage is particularly helpful when you come across an interesting article or book for an assessment that you are not currently working on; it means you will know where to find it when you do need it!

Ideally you should try to find a table in your home of a comfortable height, one that gives you enough room for the papers and books you need to access as you type. Will you be able to plug your laptop into a nearby socket and, if you like music in the background, is there a CD player nearby? You should also have a comfortable chair, and good light to work by. This may all seem like a distraction from the task in hand, but once you have established your study area, you will not need to worry about it again. Without careful preparation, 'settling down to study' can involve rituals which are time-consuming and irrelevant.

Time management

When you first decide to embark on any new venture, particularly studying for a degree, you may try to estimate how much time will be involved. I am often asked by prospective candidates how much time they will need to put aside for study. This is a very difficult question to answer as everyone reads, writes and processes information at a different speed. As a rough guide, you will probably need the same number of hours for private study as you spend in lectures.

Ideally, you should try to get the backing of your family and your work colleagues. Studying is going to affect all areas of your life and it is best for everyone to be aware of this. You may need to change your shift patterns at work, or get a relative to care for your children while you complete a written assignment at the weekend. Get these people on your side from the beginning – negotiate with them and encourage them to appreciate the ways in which your studies are going to benefit you all!

When do you feel best able to study? Some people feel fresh and alert first thing in the morning and prefer to wake early and do a few hours of study before work. Others like to study at night when everyone else is asleep and the environment is quiet. It is important to build up a study routine and to stick with it whenever possible. Initially, you should make a study calendar:

> ### PAUSE FOR THOUGHT
>
> Were you asked at your pre-course interview how you planned to fit studying in with your personal and career commitments? (If not, think about it now.)
>
> What did you answer?
>
> Were you being realistic?

	Very early morning	Morning	Afternoon	Evening	Night
Monday					
Tuesday					
Wednesday					
Thursday					
Friday					
Saturday					
Sunday					

- First, write in the times when you have other commitments – this will highlight the opportunities that are available for study.
- If you do sport/exercise, put in regular slots on the calendar. If you do not exercise, start now – it increases your energy levels and is a great de-stressor.
- Now put in five regular study periods when you will revisit your lecture notes, read and plan for assessment tasks.
- Finally, include some leisure time – without it you will burn out and your family and friends may never speak to you again!

You should be realistic about the time you can give to study. If your first timetable proves to be unachievable, adjust it accordingly. Once you have established a regular study routine, you will no longer need the timetable. However, if you feel that you are beginning to slow down or procrastinate, resurrect your last timetable, make adjustments and get back on track.

You will probably find that when working on essays and other important assessment tasks your study time will increase significantly. However, if you have been working steadily across the term, giving yourself reading and thinking time (as per your timetable), you will be much better prepared for assignments, and therefore you will be under less pressure in the run-up to the hand-in dates.

It is very easy to keep putting work off until tomorrow. A number of students have explained to me that they 'work best under pressure' and cannot get down to writing an essay until the deadline is looming. I am sceptical about this attitude – while there are a few lucky individuals who can sit down and write a perfectly reasonable essay with little preparation, most of us have to work hard to achieve our academic goals. In my experience, students who 'work best under pressure' often submit work with pages in the wrong order, omit bibliographies and generally fail to proof-read their work thoroughly. On the other hand, students who work consistently throughout the term, preparing for assessment in advance, tend to get better grades.

Support

Make sure that you access all the human resources at your disposal. Colleagues at your workplace may well be interested in your studies. They may be very eager to help by lending books and articles from career-development interests of their own. Your studies may also generate discussion among the staff and encourage everyone to examine long-established work practices. These debates can help you to think through new ideas and strengthen your knowledge and understanding of new concepts. However, you need to be prepared for some adverse reactions – some staff may feel threatened when they see a colleague becoming more knowledgeable or empowered.

You should look out for people who are prepared to read through drafts of your assignments, listen to you practice presentations and give you constructive feedback. These may be friends, work colleagues or family members. They do not need to have an in-depth understanding of early years content, but they will be able to tell you whether you are expressing yourself clearly. Also, find someone in your student group who you feel you could work with as a study buddy. You can share books, take notes for each other when you have an unavoidable absence and discuss key issues together. Plan your assessed work separately, but spare some time later to provide each other with feedback.

MAKING THE MOST OF LECTURES

Lectures are a crucial part of your programme of study. They:

· indicate what you are expected to learn
· help you to explore new ideas and concepts
· encourage debate
· are a stepping-off point for further study/reading.

In my experience, students who attend lectures regularly generally achieve the best results. Regular attendees are conscientious, and probably recognise that even the most tedious of lectures contain some nuggets of information. Borrowing notes from a fellow student afterwards is never the same as being there and experiencing the lecture and discussion first-hand.

Preparation

Look in your handbook before you go to a lecture – there should be a synopsis of what will be covered during the session. Reading this in advance will help you to put the lecture into a framework:

· What do you already know about the subject?
· Have you read anything on it?
· What do you particularly want to find out?
· Were you given a task in the previous session to bring to this lecture?

This preparation will put you in the right frame of mind, help you to leave your other commitments at the lecture-room door and enable you to settle quickly into study mode. By focusing in advance on the topic under discussion, you will be more able to put any personal or work issues to the back of your mind.

Taking notes

Taking notes is a highly individual activity.

It would be nice to think that we could go to an exciting lecture on a stimulating and thought-provoking subject, and that this would be sufficient for us to remember all the important issues. The reality is that we remember only a very small proportion of what we hear when we are in a passive mode, such as sitting in a lecture. Just listening is not enough – this is why it is so important to take good notes.

Some students try to write down *everything* their lecturer says. Clearly, this is not a practical strategy. Students who attempt this are setting themselves a mammoth task, which will reap few rewards. They are so busy taking dictation that they are not thinking about what is actually being said and are unable to digest much information. In all likelihood, when they go back and re-read their notes it will be like discovering them for the first time – they may as well have sat at home with a good textbook.

Jotting down keywords is a good strategy as long as they *are* the keywords! You need to listen very carefully, and be able to judge which are the most important of the stream of words coming from the lecturer's mouth. This is where your lecture preparation will help you – you do not need to write lots of notes on topics you already understand, but you do need to note down new information and concepts. You should write as briefly as possible – just enough to remind yourself of the basic facts.

It helps to develop your own shorthand, a series of symbols and abbreviations which you can use in your note taking. Some words (and suggested shorthand for them) which might crop up frequently in your lectures are:

- 'ch' for 'children'
- 'EY' for 'early years'
- 'P' for 'parent'.

Examples of other useful symbols are:

- = for 'is'
- -> for 'leading to'
- + for 'and'
- < for 'less than'
- > for 'more than'.

PAUSE FOR THOUGHT

Think about how you take notes in lectures and meetings.

Do you sit back and listen?

Do you try to write down everything that is said?

Do you jot down a few keywords?

Do you write down what appears on the lecturer's slides?

Finally, be aware of the main headings and structure of the lecture – in other words, take your cues from the lecturer. When planning a lecture, they will have considered which are the major areas they wish to cover (main headings). They will then make a number of points (possibly displayed as a series of bullet points) to describe and explain these ideas or major concepts and also bring in different perspectives and theoretical viewpoints. They may use overhead projector transparencies (OHT), PowerPoint® slides or provide a handout with a summary of the lecture. All these materials will help you to organise material under the headings that the lecturer has used, and thus achieve a logical and comprehensive set of lecture notes.

Most importantly, always revisit your notes after the lecture. Build this into your study programme and make it a priority to read through your notes within 24 hours, while the ideas are still fresh in your mind. Highlight sections, underline key ideas and, best of all, if time allows, rewrite your notes. Rewriting your notes forces you to digest the subject matter again, and is therefore a highly effective way to consolidate and strengthen your understanding. Doing this will ensure that you have fully understood what was discussed in the lecture. It also enables you to identify any gaps in your knowledge, recall any areas of weakness or confusion that you did not have time to record in the lecture and recognise what you need to research further.

Here are some key points to keep in mind when taking notes:

- use headings (preferably those used by the lecturer)
- frame, circle or highlight particular ideas
- use capitals to emphasise the most important issues
- underline points of particular interest
- mark (asterisk) sections you do not understand and need to clarify
- use colours to signify different types of ideas
- if you feel confident in their use, make mind maps (Buzan 2002; see below, 'Diagrammatic methods', pp. 238–40).

Listen, think and debate

Make sure that you are as active as you can be during a lecture:

- listen carefully
- think about what is being said
- check your understanding
- use every opportunity you are given to discuss ideas
- make links whenever possible to previous knowledge and experiences.

If you have a retiring nature or are lacking in confidence you may not wish to make contributions to general class discussions, but do ensure that you make the most of opportunities to express your ideas in small-group work.

Active learning

Learning theories suggest that we learn and retain more when we are actively involved – this type of deeper learning can be achieved through group work. However, do you actually take notes when feedback is given from this type of group work? If not, you should endeavour to do so in future.

Always be proactive in discussion and seminar groups; groups set their own pace – remember that a discussion is only as good as its participants' contributions. Try to ensure that group work is not dominated by the most outgoing students – they do not necessarily know more than everyone else (even though they may think they do!).

Class discussions and seminars are very good practice for writing academic essays. They mirror the process of exploring a topic and considering a variety of theoretical standpoints. Debating with other students, who do not always share your views, will help you articulate and develop your arguments and encourage you to compare and contrast opposing views.

READING

Finding relevant material

There is a wide range of literature now available on the subject of child development and the early years, and you will need to be selective when researching this material to support your studies.

The first place to start is with the course materials and individual module handbooks that you receive from your tutors. Every module should have a list of recommended reading, which will include books, journal articles and possibly websites.

REFLECTIVE ACTIVITY

Make a list of the problems you have experienced (or could experience) trying to get the books you need for your assessments. This might include difficulties such as:

- cannot afford to buy many books as they are expensive
- too many students, not enough library copies of key texts
- difficulties in getting to the college library out of work hours
- text on reading lists are unavailable.

Accessing all the books you need is tricky, but there are some steps you can take to make it a little easier. Books can be expensive, but you may be able to share the cost with your study buddy. Decide together on a couple of particularly useful key texts and buy one each to share.

It is an unfortunate fact that college and university libraries cannot possibly hold sufficient copies of key texts for all their students to borrow. However, you can be proactive in requesting that:

- reading lists are made available well in advance so that you can order copies from bookshops or your local library
- staff in the library/resource centre are informed well in advance about changes to module reading lists
- one or more copies are held as reference-only copies (in this way, the key texts should always be available when you visit the college library, even if you can't take them away)
- your fellow students are reminded to use a book as soon as they borrow it and return it as quickly as possible – a book sitting unread on a shelf does not constitute knowledge!

Finally, find out the opening hours of all the libraries/resource centres that you may wish to visit and work out how they fit into your timetable (discussed earlier). It may be helpful to designate actually a particular evening for studying in a library. Do not restrict yourself to the college library where you are studying – you should be able to use other college and university libraries, at least for reference purposes. Many institutions have long opening hours during term-time, including weekends, and borrowing books over vacation periods may entitle you to longer loans.

You should plan your library visit in advance: have a specific purpose in mind, make sure that you have the module reading list and a notebook with you. If possible, look on the library website or telephone beforehand to check the availability of the books you want.

Choosing books

Choosing books from a wide selection can be very confusing – there are so many books and so little time. Run through the following checklist and always be very clear what you are searching for:

- read the synopsis on the back cover
- look through the list of chapter headings
- scan the index looking for key theorists, topics, concepts etc.
- select a chapter and read the first paragraph (this should help you to decide whether it is worth reading further)
- concluding paragraphs usually give a good summary of the discussion.

Using a textbook is not like reading a novel – you should not expect to read it from cover to cover (unless it is absolutely fascinating). It is a sad fact that when you are studying you need to be very pragmatic and only read what is absolutely necessary.

There are several important skills which will help you to locate quickly the information you are searching for:

- try to increase the speed of your reading – you can practise this skill while reading the newspaper or a novel
- skim – this entails reading very quickly to get a general impression (this will tell you whether it is worth re-reading more fully to get the detail of the author's ideas and argument)
- scan – this entails looking out for particular headings and keywords, to see whether the author explores the topic you are particularly interested in
- reading for meaning – slower reading which helps you to understand the author's argument and assimilate new information.

Making notes

- Always have a pen and notebook with you when you read.
- Be careful to record the *full* bibliography of anything you make notes on (see below, 'References and bibliographies', pp. 244–7, for more on the importance of noting all bibliographical details as you read).
- Ensure that you indicate clearly which are direct quotes and which you have summarised in your own words.
- Make a note of the page number as you may wish to revisit this material again later.
- Always check the publication date of the material you are reading – remember that some information, for example, social trends and statistics, dates very quickly.
- Be very careful about the accuracy of material found on the Internet. It may be the work of an eminent academic or part of an essay written by a first-year undergraduate student (who may not have checked their sources and/or got a poor mark!).

ESSAY WRITING

Preparation

Essay writing is a very important part of your studies. It is here that you are able to demonstrate your understanding and knowledge of an area of the programme. Preparation is the most crucial aspect of successful essay writing. You will need to:

- unpick the question to clarify exactly what you are being asked to do
- highlight the key words in the question and keep checking that you are addressing them during your preparation
- re-read the course documents to remind yourself of the learning outcomes for the module (these may be used as a marking scheme)
- ask your tutor any questions that you have about the assessment criteria
- look back at your lecture notes to remind yourself of the appropriate material
- think about the group discussions you have taken part in (what were the major issues that arose during these debates?)
- look at your own books and check whether they cover the topic
- prepare a list of issues that you will need to research further
- go to the library and take *very* careful notes (see Reading, above, pp. 235–7).

Diagrammatic methods

Once you have all the information at your fingertips you are ready to begin planning the essay. You may already have your own tried and tested ways of essay planning, but you could also consider using a diagrammatic method, such as a mind map (Buzan 2002) or Bourner and Race's (1995) suggestion of 'laying an egg' (which hatches ideas!). Opposite you can see the diagram that I used to brainstorm my plans for this appendix.

I started with four main spokes or headings ('Starting out', 'Lectures', 'Reading' and 'Writing'), which were then further divided. If you look at the original plans for this section, 'Writing', you can see that I thought of four areas: finding a voice, types of writing, drafts and preparation. However, it was clear that the last two warranted major subsections in their own right. Working diagrammatically helped me to get my initial ideas down on paper quickly. I was then able to refine and add to the plan (and you will notice that in the end I decided not to write about 'finding a voice').

When you are planning an essay or presentation, you may find it useful to go on to make a number of more detailed maps or eggs for each area of your original diagram. These more detailed plans could include notes on specific authors or theorists and the titles of books (with references) which you are considering using to support your argument. You should always try to provide a balanced approach in any essay or presentation. Therefore, each subheading on your plan should have further spokes, outlining the pros and cons of a particular theory, concept or argument, for example.

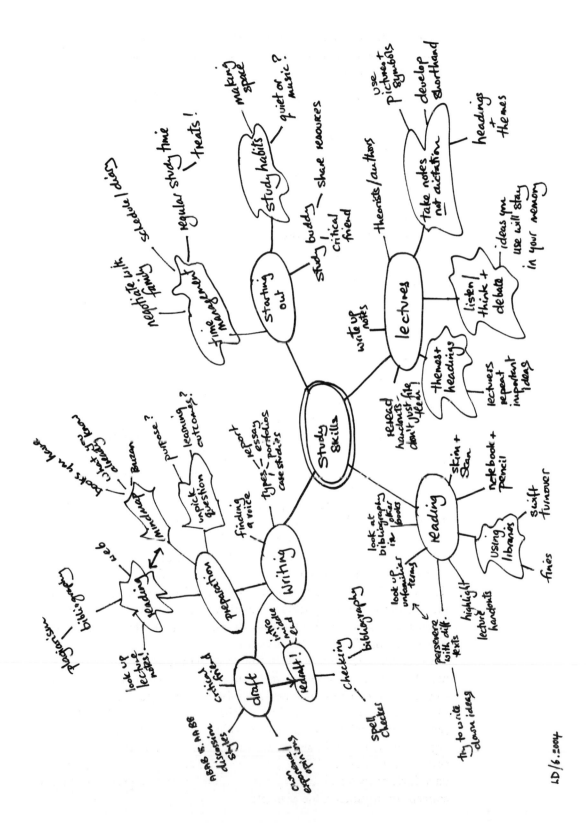

LD/6.2004

This type of detailed planning might seem time-consuming, but once you have the main ideas mapped out it will be very easy to begin writing your first draft. Each spoke will constitute one or two paragraphs in your essay, and you can use the original diagram to consider how to order the ideas (or paragraphs) in a logical sequence.

Draft, draft and redraft!

Very few of us can sit and write even the most simple communication without drafting and revising it. Clearly we do not edit our shopping lists or messages to friends, but most formal types of communication require some editing. (How many times have you left a message on someone's answer machine and wished that you could go back and re-record it?)

Beginning a piece of work can feel quite daunting. However, using diagrammatic or other methods of planning will help you to organise your material and feel confident about actually starting the writing process. It is useful to have considered the order in which you are going to present the ideas. Go back through your notes or look at your diagram and pencil in numbers to indicate the sequence you think would work best.

There are no hard-and-fast rules about how to organise your essay. Early paragraphs introduce key issues and set the scene, and the final section should draw together your ideas/argument into a tidy conclusion. It is very startling for a reader if your work stops abruptly; when I am marking essays, I sometimes find myself turning the page to look for a conclusion that the candidate has not written. It often indicates that the student has run out of words or time, or that they have not reflected sufficiently on what they have learnt from their studies.

Style

I was puzzled when I first returned to study and was advised to present an 'argument' in my essays. It took me a while to understand that I was being asked to analyse, debate and consider critically the ideas and concepts I was writing about. An academic essay should not consist of your homespun philosophy and opinions on a subject. It is very important that you underpin your discussion with reference to your reading, using the ideas of authors and theorists to support your argument. This does not mean that you cannot use your own experiences and opinions to illustrate ideas or challenge those of others, but do ensure that these do not dominate the essay.

Grades

Purely descriptive essays read like a narrative; they tell a story and take the reader through an exploratory journey. However, most academic essays require you to present an argument, posing interesting questions

REFLECTIVE ACTIVITY

Look at the marking criteria in your course handbook. There will probably be a breakdown of how the specific grades are awarded (ranging from fails through to distinction-level marks).

Look carefully at the requirements for a minimum pass (a D, or third-class mark), and then compare these with the description for a distinction (an A, or first-class mark). Write down what you think are the major differences.

Now consider the difference between a 'good' pass (a B, or upper-second-class mark) and a distinction (an A, or first-class mark). Again, write down how the criteria differ.

and demonstrating different viewpoints. A descriptive essay will usually only rate as a pass; the more analytical the debate or discussion is, the higher the grade awarded is likely to be.

You will have noticed that the higher grades require, not more information, but a more complex discussion of the material. An average essay may contain the same basic information as the distinction-level essay, but the final grade relates to the way in which the writer demonstrates their real understanding of the topic. Skilful use of the material you have researched shows that you have a genuine understanding of the issues, and have reflected on them rather than just paraphrasing what you have read.

There are two distinct ways of presenting an argument in the main body of an essay. For example, if you were considering the theories of language development proposed by Piaget (P) and Vygotsky (V), you could either write about them separately (P1, P2, P3, P4; then V1, V2, V3, V4 etc.) or weave their ideas on particular issues together, showing where they held similar views and where they differed (P1+V1; P2+V2; P3+V3 etc.) This second method is more complex, but it is also more effective because it makes an immediate comparison between specific aspects of the individual theories.

Essay tips

Introduction

- Explain what you are planning to do in the essay (you can compose this after you have written the rest of the essay).
- The introduction should indicate how you will be meeting the learning outcomes – but make sure you do this in a subtle way! Do not just paraphrase the criteria.

Paragraphs

- A sentence is not a paragraph!
- Usually, a paragraph should begin with an opening statement. The sentences that follow will then illustrate or debate this idea.
- A new idea deserves a new paragraph.
- Keep paragraphs to about four sentences long – if the paragraph seems to be growing beyond that, it is probably time to start a new one.
- Use connecting words to bridge the gap between paragraphs to help the fluency of your ideas (e.g. 'however', 'thus', 'on the other hand', 'furthermore', 'despite'). This gives your argument a logical structure and coherence.

Quotations

- Always ask yourself why you feel the need to use the author's exact words. Sometimes it *is* appropriate, particularly if it would be hard for you to express their idea as clearly.
- However, try not to use long quotations in your essays – one sentence or phrase should be sufficient.
- Always lead into a quote (using words such as 'suggests', 'concludes', 'believes', 'explains' etc.) and ensure that you make it part of your discussion.
- Do not just leave a quote dangling in the middle of the page, leaving the reader to decide which paragraph it belongs to and what point you are making with it.
- It is often better to paraphrase an author's idea, making sure that you indicate the reference clearly.
- Always include the page number(s) and date of the work.

Appendices

- Appendices enable you to include additional material that will not count in the word limit.
- You can include short documents or letters, transcripts or observations you have collected, or other material that is too lengthy to go in the essay.
- Everything that is in the appendix *must* be relevant to the essay.
- Do not be tempted to fill appendices with all the pamphlets and materials you have collected while doing your research – only include material that is relevant.
- Each document needs a separate appendix; they should be numbered in the *order that they appear* in your essay.

- Refer to them as follows: (see appendix 6). Leave the numbers blank until your work is almost finished. Once you are sure of the order they will appear in the final document, then go back and number them in the order of appearance in your essay.

Conclusion

- Your conclusion should pull the essay together, making a tidy ending.
- Briefly recap the *main* points you have presented.
- You may include recommendations or consider the impact this new understanding may have on your professional practice.

Word limits

One of the difficulties of writing academic essays is keeping within the word limits. Frequently, you will have collected so much material that it is hard to know what is most essential – to take the analogy of film production, be prepared to leave some ideas on the cutting-room floor.

I have had countless discussions with students who find themselves in this predicament. Students who leave their writing to the last minute often panic when they realise that they have too many words and cut out whole paragraphs. The danger is that they may have removed an important section and this may be reflected in their final grade.

Tips for reducing the word length

- Check that *everything* you have written is directly related to the essay title.
- Re-read the assessment criteria and learning outcomes for the module. Use these as a checklist.
- Check to see if you have repeated yourself; the same supporting material may have been used in several places – decide where it is most relevant.
- Proof-read your work carefully and look out for where you could use one word instead of three!
- If you are really desperate, try turning sentences round so that they use fewer words.

Polishing your work for submission

You will rarely sit down and write an essay in one sitting. It is useful to read through the previous day's work before you begin writing new material. This has two benefits: first, you are proofreading the section you have already written, and second, it helps you to begin the new work using the same style or 'voice'. Later, when you are at the redrafting stage, ask a friend or colleague to read your work and give you some feedback. A fresh perspective can be extremely useful, as it is often difficult to step back and see our own weaknesses, especially when we have put so much effort into a project. Take their comments as helpful feedback, not criticism!

When you feel happy with your final draft (and remember, like an artist, you will always feel that there is room for improvement!) you should go through this checklist:

- ensure you are within the word limit
- use a spell-checker if possible
- insert page numbers
- check that the page layout meets the programme specifications (e.g. you may be asked to use double spacing; put your name and/or candidate number as a header on every page)
- locate the places where you have referred to appendices and check that they are numbered correctly
- the very last task before submission is to read through your work and check that every reference appears in the bibliography section.

One last piece of advice – *do not leave things to the last minute*!

Plan to complete your work *a couple of days before* the submission date. Computers and printers (and general life events) have a nasty habit of trying to trip you up at the last minute!

REFERENCES AND BIBLIOGRAPHIES

Bibliography refers to any literature – books, journal articles, websites – that you have read as part of your research on a given topic. Once you mention the book, author or idea in your writing, it becomes a *reference*.

Literature, in whatever form, is the property of the person who conceived it; this is why you must be sure to reference correctly. In the course of your studies you will need to read widely, but you must not pass off other people's ideas as your own. Plagiarism is taken extremely seriously in higher education establishments. If tutors suspect that your assessed work is not your own, they will investigate; if you have been copying other people's published (or unpublished) work, or if large parts of an essay are lifted straight from a textbook, you are likely to be taken off the programme.

However, your essays and presentations must be based on your reading. This means that a delicate balance needs to be struck between referring to the ideas of others without flouting copyright and plagiarism rules. You cannot write an essay without substantiating your sources. Therefore, you may choose to summarise or paraphrase an author's work, or you may decide to use their actual words. If you quote the actual words you must put them in quotation marks and indicate the source (including the page number). It may be helpful to think of this process as a copyright issue – particular ideas, phrases or sentences are unique to the author in the same way that the commercial products we buy are protected by copyright laws.

The rules for referencing are relatively simple, and yet so many students I have taught find it hard to implement them correctly. Many colleges and universities in the UK use what is known as the Harvard system, but you should check your student handbook to ensure that you use the method preferred by your college or university.

Reference versus bibliography section

Another issue which can differ between institutions is whether you need a reference section *and* a bibliography at the end of your work. Just to confuse matters further, some examining bodies call the reference section the bibliography. Once again, look in your course material to check the specific requirements and ensure that you know which headings are preferred. If you are asked to produce two separate sections, the distinction is that *references* have been referred to in your work, while a *bibliography* includes books which you have read as background material, but have *not* referred to. In most undergraduate essays all the material is referenced; it is much more likely that a dissertation or project will require a differentiated list containing a fuller bibliography. Avoid the urge to put in the titles of texts you have not actually read!

The information that you should always list is as follows:

Author's surname and initials	Date of publication	Title (and edition, if relevant)	Place of publication	Publisher	Page(s) referenced

This information must always be collected when you are researching for your essays, seminars and presentations. You could use or adapt this table to help you to remember what information you need to gather.

Using references in an essay or report

You only need to give the surname of the author and the publication date in the main body of your essay – the full reference will appear at the end of your essay. Let us take the following book as an example:

Author's surname and initials	Date of publication	Title (and edition, if relevant)	Place of publication	Publisher	Page(s) referenced
Rowntree, D.	1998	*Learning How to Study. A Realistic Approach*	London	Warner Books	

In your essay you would simply refer to Rowntree (1998), but in the reference or bibliography section at the end of the essay, if using the Harvard system, you should reference it as follows (the title of the book should be in italics):

Rowntree, D. 1998: *Learning How to Study. A Realistic Approach.* London: Warner Books.

So far so simple! Now let us consider some more complicated references.

	In the main body of your essay	In the bibliography/ reference section
One author	Rowntree (1998)	Rowntree, D. 1998: *Learning How to Study. A Realistic Approach.* London: Warner Books.
Two authors	Bourner and Race (1995)	Bourner, T. and Race, P. 1995: *How to Win as a Part-time Student* (2nd edn). London: Kogan Page.
More than two authors	Gopnik *et al.* (1999)	Gopnik, A., Meltzoff, A. and Kuhl, P. 1999: *How Babies Think.* London: Weidenfeld & Nicolson.
A chapter from an edited book	Mukherji (2005)	Mukherji, P. 2005: 'The importance of health', in Dryden, L. *et al.*, *Essential Early Years.* London: Hodder Arnold.
A quote about another author within a text	Lalonde (1974, cited in Mukherji 2005)	Mukherji, P. 2005: 'The importance of health', in Dryden, L. *et al.*, *Essential Early Years.* London: Hodder Arnold. (i.e. Lalonde will not appear in the bibliography)
Newspaper article	Furedi (2004)	Furedi, F. 2004: 'Plagiarism stems from a loss of scholarly ideals', *Times Higher Education Supplement*, 6 August 2004.
Journal article	Dryden *et al.* (2003)	Dryden, L., Hyder, T. and Jethwa, S. 2003: 'Assessing individual oral presentations', in *Investigations in University Teaching and Learning*, vol. 1, no. 1, 79–83.
Internet	Stainthorp (2003)	Stainthorp, R. 2003: 'Use it or lose it'. http://www.literacytrust.org.uk/Pubs/stainthorp.html (accessed October 2004).

Paraphrasing and quoting

Let us consider how to use references in an essay. Below are two examples of how to make reference to Helen Fielding's novel, *Bridget Jones's Diary* (full reference: Fielding, H. 1996: *Bridget Jones's Diary: A Novel*. London: Picador).

In an essay I could write either:

Bridget Jones (Fielding 1996) suggests that in her experience the way to attract a man's affection is to appear disinterested in him.

Or I could write:

Bridget Jones (Fielding 1996) writes in her diary, 'Can officially confirm that the way to a man's heart these days is not through beauty, food, sex, or alluringness of character, but merely the ability to seem not very interested in him.' (p. 73).

In the first example, I have extracted and then paraphrased the major idea expressed by Bridget, the diary writer. In the second, I have used a direct quote from the text.

REFLECTIVE ACTIVITY

Make a list of the differences between the two examples given above. Consider the way that most words have been replaced by synonyms (i.e. with the same meaning) so that the author's original words have not been repeated, and also how the order of the sentence has been changed.

You can practise this skill using any current reading. For example, read a newspaper article and then write about it:

- start by summing up the whole article in a couple of sentences
- now take a couple of important sentences and paraphrase them (express them in your own words).

To summarise, references are extremely important for two reasons: first, they show that you have read and understood important literature in a particular area of study, and second, they ensure that you avoid plagiarism.

GIVING PRESENTATIONS

Many courses now include presentations as part of the formal qualification assessment. Part of the reason for this is that many jobs now require people to give presentations, and it can be helpful for students to practise these skills. However, I have found that students are often much more anxious about giving a presentation than about preparing written work. This should not be the case. A presentation is actually an opportunity to give a short talk on an area of interest, and allows you to give a more personal and informal account of your learning than an essay.

Planning

Planning for a presentation is very similar to planning for a short essay; a little material goes a long way when you are presenting it verbally to an audience. You should follow the same kind of procedures as for essay writing (see above, Essay writing, pp. 237–44):

- think carefully about the assessment criteria
- check the assessment criteria and regularly remind yourself of the learning outcomes for the module
- gather the information and keep thorough notes
- like an essay, a presentation must have an introduction and a strong conclusion
- make a plan, using a diagrammatic structure
- limit yourself to a small number of main points you wish to make (maybe five)

PAUSE FOR THOUGHT

How do you feel about presenting to an audience? If the thought of talking to a group makes you feel anxious, what is it that concerns you?

There are actually a number of advantages to making a presentation, as opposed to writing an essay, which should outweigh your anxiety:

- you usually get to choose the exact topic (within certain boundaries)
- you will probably need to gather a lot less material
- it is a more personal, less academic account of your understanding
- it will probably take less time to prepare
- there is no need for proofreading!

- carefully consider the order in which you are going to discuss these points (clarity is very important if you are to keep the audience's attention)
- consider how visual aids can be used to enhance your presentation.

Preparation

Once you have designed the plan and gathered your supporting evidence (references to your reading, major theorists, anecdotes from your own professional experience etc.) transpose your notes onto a series of index cards, using a separate card for each new idea. This method has an additional benefit, since you can shuffle the cards around until you feel happy with the order.

You could write out your notes in longhand and read them to your audience. However, it is much better to make notes on the cards, which will act as prompts when you give your presentation. This method will allow you to maintain good eye contact with your audience and establish a friendlier rapport. Remember that when you are presenting to a group of your fellow students, they have probably had to sit for quite a considerable length of time listening to a whole series of presentations. It is quite dull to watch someone read an essay to you! The more you can engage the audience's attention and interest, the more confident you will feel in the delivery of your material.

Visual aids

Visual aids are there to support, illustrate and enliven your talk. You can use:

- posters
- photographs
- artefacts (toys, models etc.)
- overhead projector transparencies (OHTs)
- PowerPoint® slides
- tape recordings
- video or DVD clips
- a whiteboard or flip chart to present material as part of your delivery.

It is very helpful for the audience if you introduce your presentation by providing a list of the main issues you plan to cover – these can be displayed on a poster or screen (using OHTs or PowerPoint® slides). In some cases you may be asked to provide a handout, which will subsequently be used as evidence of your presentation. This could include a bibliography which your fellow students might find helpful.

If you intend to use electronic visual aids, be sure to check that the equipment will be available in the room you are presenting in, and get there very early to test things out. The video clip which works smoothly in your home VCR may have a different tracking to the one at the college. It is a good idea to have paper versions of PowerPoint® slides and OHTs, just in case the technology lets you down.

Try to avoid passing round interesting material during your talk, as this will distract people's attention from what you are saying. However, it is a good idea to point to interesting posters or hold up colourful artefacts and other materials during your presentation, which the audience will be able to look at in more detail after your talk. Visual aids used correctly can really enhance a good presentation, but they will not make up for poor research!

Timing

Timing is crucial in a presentation and is often one of the hardest things to gauge. Once all your notes are ready, you will need to practise at home. There are two reasons why this is so important: first, it allows you to rehearse your delivery and build up your confidence, and second, you can find out whether you have too much or too little material. You may be surprised at how much longer it takes to read aloud a short passage than it does to read it in your head. You really do need to get the timing right, as you are likely to be penalised if you run over the allotted time. Audiences also tend to get restless if they have to sit through very long presentations, or if you run over into their precious lunch hour!

Presenting to an audience

- Speak clearly.
- Try to look as if you are enjoying yourself – enthusiasm is catching.
- Try to make the delivery lively; you can use humour.
- Always face the audience and maintain as much eye contact as possible.
- Try not to rush – you will make mistakes and become flustered. Speak slowly and clearly.
- Use your visual aids to help the audience; they should not be a distraction.
- Wear something that makes you feel good and helps to boost your confidence.
- Most importantly, remember that the audience are your peers. They are going to be receptive to your ideas, without being critical.

Group presentations

If you are asked to work in a group to prepare a presentation, ensure that you capitalise on individual talents and expertise. Brainstorm a plan of action and then consider how to divide up the workload in the most efficient way. One member of the group may be excellent at researching while another has artistic talents. You need to check with your tutor whether all the group members are required to speak, or whether the most confident can deliver the presentation on behalf of the group. Meeting up to plan and rehearse can be difficult if you are studying part-time. In this case, it may be better for each person to be responsible for a particular section of the presentation.

FURTHER READING

Bourner, T. and Race, P. 1995: *How To Win as a Part-time Student* (2nd edn). London: Kogan Page.

Crème, P. and Lea, M. R. 2003: *Writing at University: A Guide for Students* (2nd edn). Buckingham: Open University Press.

Fairbairn, G. J. and Fairbairn, S. 2001: *Reading at University. A Guide for Students*. Buckingham: Open University Press.

Greetham, B. 2001: *How To Write Better Essays*. Hampshire: Palgrave.

Seinfeld, S. and Burns, T. 2003: *Essential Study Skills: The Complete Guide to Success at University*. London: Sage Publications.

BIBLIOGRAPHY

CHAPTER 1 LAUNCHING INTO LEARNING

Aubrey, C., David, T., Godfrey, R. and Thompson, L. 2000: *Early Childhood Educational Research*. London and New York: Routledge Falmer.

Belbin, R. Meredith 2003: *Management Teams: Why They Succeed or Fail* (2nd edn). Oxford: Butterworth-Heinemann.

Brookfield, S. D. 1995: *Becoming a Critically Reflective Teacher*. San Francisco: Jossey-Bass.

Bruner, J. 1975: 'From communication to language: a psychological perspective'. *Cognition* 3, 225–89.

Colwell, S. 1998: 'Mentoring, socialisation and the mentor/protégé relationship [1]'. *Teaching in Higher Education* 3 (3), 313–25.

Costa, A. and Kallick, B. 1993: 'Through the lens of a critical friend'. *Educational Leadership* 51 (2), 49–51.

Dewey, J. 1933: *How We Think: A Restatement of the Relation of Reflective Thinking in the Educative Process*. Chicago: Henry Regnery.

Dunn, R. S. and Dunn, J. K. 1978: *Teaching Students Through Their Individual Learning Styles: A Practical Approach*. Englewood Cliffs, NJ: Prentice Hall.

Gardiner, C 1998: Mentoring: towards a professional relationship. *Mentoring and Tutoring* 6, 77–84.

Hayes, N. and Orrell, S. 1993: *Maslow in Psychology: An Introduction*. London: Longman Group UK Ltd.

Honey, P. and Mumford, A. 1992: *A Manual of Learning Styles*. Maidenhead: Peter Honey Publications.

Kolb, D. A. 1984: *Experiential Learning – Experience as the Source of Learning and Development*. Englewood Cliffs, NJ: Prentice Hall.

Peters, J. M. 1994: 'Instructors as researchers-and-theorists: faculty development in a community college', in Benn, R. and Fieldhouse, R. (eds), *Training and Professional Development in Adult and Continuing Education*. Exeter: CRCE.

Piaget, J., Garbain, M. and Garbain, R. 2001: *The Language and Thought of the Child*. London: Routledge.

Pollard, A. 2002: *Reflective Teaching: Effective and Evidence Informed Professional Practice*. London and New York: Continuum.

Rosenshine, B. and Meister, C. 1992: 'The use of scaffolds for teaching higher-level cognitive strategies'. *Educational Leadership* 49 (7), 26–33.

Schon, D. 1983: *The Reflective Practitioner*. San Francisco: Jossey-Bass.

Usher, R. and Edwards, R. 1994: *Postmodernism and Education*. London: Routledge.

CHAPTER 2 THE IMPORTANCE OF HEALTH

Acheson, D. 1998: *Independent Inquiry into Inequalities in Health Report*. London: The Stationery Office.

Black, D. *et al.* 1980: *Inequalities in Health: Report of a Research Working Group*. London: DHSS.

BMA 1999: *Growing Up in Britain: Ensuring a Healthy Future for our Children*. London: BMA Publications.

Bradshaw, J. 2002: *The Well-being of Children in the UK*. London: Save the Children.

Child Accident Prevention Trust 2003: 'Children's accidents – facts and figures'. http://www.capt.org.uk (accessed October 2004).

David, T., Goouch, K., Powell, S. and Abbott, L. 2003: *Birth to Three Matters: A Review of the Literature, Compiled to Inform the Framework to Support Children in their Earliest Years*. Nottingham: DfES Publications, ch. 6.

Deckelbaum, R., 2002: *Nutrition Today Matters Tomorrow: A Report from the March of Dimes Task Force on Nutrition and Optimal Human Development*. http://www.marchofdimes.com/aboutus/681_1926.asp (accessed October 2004).

DfES 2000: *Curriculum Guidance for the Foundation Stage*. Sudbury: QCA Publications.

DfES 2001: *Promoting Children's Mental Health within Early Years and School Settings*. Nottingham: DfES Publications.

DfES and the Sure Start Unit 2003: *Birth to Three Matters: A Framework to Support Children in their Earliest Years*. Sudbury: DfES Publications.

DoH 2002: *Tackling Health Inequalities 2002 Cross-Cutting Review*. London: The Stationery Office.

DoH 2003: *Tackling Health Inequalities: A Programme for Action*. London: The Stationery Office.

Downie, R. S., Tannahill, C. and Tannahill, A. 1996: *Health Promotion: Models and Values* (2nd edn). Oxford: Oxford University Press.

Ewles, L. and Simnet, I. 1999: *Promoting Health: A Practical Guide*. London: Bailliere Tindall.

Fieldhouse, P. 1996: *Food and Nutrition Customs and Culture* (2nd edn). Cheltenham: Nelson Thornes.

Graham, H. and Power, C. 2004: *Childhood Disadvantage and Adult Health: A Life Course Framework*. Health Development Agency NHS, http://www.hda.nhs.uk/evidence (accessed October 2004).

Hall, D. and Elliman, D. 2003: *Health for All Children*. Oxford: Oxford University Press.

Hamlyn, B., Brooker, S., Oleinikova, K. and Wands, S. 2000: *Infant Feeding Survey*. London: DoH.

Health Education Board for Scotland 2003: 'Health promotion training needs among early years childcare and education providers' (Research in brief no. 8). http://www.hebs.com/research/pd/ (accessed October 2004).

Hyder, T. and Mukherji, P. 2004: *Aspects of Health Promotion. Distance Learning Handbook*. London: London Metropolitan University.

Jacobson, B., Smith, A. and Whitehead, M. (eds) 1991: *The Nation's Health: A Strategy for the 1990s* (revised edn). London: King Edward's Hospital Fund, 114.

Karnes, T. 2004: 'Health, nutrition and safety', in Bremner, G. and Fogel, A. (eds), *Blackwell Handbook of Infant Development*. Oxford: Blackwell Publishing, ch. 25.

Lalonde, M. 1974: *A New Perspective on the Health of Canadians*. Ottawa: Government of Canada.

Naidoo, J. and Wills, J. 2000: *Health Promotion Foundations for Practice* (2nd edn). Edinburgh: Bailliere Tindall, Harcourt Publishers Ltd (in association with the Royal College of Nursing).

National Alliance for Equity in Dental Health 2000: *Inequalities in Dental Health: A Briefing Paper*. Manchester: British Fluoridation Society.

NCH 2004: 'Going hungry: the struggle to eat healthily on a low income'. http://www.nch.org.uk/goinghungry/ (accessed October 2004).

Office for National Statistics 2004a: *The Health of Children and Young People*. London: HMSO.

Office for National Statistics 2004b: *Annual Review of the Registrar General on Childhood: Infant and Perinatal Deaths in England and Wales*. London: HMSO.

Parliamentary Office of Science and Technology 2003: *Improving Children's Diet*. Report 199, September. London: POST.

Rutter, M. and Smith, D. J. (eds) 1995: *Psychosocial Disorders in Young People: Time, Trends, and their Causes*. Chichester: Wiley.

Sebire, N. J., Jolly, M., Harris, J. P., Wadsworth, J., Joffe, M., Bear, R. W., Regan, L. and Robinson, S. 2001: 'Maternal obesity and pregnancy outcome: a study of 287,213 pregnancies in London'. *International Journal of Obstetrics and Related Metabolic Disorders* 25 (8), 1175–82.

Spencer, N. 2000: *Poverty and Child Health*. Oxford: Radcliff Medical Press.

The United Kingdom Parliament 2004: *Summary of the Select Committee of Health Third Report on Obesity*. London: The Stationery Office.

Tones, K. and Tilford, S. 2001: *Health Promotion, Effectiveness, Efficiency and Equity* (3rd edn). Cheltenham: Nelson Thornes.

Thompson, M., Petticrew, M. and Morrison, D. 2001: 'Health effects of housing improvement: systematic review of intervention studies'. *British Medical Journal* 323, 187–90.

UNICEF 2000: *The State of the World's Children*. http://www.unicef.org (accessed October 2004).

World Health Organization 1946: *Constitution*. Geneva: WHO.

World Health Organization 1984: *Health Promotion, a Discussion Document on the Concepts and Principles*. Copenhagen: WHO Regional Office for Europe.

World Health Organization 2004: *Global Strategy for Infant and Young Child Feeding*. Geneva: WHO.

CHAPTER 3 LANGUAGE AND LITERACY

Alladina, S. 1995: *Being Bilingual*. Stoke-on-Trent: Trentham Books.

Baker, C. 2002: *Foundations of Bilingual Education and Bilingualism* (2nd edn). Clevedon: Multilingual Matters Ltd.

Barratt-Pugh, C. 2000: *The Socio-cultural Context of Literacy Learning*, in Barratt-Pugh, C. and Rohl, M. (eds), *Literacy Learning in the Early Years*. Buckingham: Open University Press.

Bee, H. 1997: *The Developing Child* (8th edn). Harlow: Longman.

Bernstein, B. 1975: *Class, Codes and Control Vol. 3 Towards a Theory of Educational Transmission* (2nd edn). London: Routledge and Kegan Paul.

Bettelheim, B. 1975: *The Uses of Enchantment. The Meaning and Importance of Fairy Tales*. London: Thames and Hudson.

Bissex, G. 1980: *GNYS AT WRK: A Child Learns to Write and Read*. Harvard, MA: Harvard University Press.

Browne, A. 1999: 'Developing Writing' in Marsh, J. and Hallet, E. (eds), *Desirable Literacies: Approaches to Language and Literacy in the Early Years*. London: Paul Chapman.

Bruner, J. 1985: *Child's Talk. Learning to Use Language*. London: Norton.

Bryant, P. E., Bradley, L., MacLean, M. and Crossland, J. 1989: 'Nursery rhymes, phonological skills and reading'. *Journal of Child Language* 16, 407–28.

Chomsky, N. 1965: *Aspects of Theory of Syntax*. Cambridge, MA: MIT Press.

Clay, M. M. 1991: *Becoming Literate. The Construction of Inner Control*. Auckland, New Zealand: Heinemann.

Cummins, J. 1976: 'The influence of bilingualism on cognitive growth: a synthesis of research findings and explanatory hypotheses'. *Working Papers in Bilingualism* 9, 1–43.

Cummins, J. and Swain, M. 1986: *Bilingualism in Education*. Harlow: Longman.

DfEE 1998: *The National Literacy Strategy*. Framework for Teaching. London: DfEE.

DfEE/QCA 2000a: *Curriculum Guidance for the Foundation Stage*. London: DfEE.

DfEE/QCA 2000b: *English. The National Curriculum for English Key Stages 1–4*. London: DfEE.

Dombey, H. 1992: *Words and Worlds. Reading in the Early Years of School*. Sheffield: NATE.

Drury, R. 2004: 'Samia and Sadaqat Play School. Early bilingual literacy at home', in Gregory, E., Long, S. and Volk, D. (eds), *Many Pathways to Literacy*. London: Routledge.

Garton, A. and Pratt, C. 2002: *Learning to Be Literate. The Development of Spoken and Written Language* (2nd edn). Oxford: Blackwell.

Godwin, D. and Perkins, M. 2002: *Teaching Language and Literacy in the Early Years* (2nd edn). London: David Fulton.

Gopnik, A., Meltzoff, A. and Kuhl, P. 1999: *How Babies Think*. London: Weidenfeld and Nicolson.

Gregory, E., Williams, A., Baker, D. and Street, B. 2004: 'Introducing literacy to four year olds: creating classroom cultures in three schools', in *Journal of Early Childhood Literacy* 4 (1), April.

Gussin Paley, V. 1981: *Wally's Stories*. London: Harvard University Press.

Gussin Paley, V. 1986: *Mollie Is Three. Growing Up in School*. London: University of Chicago Press.

Hall, D. 1995: *Assessing the Needs of Bilingual Pupils*. London: David Fulton.

Hall, N. and Robinson, A. 2003: *Exploring Writing and Play in the Early Years* (2nd edn). London: David Fulton.

Hallet, E. 1999: 'Sign and symbols: environmental print', in Marsh, J. and Hallet, E. (eds), *Desirable Literacies. Approaches to Language and Literacy in the Early Years*. London: Paul Chapman.

Halliday, M. A. K. 1975: *Learning How to Mean. Explorations in the Development of Language*. London: Arnold.

Heath, S. B. 1983: *Ways with Words, Language, Life and Work in Communities and Classrooms*. Cambridge: Cambridge University Press.

Hester, H. 1990: *Patterns of Learning*. London: CLPE.

Karmiloff, K. and Karmiloff-Smith, A. 2001: *Pathways to Language. From Fetus to Adolescent*. London: Harvard University Press.

Kellogg, R. 1979: *Children's Drawings, Children's Minds*. New York: Avon.

Kenner, C. 2000: *Home Pages. Literacy Links for Bilingual Children*. Stoke-on-Trent: Trentham Books.

Krashen, S. D. 1981: *Principles and Practice in Second Language Acquisition*. London: Prentice Hall International.

Marsh, J. and Millard, E. 2000: *Literacy and Popular Culture: Using Children's Culture in the Classroom*. London: Paul Chapman.

Matthews, J. 1994: *Helping Children to Draw and Paint in Early Childhood. Children and Visual Representation*. London: Hodder and Stoughton.

Meek, M. 1991: *On Being Literate*. London: Bodley Head.

Moore, M. and Wade, B. 1998: *A Gift for Life: Bookstart: The First Five Years*. London: Bookstart.

Nutbrown, C. 1997: *Recognising Early Literacy Development. Assessing Children's Achievements*. London: Paul Chapman.

Piaget, J. 1959: *The Language and Thought of the Child*. London: Routledge.

Riley, J. L. 1999: *The Teaching of Reading at KS1 and Before*. Cheltenham: Stanley Thornes.

Rivalland, J. 2000: 'Linking literacy learning across different contexts', in Barrat-Pugh, C. and Rohl, M. (eds), *Literacy Learning in the Early Years*. Milton Keynes: Open University Press.

Sacks, O. 1990: *Seeing Voices. A Journey into the World of the Deaf*. California: University of California Press.

Sedgwick, F. 2001: *Teaching Literacy*. London: Continuum.

Sheridan, S. R. 2004: *Scribbles*: 'The missing link in a bio-evolutionary theory of human language with implications for human consciousness'. www.drawingwriting.com/scribb2.pdf (accessed October 2004).

Siraj-Blatchford, I. and Clarke, P. 2000: *Supporting Identity, Diversity and Language in the Early Years*. Buckingham: Open University Press.

Tizard, B. and Hughes, M. 1984: *Young Children Learning. Talking and Thinking at Home and School*. London: Fontana.

Tough, J. 1977: *The Development of Meaning. A Study of Children's Use of Language*. London: George Allen & Unwin.

Vygotsky, L. 1986: *Thought and Language*. Cambridge, MA: MIT Press.

Waterland, L. 1988: *Read With Me. An Apprenticeship Approach to Reading*. Stroud: Thimble Press.

Wells, G. 1987: *The Meaning Makers: Children Learning Language and Using Language to Learn*. London: Hodder and Stoughton.

Whitehead, M. R. 1997: *Language and Literacy in the Early Years*. London: Paul Chapman.

Wood, D. 1988: *How Children Think and Learn*. Oxford: Blackwell.

Zalewski, D. 2002: 'Even blind people can draw'. *The New York Times Magazine*, 15 December.

CHAPTER 4 WORKING WITH YOUNG CHILDREN

Athey, C. 1990: *Extending Thought in Young Children*. London: Paul Chapman Publishing.

Bennett, J. 2003: 'Starting strong: the persistent division between care and education'. *Early Childhood Research* 1 (1), May, 21–48. London: Sage.

Blakemore, C. 1998: 'Brain development and research findings' (unpublished conference paper). Pen Green Centre: Early Years Conference, 28 January.

Blakemore, C. 2000: 'Early learning and the brain' (unpublished paper). RSA Lecture, 14 February.

Bowlby, J. 1969: *Attachment and Loss*. Vol.1 Attachment. London: Hogarth Press.

Bowlby, J. 1988: *A Secure Base: Clinical Applications of Attachment Theory*. London: Routledge.

Bowlby, R. 2002: 'Beyond attachment' (unpublished paper). Harrogate: RNIB Conference, June.

Bredekamp, S. and Copple, C. (eds) 1997: *Developmentally Appropriate Practice in Early Childhood Programs*. Washington, DC: National Association for the Education of Young Children.

Bruce, T. 1987 (revised 1997): *Early Childhood Education*. London: Hodder and Stoughton.

Bruce, T. 1991: *Time to Play in Early Childhood Education*. London: Hodder and Stoughton.

Bruce, T. 2001: *Learning Through Play: Babies, Toddlers and the Foundation Years*. London: Hodder and Stoughton.

Bruce, T. and Meggitt, C. 2002: *Child Care and Education* (3rd edn). London: Hodder and Stoughton.

Carnegie Foundation 1994: *Starting Points: Meeting the Needs of our Youngest Children*. New York: Carnegie Corporation.

Carter, R. 1999: *Mapping the Mind*. London: Seven Dials.

Cousins, J. 1999: *Listening to Four Year Olds: How They Can Help Us Plan Their Care and Education*. London: National Children's Bureau.

David, T. *et al.* 2002: *Review of the Literature to Support Birth to Three Matters: A Framework to Support Children in their Earliest Years*. London: DfES.

DfES 2001: *National Standards for Under-eights in Day Care and Childminding*. London: DfES.

DfES 2002: *Birth to Three Matters: A Framework to Support Children in their Earliest Years*. London: DfES.

Elfer, P. 2001: 'Attachment and the role of the key person' (unpublished paper). Hammersmith: Focus on Mental Health, From Birth to Primary School, 15 June.

Elfer, P., Goldschmied, E. and Selleck, D. 2003: *Key Person Relationships in Nursery*. London: Sage.

Forbes, R. 2004: *Beginning to Play: Young Children from Birth to Three*. Maidenhead: Open University Press.

Goldschmied, E. and Jackson, S. 1994: *People Under Three: Young Children in Day Care*. London and New York: Routledge.

Goleman, D. 1996: *Emotional Intelligence: Why it Can Matter More than IQ*. London: Bloomsbury.

Gopnik, A. Meltzoff, A. and Kuhl, P. 1999: *How Babies Think: the Science of Childhood*. London: Weidenfeld and Nicolson.

Goswami, U. 1998: *Cognition in Children*. Sussex: Psychology Press Limited.

Greenfield, S. 1999: 'The state of the art of the science of brain research' (unpublished paper). London: Learning and the Brain Day Conference, The Royal Institution, 23 November.

Greenfield, S. 2000: *Brain Story*. London: BBC Worldwide Ltd.

Greenman, J. and Stonehouse, A. 1997: *Prime Times: A Handbook for Excellence in Infant and Toddler Programs*. Melbourne, Australia: Longman.

Griffin, B. 1997: 'The child should feel "good enough" – nurturing a sense of self in young children', in Abbot, L. and Moylett, H. (eds), *Working with the Under-3s: Responding to Children's Needs*. Buckingham: Open University Press.

Gross, R. 1997: 'Attachment theory extensions and applications'. *Psychology Review* 4 (2), 10–13.

Gussin Paley, V. 1992: *You Can't Say You Can't Play*. Harvard, MA: Harvard University Press.

Hopkins, J. 1988: 'Facilitating the development of intimacy between nurses and infants in day nurseries'. *Early Childhood Development and Care* 33, 99–111.

Jackson, D. 2002: *Baby Wisdom: The World's Best-kept Secrets for the First Year of Parenting*. London: Hodder and Stoughton.

Jensen, C. 1994: 'Fragments for a discussion about quality', in Moss, P. and Pence, A. (eds), *Valuing Quality in Early Childhood Services*. London: Paul Chapman Publishing.

Kellmer Pringle, M. 1980 (1974): *The Needs of Children* (2nd edn). London: Hutchinson.

Kotulak, R. 1997: *Inside the Brain. Revolutionary Discoveries of How the Mind Works*. Kansas City, MO: Andrews McMeel Publishing.

Laevers, F., Vandenbussche, E., Kog, M. and Depondt, L. 1997: 'A process-oriented child monitoring system for young children'. *Experiential Education Series* 2. Centre for Experiential Education.

Lancaster, P. 2003: *Listening to Young Children* (resource pack). Maidenhead: Open University Press.

Manning-Morton, J. and Thorp, M. 2001: *Key Times – A Framework for Developing High Quality Provision for Children Under Three Years Old*. London: Camden Under Threes Development Group and The University of North London.

Manning-Morton, J. and Thorp, M. 2003: *A Time to Play: Playing, Growing and Learning in the First Three Years of Life*. Maidenhead: Open University Press.

Moser, C. 1999: 'A fresh start: improving literacy and numeracy for adults. Summary and recommendations of the working group'. London: DfES.

Murray, L. and Andrews, E. 2000: *The Social Baby*. Richmond: The Children's Project.

Penn, H. 1999: 'How should we care for babies and toddlers? An analysis of practice in out-of-home care for children under three'. Childcare Resource and Research Unit, Occasional Paper 10 (iv), 66, Centre for Urban and Community Studies, University of Toronto, June.

Piaget, J. 1962: *Play, Dreams and Imitation in Childhood*. London: Routledge and Kegan Paul.

Piaget, J. and Inhelder, B. 1969: *The Psychology of the Child*. London and Henley: Routledge and Kegan Paul.

Pugh, G. (ed.) 1996: *Contemporary Issues in the Early Years*. London: Paul Chapman Publishing Ltd.

Purves, L. and Selleck, D. 1999: *Tuning into Children: Understanding a Child's Development From Birth to 5 years* (pocket book and audio tapes to accompany series). London: National Children's Bureau/BBC Education/BBC Radio 4.

QCA 2000: *Curriculum Guidance for the Foundation Stage*. London: DfEE/QCA.

Rutter, M. 1981: *Maternal Deprivation Reassessed* (2nd edn). Middlesex: Penguin Books.

Selleck, D. 1997: 'Baby art: art is me', in *Reflections on Early Education and Care. Inspired by Visits to Reggio Emilia*, Italy. London: BAECE.

Selleck, D. 2001: 'Being under three years of age: enhancing quality experience', in Pugh, G. (ed.), *Contemporary Issues in the Early Years*. London: Paul Chapman Publishing Ltd.

Selleck, D. and Griffin, S. 1996: 'Quality for under threes', in Pugh, G. (ed.), *Contemporary Issues in the Early Years*. London: Paul Chapman Publishing Ltd.

Sheridan, M. 1973: *Children's Developmental Progress from Birth to Five Years*. NFER.

Sheridan, M., Frost, M., Sharma, A. (eds) 1997: *From Birth to Five Years: Children's Developmental Progress*. London: Routledge.

Shore, R. 1997: *Rethinking the Brain: New Insights into Early Development*. New York: Families & Work Institute.

Steele, H. 2001: 'Intergenerational patterns of attachment: recent findings from research' (unpublished paper). Pen Green Children's Centre: Reflexive Relationships: Encouraging Positive Parent–Child Interactions, 24 March.

Thorp, M. 2003: 'A time to play: playing, growing and learning in the first three years of life' (unpublished paper). London Metropolitan University: Debating Play Conference, 12 July.

Trevarthen, C. 1998: 'The child's need to learn a culture', in Woodhead, M., Faulkner, D. and Littleton, K. (eds), *Cultural Worlds of Early Childhood*. London: Routledge.

Trevarthen, C. 2000: 'Communicating so babies understand for all the senses: getting in tune with core impulses for learning' (unpublished paper). RNIB: A Curriculum for Babies Conference, June.

Trevarthen, C. 2001: 'Tuning into children: motherese and teacherese, the listening voice' (unpublished paper). Pen Green Children's Centre, 24 March.

Vygotsky, L. 1978: *Mind in Society*. Cambridge, MA: Harvard University Press.

Wells, A. 2003: 'Speaking out'. *Nursery World*, 23 January, 16.

Whalley, M. 1994: *Learning to Be Strong*. London: Hodder and Stoughton.

Whalley, M. (ed.) and the Pen Green Centre Team 1997: *Working with Parents*. London: Hodder and Stoughton.

Winnicott, D. W. 1964: *The Child, the Family, and the Outside World*. Middlesex and Victoria, Australia: Penguin.

Woodhead, M., Faulkner, D. and Littleton, K. 1998: *Cultural Worlds of Early Childhood*. London and New York: Routledge and the Open University.

CHAPTER 5 THE FOUNDATION STAGE

Aspin, D. N. 1983: 'Friedrich Froebel: visionary, prophet and healer?' *Early Child Development and Care* 12 (3 and 4).

Blackstone, T. 1971: *A Fair Start*. London: Allen Lane.

Board of Education 1936: *Nursery Schools and Nursery Classes*. London: HMSO, Educational pamphlet 106.

Braedekamp, S. (ed.) 1987: *Developmentally Appropriate Practice in Early Childhood Programs Serving Children from Birth through Age 8*. Washington, DC: NAEYC.

Bruce, T. 2001: *Learning Through Play*. London: Hodder and Stoughton.

Bruner, J. 1980: *Under Five in Britain*. London: Grant McIntyre.

Burman, E. 1994: *Deconstructing Developmental Psychology*. London: Routledge.

CACE 1967: *Children and their Primary Schools Vol. 1: The Plowden Report*. London: HMSO.

Carr, M. 2001: *Assessment in Early Childhood Settings: Learning Stories*. London: Paul Chapman.

Cox, T. (ed.) 1996: *The National Curriculum and the Early Years*. London: Falmer Press.

Curtis, A. 1986: *A Curriculum for the Pre-school Child*. Windsor: NFER.

David, T. 1998: *Researching Early Childhood Education: European Perspectives*. London: Paul Chapman Publishing.

Devlin, K. 2000: *The Maths Gene*. London: Weidenfeld and Nicolson.

DfES 1989: *The National Curriculum*. London: HMSO.

Doherty, J. and Bailey, R. 2003: *Supporting Physical Development in the Early Years*. Buckingham: Open University Press.

ECEF 1998: *Quality in Diversity in Early Learning*. London: ECEF and NCB.

Edwards, C., Gandini, L. and Forman, G. (eds) 1993. *The Hundred Languages of Children*. Norwood, NJ: Ablex.

Eliot, L. 1999: *Early Intelligence*. London: Penguin.

Froebel, F. 1887: *The Education of Man*. New York: Appleton.

Goleman, D. 1996: *Emotional Intelligence*. London: Fontana.

Green, J. A. and Collie, F. A. (eds) 1916: *Pestalozzi's Educational Writings*. London: Edward Arnold.

Giudici, C., Rinaldi, C. and Krechevsky, M. 2001: *Making Learning Visible: Children as Individual and Group Learners.* Reggio Emilia: Project Zero and Reggio Children.

Healy, J. 1999: *Failure to Connect.* New York: Simon and Schuster.

Hobson, P. 2002: *The Cradle of Thought.* London: Macmillan.

Hohmann, M. and Weikart, D. P. 1995: *Educating Young Children; Active Learning Practices for Preschool and Childcare Programs.* Ypsilanti, MI: High/Scope Press.

Inner London Education Authority 1987: *The Early Years: A Curriculum for Young Children.* London: ILEA Learning Resources Branch.

Inner London Education Authority 1990: *The Early Years: A Science Curriculum for Young Children.* London: ILEA Learning Resources Branch.

Isaacs, S. 1929: *The Nursery Years.* London: Routledge and Kegan Paul.

James, C. 1981: 'A curriculum framework for the nursery'. *Early Childhood*, July, 14–17

Jenkinson, S. 2001: *The Genius of Play.* Stroud: Hawthorn Press.

Lewis-Williams, D. 2002: *The Mind in the Cave.* London: Thames and Hudson.

Lowndes, G. A. N. 1960: *Margaret McMillan: The Children's Champion.* London: Museum Press.

Maude, P. 2001: *Physical Children, Active Teaching.* Buckingham: Open University Press.

Mazur, B. 2003: *Imagining Numbers.* London: Allen Lane/The Penguin Press.

Ministry of Education 1996: *Te WhārikiHe Whaariki Matauranga: Early Childhood Curriculum.* Wellington, New Zealand: Learning Media.

Moyles, J., Adams, S. and Musgrove, A. 2002: *Study of Pedagogical Effectiveness in Early Learning.* London: DfES, Research Report 363 (http://www.dfes.gov.uk/research/data/uploadfiles/RR363.pdf – accessed October 2004).

Murray, L. and Andrews, L. 2000: *The Social Baby.* Richmond: CP Publishing.

NACCCE 1999: *All our Futures: Creativity, Culture and Education.* Sudbury: DfEE Publications.

NNS 1999: *The Daily Mathematics Lesson.* London: DfEE.

Odam, G. 1995: *The Sounding Symbol.* Cheltenham: Stanley Thornes.

Pascal, C. and Bertram, T. 1997: *Effective Early Learning: Case Studies in Improvement.* London: Hodder and Stoughton.

Pound, L. 1989: 'Are political fights over curricula necessary?' in McLeod, F. (ed.), *Perspectives on HighScope.* Exeter: University of Exeter, School of Education.

Pound, L. 2002: 'Breadth and depth in early foundations', in Fisher, J. (ed.), *The Foundations of Learning.* Buckingham: Open University Press.

Pound, L. and Harrison, C. 2003: *Supporting Musical Development in the Early Years.* Buckingham: Open University Press.

QCA 2000: *Curriculum Guidance for the Foundation Stage.* London: DfEE/QCA.

QCA 2001: *Planning for Learning in the Foundation Stage.* London: DfEE/QCA.

QCA 2003: *Foundation Stage Profile Handbook*. London: DfES/QCA.

Ramachandran, V. S. and Blakeslee, S. 1999: *Phantoms in the Brain*. London: Fourth Estate.

SCAA 1996: *Nursery Education: Desirable Outcomes for Children's Learning on Entering Compulsory Education*. London: DES/SCAA.

Siegel, D. 1999: *The Developing Mind*. New York: Guilford Press.

Siraj-Blatchford, I., Sylva, K., Muttock, S., Gilden, R. and Bell, D. 2002: *Researching Effective Pedagogy in the Early Years*. London: DfES, Research Report 356 (http://www.dfes.gov.uk/research/data/uploadfiles/RR356.pdf – accessed October 2004).

Siraj-Blatchford, J. 2004: 'Don't be surprised by the future: the development of appropriate new learning technologies for young children', in Siraj-Blatchford, J. (ed.), *Developing New Technologies for Young Children*. Stoke-on-Trent: Trentham Books.

Temple, C., Nathan, R., Burris, N. and Temple, F. 1982: *The Beginnings of Writing* (2nd edn). London: Allyn & Bacon, Inc.

Tizard, B. 1974: *Early Childhood Education*. Windsor: NFER.

Tizard, B. and Hughes, M. 1984: *Young Children Learning*. London: Fontana.

Trevarthen, C. 1998: 'The child's need to learn a culture', in Woodhead, M., Faulkner, D. and Littleton, K. (eds), *Cultural Worlds of Early Childhood*. London: Routledge/The Open University.

van der Eyken, W. and Turner, B. 1969: *Adventures in Education*. Harmondsworth: Penguin Press.

Webb, L. 1974: *Purposes and Practice in Nursery Education*. Oxford: Basil Blackwell.

Whitbread, N. 1972: *The Evolution of the Nursery-Infant School*. London: Routledge and Kegan Paul.

CHAPTER 6 EDUCATIONAL TRANSITIONS

Anning, A. 1998: 'Appropriateness or effectiveness in the early childhood curriculum in the UK: some research evidence'. *International Journal of Early Years Education* 6 (3), 299–314.

Bennet, S. N. 2000: *Progression and Continuity in Pre-School and Reception Classes*. ESRC Report R000222791.

Brooker, L. 2002: *Starting School – Young Children Learning Cultures*. Buckingham: Open University Press.

Brostrom, S. 2002: 'Communication and continuity in the transition from kindergarten to school', in Fabian, H. and Dunlop, A. (eds), *Transitions in the Early Years*. London and New York: RoutledgeFalmer.

Bruce, T. 1987: *Early Childhood Education*. London: Hodder and Stoughton.

DfEE 1998: *Meeting the Childcare Challenge: A Framework and Consultation Document*. http://www.surestart.gov.uk/_doc/0-BB628F.doc (accessed October 2004).

DfES 1990: *Starting with Quality: Report of the Committee of Enquiry into the Quality of Educational Experiences Offered to 3- and 4-Year Olds* (Rumbold Report). London: HMSO.

DfES 2003: *DfES Analytical Services*, Early Years Census. London: DfES.

Drury, R., Millar, L. and Campbell, R. (eds) 2000: Looking at Early Years Education and Care. London: David Fulton.

Dunlop, A. and Fabian, H. 2002: 'Conclusions: debating transitions, continuity and progression in the early years', in Fabian, H. and Dunlop, A. (eds), *Transitions in the Early Years*. London and New York: RoutledgeFalmer.

Fabian, H. 2002: 'Empowering children for transitions', in Fabian, H. and Dunlop, A. (eds), *Transitions in the Early Years*. London and New York: RoutledgeFalmer.

Fabian, H. and Dunlop, A. (eds) 2002: *Transitions in the Early Years*. London and New York: RoutledgeFalmer.

Green Paper 2003 (Presented to Parliament by the Chief Secretary to the Treasury by Command of Her Majesty): *Every Child Matters*: Norwich: The Stationery Office, September.

Hargreaves, L. and Galton, M. 2002: *Transfer from the Primary Classroom*. London: RoutledgeFalmer.

House of Commons 2000: *Early Years. Volume 1. Report and Proceedings of the Committee and of the Education Sub-Committee Relating to the Report*. London: The Stationery Office.

Hughes, M. 1995: *Progression in Learning*, BERA Dialogues 11. Clevedon: Multi-lingual Matters.

Keating, I., Basford, J., Hodson, E. and Harnett, A. 2002: 'Reception teacher responses to the foundation stage'. *International Journal of Early Years Education* 10 (3), 193–203.

Lee, B. 2002: *The Role of Teaching Assistants in the Classroom*. Slough: NFER (http://www.nfer.ac.uk/research/outcome_popup.asp?theID=TAC – accessed October 2004)

Lindsey, G. and Desforges, M. 1998: *Baseline Assessment, Practice, Problems and Possibilities*. London: David Fulton.

Meadows, S. and Cashdan, A. 1988: *Helping Children Learn*. London: David Fulton.

Melhuish, E. *et al.* 1999: *Parent, Family and Child Characteristics in Relation to Type of Preschool and Socio-Economic Differences* (Effective Provision for Pre-School Education Project). London: Institute of Education, Technical paper 4.

Munn, P. 1995: 'Progression in learning, literacy and numeracy in the pre-school', in Hughes, M. (ed.), *Progression in Learning*, BERA Dialogues 11. Clevedon: Multi-lingual Matters.

Munn, P. and Schaffer, R. 1996: 'Teaching and learning in the pre-school period', in Hughes, M. (ed.), *Teaching and Learning in Changing Times*. Oxford: Blackwell.

Neuman, M. J. 2002: 'The wider context: an international overview of transition issues', in Fabian, H. and Dunlop, A. (eds), *Transitions in the Early Years*. London and New York: RoutledgeFalmer.

New, R. 1992: 'The integrated early childhood curriculum', in Seefeldt, C. (ed.), *The Early Childhood Curriculum: A Review of Current Research*. New York: Teachers College Press.

Nutbrown, C. 1997: *Recognising Early Literacy Development*. London: Paul Chapman.

Ofsted 2002: *Teaching Assistants in Primary Schools: An Evaluation of the Quality and Impact of their Work* (HMI 434). http://www.ofsted.gov.uk/publications/index.cfm?fuseaction=pubs.displayfile&id=7&type=pdf (accessed October 2004).

Ofsted 2004a: *Transition from the Reception Year to Year 1 – An Evaluation by HMI 2221*. http://www.ofsted.gov.uk/publications/index.cfm?fuseaction=pubs.displayfile&id=3655&type=pdf (accessed October 2004).

Ofsted 2004b: Ofsted News NR 2004–46, 19 May. http://www.ofsted.gov.uk/news/index.cfm?fuseaction=news.details&id=1559 (accessed October 2004).

Penn, H. 2000: *Early Childhood Services*. Buckingham: Open University Press.

QCA/DfEE 2000: *Curriculum Guidance for the Foundation Stage*. London: DfEE.

QCA 2003: *The Foundation Stage Profile Handbook*. London: DfEE.

Siraj-Blatchford, I. 2001: 'Diversity and learning in the early years', in Pugh, G. (ed.), *Contemporary Issues in the Early Years: Working Collaboratively for Children* (3rd edn). London: Paul Chapman Publishing.

Siraj-Blatchford, I. Sylva, K., Muttock, S., Gilden, R. and Bell, D. 2002: *Researching Effective Pedagogy in the Early Years* (REPEY). London: DfES, Research Report 356 (http://www.dfes.gov.uk/research/data/uploadfiles/RR356.pdf – accessed October 2004).

Spelman, B. 1979: *Pupil Adaptation to Secondary School*. Belfast: Northern Ireland Council for Educational Research, Publication No. 18.

Stephen, C. and Cope, P. 2003: 'Moving on to primary 1: an exploratory study of the experiences of transition from pre-school to primary', in *Insight* 3. Scottish Executive Education Department (http://www.scotland.gov.uk/library5/education/ins3-00.asp – accessed October 2004).

Sylva, K., Melhuish, E., Sammons, P., Siraj-Blatchford, I., Taggart, B. and Elliot, K. 2003: *The Effective Provision of Pre-School Education (EPPE) Project: Findings from the Pre-School Period*. London: DfEE, Report Brief No. RBX15-03 (http://www.dfes.gov.uk/research/data/uploadfiles/RBX15-03.doc – accessed October 2004).

Sylva, K., Roy, C. and McIntyre, G. 1980: *Child Watching at Playgroup and Nursery School*. London: Grant McIntyre.

Taylor Nelson Sofres with Aubrey, C. 2002: *Implementing the Foundation Stage in Reception Classes*. London: DFES, Research Report 350 (http://www.dfes.gov.uk/research/data/uploadfiles/RR350.doc – accessed October 2004).

Wood, L. and Bennet, N. 1997: 'The rhetoric and reality of play: teachers' thinking and classroom practice'. *Early Years* 17 (2), 22–7.

Wood, E. and Bennet, N. 2001: 'Early childhood teachers' theories of progression and continuity'. *International Journal of Early Years Education* 9 (3), 229–43.

BIBLIOGRAPHY

CHAPTER 7 EARLY YEARS AND ILT

Dewey, J. 1933: *How We Think: A Restatement of the Relation of Reflective Thinking in the Educative Process*. Chicago: Henry Regnery.

Gagne, R. M. 1978: *The Conditions of Learning*. New York: Holt, Rinehart and Winston.

Monteith, M. (ed.) 2002: *Teaching Primary Literacy with ICT*. Buckingham: Open University Press.

Ofcom 2004: 'Ofcom Internet and Broadband Update'. http://www.ofcom.org.uk/research/consumer_audience_research/telecoms/int_bband_updt/?a=87101 (April).

Piaget, J. 1959: *The Language and Thought of the Child*. London: Routledge.

Piaget, J. 1962: *Play, Dreams and Imitation in Childhood*. London: Routledge and Kegan Paul.

Siraj-Blatchford, I. and Siraj-Blatchford, J. 2003: *More Than Computers – Information and Communication Technology in the Early Years*. London: British Association for Early Childhood.

Siraj-Blatchford, J. and Whitbread, D. 2003: *Supporting ICT in the Early Years*. Buckingham: Open University Press.

Smith, A. 1996: *Accelerated Learning in the Classroom*. Stafford: Network Educational Press.

Vygotsky, L. 1978: *Mind in Society*. Cambridge, MA: Harvard University Press.

Vygotsky, L. 1986: *Thought and Language*. Cambridge, MA: MIT Press.

CHAPTER 8 MANAGEMENT, TEAMWORK AND LEADERSHIP

Bruce, T. and Meggitt, C. 2002: *Child Care and Education* (3rd edn). London: Hodder and Stoughton.

Coleman, M. 2002: *Women as Headteachers: Striking the Balance*. Stoke-on-Trent: Trentham Books.

Department for Education and Skills/National College for School Leadership 2004: *National Professional Qualification in Integrated Centre Leadership*. Nottingham: National College for School Leadership.

Edgington, M. 2004: *The Foundation Stage Teacher in Action: Teaching 3, 4 and 5 year olds* (3rd edn). London: Paul Chapman Publishing.

Elfer, P., Goldschmied, E. and Selleck, D. 2003: *Key Persons in the Nursery*. London: David Fulton Publishers.

Fox, M. 1997: The multidisciplinary assessment of under-fives with cerebral palsy. In Wolfendale, S. (ed.) *Meeting Special Needs in the Early Years*. London: David Fulton Publishers.

Goleman, D., Boyatzis, R. and McKee, A. 2002: *The New Leaders: Transforming the Art of Leadership into the Science of Results*. London: Time Warner.

Gronn, P. 2003: *The New Work of Educational Leaders*. London: Sage.

H.M. Treasury 2004: *Choice for parents, the best start for children: a ten year strategy for childcare*. London: HMSO.

Hindle, T. 1998: *Managing Meetings*. London: Dorling Kindersley.

Lindon, J. and Lindon, L. 1997: *Working Together for Young Children*. London: Macmillan Press Ltd.

Lyus, V. 1998: *Management in the Early Years*. London: Hodder and Stoughton.

QCA 2000: *Curriculum Guidance for the Foundation Stage*. London: DfEE/QCA.

Rodd, J. 1998: *Leadership in Early Childhood* (2nd edn). Buckingham: Open University Press.

Smith, A. and Langston, A. 1999: *Managing Staff in Early Years Settings*. London: Routledge.

van Maurik, J. 2004: *Writers on Leadership*. London: Penguin Business.

Whalley, M. 1994: *Learning to Be Strong*. London: Hodder and Stoughton.

CHAPTER 9 EARLY YEARS POLICY

Bertram, T. and Pascal, C. 2001: *Early Excellence Centre Pilot Programme Annual Evaluation Report*. London: DfEE.

Bowlby, J. 1953: *Child Care and the Growth of Love*. Harmondsworth: Penguin Books.

CACE 1967: *Children and their Primary Schools Vol. 1: The Plowden Report*. London: HMSO.

Carnegie Foundation 1994: *Starting Points: Meeting the Needs of our Youngest Children*. New York: Carnegie Corporation.

DfEE 1999: *Early Years Development: Partnerships and Plans*. London: DfEE.

DfES 1990: *Starting with Quality: Report of the Committee of Enquiry into the Quality of Educational Experiences Offered to 3- and 4-Year Olds* (Rumbold Report). London: HMSO.

DfES 2002: *Birth to Three Matters: A Framework for Supporting Children in their Earliest Years*. London: DfES.

DoH 1989: *Children Act*. London: HMSO.

H.M. Treasury 2004: *Choice for Parents, the Best Start for Children: a Ten-Year Strategy for Childcare*. Norwich: HMSO.

Lowndes, G. A. N. 1960: *Margaret McMillan: The Children's Champion*. London: Museum Press.

Malaguzzi, L. 1993: 'History, ideas and basic philosophy', in Edwards, C., Gandini, L. and Forman, G. (eds), *The Hundred Languages of Children*. Norwood, NJ: Ablex.

QCA 2000: *Curriculum Guidance for the Foundation Stage*. London: DfEE/QCA.

QCA 2001: *Planning for Learning in the Early Years*. London: DfES/QCA.

QCA 2003: *Foundation Stage Profile Handbook*. London: DfES/QCA.

Riley, D. 1983: *War in the Nursery*. London: Virago Press.

SCAA 1996: *Nursery Education: Desirable Outcomes for Children's Learning on Entering Compulsory Education*. London: DES/SCAA.

Siraj-Blatchford, I., Sylva, K., Muttock, S., Gilden, R. and Bell, D. 2002: *Researching Effective Pedagogy in the Early Years*. London: DfES, Research report 356.

Sylva, K. 1999: 'The role of research in explaining the past and shaping the future', in Abbot, L. and Moylett, H. (eds), *Early Education Transformed*. London: Falmer Press.

Whitbread, N. 1972: *The Evolution of the Nursery-Infant School*. London: Routledge and Kegan Paul.

CHAPTER 10 SPECIAL EDUCATIONAL NEEDS

Advisory Centre for Education (ACE) 2002: *Special Education Handbook: The Law on Children with Special Educational Needs*. London: ACE.

Beresford, B. and Oldham, C. 2002: *Housing Matters: National Evidence Relating to Disabled Children and their Housing*. Bristol: The Policy Press.

Dare, A. and O'Donovan, M. 2002: *Good Practice in Caring for Young Children with Special Needs* (2nd edn). Cheltenham: Nelson Thornes.

DfES 1978: *Special Educational Needs: Report of the Committee of Enquiry into the Education of Handicapped Children and Young People* (Warnock Report). London: HMSO.

DfES 1981: *Education Act*. London: HMSO.

DfES 2001: *Special Educational Needs Code of Practice*. Nottingham: DfES.

DfES 2003: *Statistics for Education: Special Educational Needs in England*. London: HMSO.

DfES 2004: *Removing Barriers to Achievement*. London: DfES.

DoH 1989: *Children Act*. London: HMSO.

Dyson, A. 2001: 'Special needs in the twenty-first century: where we've been and where we're going'. *British Journal of Special Education* 28 (1), March.

Lewisham Early Years Special Needs Team 2003: *Special Educational Needs: Policy, Information and Practice for Lewisham Early Years Practitioners*. London: London Borough of Lewisham.

Rathbone: *Could Do Better: An Analysis of How Well Mainstream Schools Involve the Parents of Pupils with Special Educational Needs*. Available from Rathbone, Churchgate House, 56 Oxford Street, Manchester M1 6EU (Price £5.00).

Sylva, K., Melhuish, E., Sammons, P., Siraj-Blatchford, I., Taggart, B. and Elliot, K. 2003: *The Effective Provision of Pre-School Education Project*. London: University of London, Institute of Education.

Tassoni, P. 2003: *Supporting Special Needs. Understanding Inclusion in the Early Years*. Oxford: Heinemann Educational.

Wall, K. 2003: *Special Needs and Early Years: A Practitioner's Guide*. London: Sage.

CHAPTER 11 CHILD PROTECTION

Beckett, C. 2003: *Child Protection: An Introduction*. Sage: London.

Bruce, T. and Meggitt, C. 2002: *Child Care and Education* (3rd edn). London: Hodder and Stoughton.

Children Are Unbeatable! 2004: 'Research review' (Briefing 6). http://www.childrenareunbeatable.org.uk/briefings/CAU_Briefing6.pdf (accessed October 2004).

Daycare Trust 2004: 'Childcare and child poverty'. *Childcare Facts: About Poverty*. http://daycaretrust.org.uk/mod.php?mod=userpage&menu=1002&page_id=8 (accessed October 2004).

DfES 2002: *Birth to Three Matters: A Framework to Support Children in their Earliest Years*. London: DfES.

DoH 1999: *Working Together to Safeguard Children: A Guide to Inter-Agency Working to Safeguard and Promote the Welfare of Children*. London: The Stationery Office.

DoH 2000: *Framework for the Assessment of Children in Need and their Families*. London: The Stationery Office.

DoH 2003: *What To Do if You're Worried a Child Is Being Abused*. London: The Stationery Office.

Donnellan, C. 2001: *Confronting Child Abuse Issues* 22. Cambridge: Independence.

Evans, H. 2002a: 'Emotional abuse'. NSPCC Information Briefings (NSPCC Child Protection Awareness Group). http://www.nspcc.org.uk/inform (accessed October 2004), February.

Evans, H. 2002b: 'Child neglect'. NSPCC Information Briefings (NSPCC Child Protection Awareness Group). http://www.nspcc.org.uk/inform (accessed October 2004), February.

Finch, S. 1998: *'An Eye For an Eye Leaves Everyone Blind'. Teaching Young Children to Settle Conflicts without Violence*. London: National Early Years Network.

Foley, P., Roche, J. and Tucker, S. 2000: *Children in Society: Contemporary Theory and Practice*. Basingstoke: Palgrave.

Gibson, C. *et al.* 2000: *Point of Law: The Children Act Explained*. Grimsby: The Stationery Office.

Gillham, B. 1994: *The Facts About Child Physical Abuse*. London: Cassell.

Goldschmied, E. and Jackson, S. 1994: *People Under Three: Young Children in Day Care*. London and New York: Routledge.

Green Paper 2003 (Presented to Parliament by the Chief Secretary to the Treasury by Command of Her Majesty): *Every Child Matters*: Norwich: The Stationery Office, September.

Gussin Paley, V. 1981: *Wally's Stories*. London: Harvard University Press.

Gussin Paley, V. 1992: *You Can't Say You Can't Play*. Harvard, MA: Harvard University Press.

Hewlett, S. 1993: *Child Neglect in Rich Nations*. Unicef.

Kindlon, D. and Thompson, M. 1999: *Raising Cain: Protecting the Emotional Life of Boys*. London: Michael Joseph.

Lindon, J. 1999: *Too Safe for their Own Good? Helping Children Learn About Risk and Lifeskills*. London: National Early Years Network.

Lindon, J. 2003: *Child Protection*. London: Hodder and Stoughton.

Lindon, J. and Lindon, L. 1997: *Working Together for Young Children: A Guide for Managers and Staff*. London: Thomson Learning.

Miles, R. (1994) *The Children we Deserve: Love and Hate in the Making of the Family*. London: HarperCollins.

Miller, D. 2002: 'Disabled children and abuse'. *NSPCC Information Briefings* (NSPCC Practice Development Group). http://www.nspcc.org.uk/inform (accessed October 2004), February.

Miller, J. 1997: *Never Too Young: How Young Children Can Take Responsibility and Make Decisions*. London: National Early Years Network (in association with Save the Children).

NSPCC 2000: 'Survey finds hidden victims of child abuse'. http://www.nspcc.org.uk/html/home/informationresources/hiddenchildabuse survey.htm (accessed October 2004), 21 November.

Renvoize, J. 1993: *Innocence Destroyed: A Study of Child Sexual Abuse*. London: Routledge.

Ofsted 2001: *Guidance to the National Standards Full Day Care*, Sessional Care and Childminding. London: The Stationery Office.

Ofsted 2003: *Day Care: Guidance to the National Standards: Revisions to Certain Criteria: Version 2*. London: The Stationery Office.

Ofsted 2004: *Childminding: Guidance to the National Standards. Revisions to Certain Criteria: Version 2*. London: The Stationery Office.

Practical Professional Childcare 2003: 'Can't Smack Won't Smack'. Leamington Spa: Step Forward Publishing, November.

Steele, H. 2001: 'Intergenerational patterns of attachment: recent findings from research' (unpublished paper). Pen Green Children's Centre: Reflexive Relationships: Encouraging Positive Parent–Child Interactions Conference, 23 March.

Taylor, J. and Woods, M. (eds) 1997: *Early Childhood Studies: An Holistic Introduction*. London: Arnold.

United Nations 1990: *Convention on the Rights of the Child*. http://www.ohchr.org/english/law/crc.htm (accessed October 2004).

Willow, C. and Hyder, T. 1998: *It Hurts You Inside. Children Talking About Smacking*. London: National Children's Bureau and Save the Children.

APPENDIX: STUDY SKILLS

Buzan, T. 2002: *How To Mind Map: The Ultimate Thinking Tool That Will Change Your Life*. London: HarperCollins.

Fielding, H. 1996: *Bridget Jones's Diary: A Novel*. London: Picador.

NAME INDEX

SUBJECT INDEX